STANLEY I PRESUME

Also by Stanley Johnson

STANLEY JOHNSON

Stanley I Presume

Pembroke Branch Tel. 6689575

FOURTH ESTATE · *London*

First published in Great Britain in 2009 by
Fourth Estate
An imprint of HarperCollins*Publishers*
77–85 Fulham Palace Road
London W6 8JB

Visit our authors' blog: www.fifthestate.co.uk
LOVE THIS BOOK? WWW.BOOKARMY.COM

1

A catalogue record for this book is
available from the British Library

HB ISBN 978-0-00-729672-9

Typeset in Minion by G&M Designs Limited,
Raunds, Northamptonshire

Printed in Great Britain by Clays Ltd, St Ives plc

Mixed Sources
Product group from well-managed
forests and other controlled sources
www.fsc.org Cert no. SW-COC-1806
© 1996 Forest Stewardship Council
FSC

FSC is a non-profit international organisation established to promote the
responsible management of the world's forests. Products carrying the FSC
label are independently certified to assure customers that they come
from forests that are managed to meet the social, economic and
ecological needs of present and future generations.

Find out more about HarperCollins and the environment at
www.harpercollins.co.uk/green

In memory of my parents

CONTENTS

ONE

A Plane Crash; Fishcakes for Breakfast

My mother was by nature an optimist. She was always ready to look on the bright side of life. I remember being woken by her one night when I was about four years old. My father was a pilot in the RAF during the war and we were living in a little cottage near the runway at Chivenor in north Devon where his squadron was posted.

'Look, darling! Come quickly!' She hustled me to the window. 'There is a wonderful bonfire on the runway! A plane has crashed and, quite soon, the depth charges will explode!'

I can't remember whether the depth charges did explode that night, but I recall the knock on the door the next morning.

It was the RAF padre. He took off his hat as he spoke.

'Mrs Johnson? I'm afraid I've some bad news. Your husband …'

As it turned out, the spectacular plane crash we had witnessed the previous night had actually involved my father, returning home from trying to spot enemy U-boats in the western approaches. One of the engines on his Wellington bomber had apparently 'feathered', whatever that meant, causing him to lose height on the final approach. As a result he had clipped a telegraph pole and crashed on the runway. In the resulting conflagration he had been severely burned.

'The good news,' the padre continued, 'is that your husband is still alive.'

My mother thrust her chin out and her eyes glinted. 'I didn't doubt it for a moment.'

'Daddy's crash' was one of the milestones of my childhood. My father in fact ended up losing height in more senses than one. He received extensive plastic surgery (and a DFC for extricating his crew from the burning plane) and spent the rest of his life with one leg two

1

inches shorter than the other. The hospital treatment took time and it was not until 1947 that he was finally demobilized.

My mother's name was Irène, but most of her life she was known as 'Buster', a nickname she acquired at Cheltenham Ladies' College, which she attended in the early 1920s. I once asked her why her schoolmates called her Buster.

'Because I was rather large at school, darling. The girls thought it funny.'

My mother obviously thought it funny too because she laughed at the memory. She didn't appear to hold a grudge against her school-mates. On the contrary, she gave every impression of having enjoyed her days at Cheltenham. I still have her lacrosse stick.

Going up to Oxford in 1926, she read French and Russian at St Hugh's and took a perfectly respectable second at a time when female undergraduates at Oxford were still something of a rarity. She gained a half-blue at judo and would, I am sure, have been quite ready to demonstrate her proficiency should the need arise. As things turned out, she lived over half her life (forty-six years out of eighty) on our Exmoor farm where opportunities for 'throwing one's opponent', as she put it, were few and far between, though there were often runaway sheep to be tackled.

She met my father in Egypt before the war. She was tutoring; he was working on a farm in the Nile Delta belonging to a Swiss uncle. According to my mother, she snared him over a shove-halfpenny board.

'Your father was keen on the game and I was keen on him. Since I had the only shove-halfpenny board in Cairo, I knew he had to come to my flat to play. Mind you, I wasn't very good. Your father would some-times play his right hand against his left to give himself a better game.'

They returned to England and were married in 1936. My father found a job in a timber-broking firm and, as the war clouds gathered, my mother had two children in quick succession, namely my brother Peter and my sister Hilary.

The family was living at the time in my maternal grandfather's house near St Ives in Cornwall. Grandpa had fought in the First World War and had lived in Bromley, Kent, with a holiday home in Carbis Bay, near St Ives, which became his principal residence when the Second World War broke out.

Grandpa's wife, born Marie-Louise de Pfeffel, was French and my mother was very proud of her French ancestry, as am I. When I was growing up, she pressed me on more than one occasion to explore the possibilities of claiming a French barony which she believed might be able to be passed through the female line. Her mother's father was Baron Hubert de Pfeffel. He owned a large house in Versailles, in the Avenue de Paris, which used to belong to Madame du Barry, Louis XV's mistress. My mother was born there in 1907.

'*Relever le titre* – resurrect the title' was the way she put it. I remember pointing out that if anyone was to claim a French title, it should be my elder brother, Peter, not I.

Years later, when I was a member of the European Parliament, I escaped from a tedious session in Strasbourg to visit Colmar, where some of my French ancestors originated. My wife, Jenny, was with me and we had lunch in a handsome medieval building, which bears the title Restaurant Pfeffel.

The particular Pfeffel who is commemorated in this tasty eating house is a blind poet, known as Gottlieb Konrad, or, in the French version of his name, Théophile-Conrad. Being a versatile man, in spite of his disability, he also seems to have established a famous military academy in Colmar.

Apart from the brasserie, there is a Square Pfeffel in Colmar. There was also, we were told, a statue of the poet. This was bombed in the First World War, but restored in time for the Second World War when unfortunately it was once again destroyed, this time without being rebuilt.

I have only the haziest recollections of my French grandmother, Marie-Louise Williams (née Pfeffel), who died of an allergic reaction to a bee sting before the war ended but she was, it seems, aware of my arrival – on 18 August 1940. My mother once described the circumstances of my birth to me.

'It was already late at night. I told your granny that you were on the way. Granny told Grandpa and Grandpa called for William. William barely had time to get Poppy out of the garage to run me into Penzance before you arrived!'

William was my grandfather's chauffeur and Poppy was Grandpa's red Daimler which, owing to fuel rationing, saw very few outings during the course of the war, though getting me to the hospital on time clearly qualified as an allowable excursion.

With hindsight, I am aware that 18 August 1940 was one of the high points of the Battle of Britain. For my birthday a few years ago, my (younger) daughter, Julia, gave me a copy of *The Times* which recorded the demise of more than three hundred German fighter planes on that one afternoon of 18 August, as against the loss of fewer than one hundred British aircraft. Newly swaddled in Penzance general hospital, I knew nothing of these great events. I didn't even know that there was a war on.

William took Poppy out of the garage again a few days later to bring my mother and me back from hospital. We returned to my grand-father's house, known as Trevose View because on a clear day you could see the lighthouse at Trevose Head. My birth certificate records my name as Stanley Patrick Johnson, the Stanley being in Grandpa's honour. Where the Patrick came from remains a mystery to me. If my mother ever explained, I have forgotten.

With my father assigned on active duty to RAF Coastal Command, my mother spent extended periods during the war at her parents' Cornish home. I have already said that I don't have much recollection of my French grandmother, Marie-Louise. *Par contre*, as she might have said, my memories of Grandpa Stanley are vivid.

Stanley Williams came of solid yeoman stock. His great-grand-father, Amos Williams, farmed at Ashway, high above the River Barle near Dulverton on Exmoor, a few miles from where, a century later, we would buy our own farm (though on the Exe, not the Barle).

Amos is buried in Dulverton churchyard, as are other members of the Williams family. But one of Amos's sons, George Williams, left his father's Exmoor farm to seek his fortune in London. In this he was successful, being apprenticed to a draper and in due course marrying the boss's daughter. George Williams went on to found the Young Men's Christian Association (YMCA), received a knighthood from Queen Victoria and the Freedom of the City of London from the Lord Mayor and Aldermen. He died in 1905, enjoyed (if that is the right word) a well-attended funeral and is buried in the crypt of St Paul's Cathedral.

The family prospered. George Williams's grandson Stanley (my grandfather) was sent to Harrow, where – according to my mother – he held the record, unchallenged for a considerable period, for the longest throw of a cricket ball. He then went up to Lincoln College, Oxford, where he did not excel academically.

I remember Grandpa explaining that his own father had taken the view that a young man blessed with a place at Oxford shouldn't fritter away his opportunities by spending too much time on his studies.

'Pater took me to see my tutor, that first day at Oxford,' Grandpa recalled. 'He told me he would be disappointed if I didn't get a fourth!'

In the event, Grandpa went one better (or worse). He missed any kind of honours completely, obtaining instead a pass degree in law, a considerable feat. His copy of Justinian, pages scrupulously still uncut, is on the shelf outside the new bathroom at Nethercote, our farm on Exmoor. (I shall come to Nethercote shortly.)

After surviving the First World War, Stanley went into Lloyd's. For a time he was an active 'name'.

My cousin Colin Williams, whose grandfather, Stanley's brother, was killed in the First World War, while his father was killed in the second and who has himself made a career in the City as a minerals trader, explained to me recently that, at least where Lloyd's is concerned, the adjective 'active' is itself a relative term.

'Basically, as I understood it, your grandfather Stanley would catch the 10.30 a.m. from Bromley, where he lived with your grandmother and what he termed "the brood". The train would arrive at London Bridge some time after eleven, when your grandfather would walk to Lloyd's. He would spend an hour or so at Lloyd's, writing a letter or whatever, then he would go to Simpson's in Cornhill Street for lunch.'

Colin explained that my grandfather was in fact teetotal, having taken the pledge during his undergraduate years after one too many nights of excess.

'But that didn't mean Grandpa Stanley didn't have a perfectly good lunch. Remember, in those days the Cornhill Simpson's had a full-size billiard table downstairs. Your grandfather was an excellent player. He'd probably leave Simpson's around three, walk back to London Bridge and arrive home in Bromley well before five.'

Not long ago, my cousin Colin invited me to Simpson's for lunch. With extensive business interests in Russia, he had been helping my youngest son, Max, get a Russian visa, so Max came along too. The three of us sat in one of the antique wooden booths, which, I imagined, hadn't changed for centuries, and toasted Grandpa Stanley with silver tankards of ale.

Later, we went downstairs to the room where the billiard table used to be, now serving as an overflow dining area. It wasn't difficult to imagine Grandpa whiling away the afternoon until he could decently call it a day.

The outbreak of the Second World War enabled Grandpa to call it a day in a rather more comprehensive way. He ceased to be an 'active' name at Lloyd's, retiring to Cornwall to await the arrival (with the customary three-year delay in the accounts) of the latest dividend statement.

My mother was the eldest of his four daughters (he had no sons). All his daughters, with their respective families, visited him at Trevose View, though the main burden of looking after him when his wife died fell on the youngest daughter, Nikki (then unmarried). Poppy, the red Daimler, was super-annuated after the war and William, the chauffeur, moved on. But the housekeeper, Jessie, was very much a fixture.

Even after we bought Nethercote, our farm in west Somerset, my mother would take us children on regular summer trips to Cornwall to stay with Grandpa.

By then – I am talking about the early fifties – there were four Johnson siblings, my younger sister, Gillian Marie-Louise, having been born at the end of 1944.

Jessie was a cook as well as a housekeeper. One of her specialities was fishcakes. We would come down to breakfast, my grandfather Stanley sitting at the head of the table with a splendid view over the hydrangeas towards Trevose Head and the occasional gannet flying far out to sea. My mother would sit on his right and the four children would range themselves round.

'Fishcakes today!' Grandpa would inform us. He would ring the bell and Jessie would push a steaming plate through the hatch.

Having a smattering of schoolboy Greek, Grandpa would take the spatula and give a quick tap on each fishcake, shouting as he did so 'alpha, beta, gamma, delta, epsilon, zeta …'

If you spotted a fishcake you fancied, you had to call out the right letter (in Greek of course) and, provided none of your siblings had beaten you to it, that particular succulent item, crisply fried, with a light golden brown tan overall, was yours.

Grandpa was a thrifty soul. He elevated beachcombing into a high art. Two or three days a week he would set out on a long walk to the beaches of Lelant or Hayle, returning with a canvas sack filled with bits of driftwood or lumps of coal washed up by the tide.

As we grew older, he would invite us to accompany him. The quickest route to the Hayle estuary was along the single-track branch line running from St Erth to St Ives. I remember hopping from sleeper to sleeper between the shiny rails, then stepping smartly to the side to let the train go by. Sometimes, when you were in the deep cutting between Carbis Bay and Lelant, you would hear the chug of the engine and the shrill whistle long before you saw the train. Or you could put your ear to the rail and sense the vibrations even earlier.

Occasionally, Grandpa would find large white shells on the beach and he would pop these in his canvas bag too. Over time, he amassed quite a collection which he used to form the words CARBIS BAY on the grassy embankment of the nearest station to our house.

'People come here from all over, even from Birmingham,' he would say. 'Now they know which station to get off at.'

The shells are still in place today, serving their intended purpose since, amazingly, the St Erth to St Ives train has survived despite regular attempts to close it down, a fate to which many similar branch lines have long since succumbed.

My grandfather died in 1955. By then I was already in my second year as a boarder at Sherborne School in Dorset. I remember reading the notice of his death in the *Daily Telegraph* before having word of it from my parents. When I did hear from home, it was, unusually, a letter from my father. I say 'unusually' because on the whole it was my mother who wrote the weekly letter, most often giving news of events on the farm.

'Grandpa was a very decent chap,' my father wrote. 'There were not many like him around.'

My mother, a great hoarder, kept all our letters home. Not long ago, my sister Gillian (more often called by my parents 'Birdie', because apparently as an infant she opened her mouth to be fed like a baby bird) handed me a bag of letters which she had found among my mother's possessions. On inspection, I discovered they were on the whole unilluminating communications which I had sent home over the years – from prep school, public school, university and even, with diminishing frequency, from the great wide world beyond.

Flipping through them, I found one dated Sunday 5 November. It read: 'Dear Mummy and Daddy. Thank you for the news. I am very sorry indeed and await further details. Daddy's letter was no shock as we had already seen the news in Wednesday's *Telegraph*. Pete [my brother] showed it to me.'

I went on to say: 'Man's life is three score years and ten, and Grandpa was 75! November 12th is an away match for the 1st and a home match for the 2nd, in which Pete will be playing.'

It is now more than fifty years since Grandpa died. As I look back, I can't help feeling that my response to the news that he had been summoned to that great billiard table in the sky, at least as recorded in the weekly letter home, was more than a little laconic. All his grandchildren were tremendously fond of him. I certainly was. And his investments in Lloyd's had paid my school fees.

TWO

Stanley Blake Walks to Bampton

With my grandfather's financial assistance, my parents bought a small-holding near Horsell in Surrey, called Parley Brook House. The house had a garden and paddock in which we kept livestock of various kinds including pigs and poultry. For a time, my father resumed his pre-war life as a timber broker in the City, while trying to keep an eye on the animals at the same time.

Each evening, on returning from London to Surrey, he would drive an old open Lancia Lambda around various restaurants in the Woking area collecting vegetable and other waste which he would then boil up in an iron vat and serve as swill to the pigs. It frequently fell to us children to keep the fire going under the vat, by feeding it with logs and brushwood. Failure to do so, my father explained, meant that the swill would not be properly cooked and the pigs would suffer.

I remember one spectacular eruption when my father, returning home from the pub for Sunday lunch, discovered we had let the fire go out. He was an immensely strong man and for a moment it seemed as though he was going to pick up the entire dining-room table, laden as it was with crockery, cutlery and the Sunday roast, and hurl it across the room. In the event, he brought the carving knife hard down on the table, causing splinters to fly.

My mother had a fine sense of drama. Far from being disconcerted, she applauded.

'Bravo, Johnny!' she exclaimed.

She later explained to us that my father had been in a bad mood not so much because of our own lapses but because he couldn't stand working in London.

'He simply hates it,' she said.

9

In spite of the drama, I could see that she was entirely on my father's side. She knew that there was nothing my father wanted more than to be a full-time farmer. He was an outdoor man through and through and the sooner he could get back to the land, the happier she knew he would be.

It was obvious to me as a child that my father's happiness was, for my mother, a paramount consideration. She once confessed to me, rather wistfully, that she had hoped, with her university education and knowledge of languages, that she might marry a diplomat.

'I could rather see myself being an ambassador's wife.'

In that case, I remember thinking, she had picked the wrong man. Owing to family circumstances that I shall later explain, my father had had to leave school at the age of thirteen. He had then worked on a farm in Dorset, before leaving as a young man for Canada. He didn't, as far as I knew, possess any formal academic qualification, except possibly a school leaver's certificate. Even if he had wanted to, which he plainly didn't, there was no way my father could have been a British diplomat of the traditional pinstriped variety.

While my father grew increasingly frustrated with a suburban existence (even though there were still plenty of open vistas in post-war Surrey) my brother and I went off to prep school in deepest Devon.

It is in fact entirely thanks to our having been sent off to Ravenswood School, Stoodleigh, near Tiverton, in Devon, that my father was at last able to escape the life he loathed in London and, at the age of forty, take up an existence he had always longed for, namely running his own farm on Exmoor, about as remote a part of the country as could then be imagined.

Did my mother ever regret moving so far away from the bright lights? If she did, she put those regrets resolutely behind her. Her job, as she saw it, was to stand by her man and, if he wanted to be an Exmoor farmer, then that was what she wanted too. It was a question of 'whither thou goest, I go and what thou doest, that I will do'.

The purchase in 1951 of West Nethercote, a 250-acre hill farm in the parish of Winsford, west Somerset, has probably been the single most important determinant of my life and of the kind of person I am.

When my parents were still alive, and we were all sitting around the table with some farm task (haymaking or shearing, for example) satisfactorily accomplished, my father might on occasion take his pipe out of his mouth and venture into the historical subjunctive.

'But what if old Stanley Blake hadn't walked into the White Horse in Bampton that evening?'

The White Horse, Bampton, was a pub where my parents would stay on their annual visit to see my brother and me at school. In those days, exeats were not part of the school calendar. Your parents sent you off to school at the beginning of term and they certainly didn't expect to see you until the holidays. In any case, if you lived in Surrey and went to school in Devon going home at weekends or for half-term simply wasn't practical.

During the course of these visits, my father became friendly with the White Horse's landlord, one Mr Collacott. He must have told Collacott how much he hoped to start farming in the West Country because one day in the summer of 1951, soon after the parental appearance at Ravenswood School's annual Sports Day, Mr Collacott telephoned to say that an old boy called Stanley Blake had walked into the pub from his farm on Exmoor (ten miles as the crow flies, more by road) and in the course of a long evening at the bar had intimated that he was think-ing of selling up.

Next day, my father took the day off from the unloved timber brokers, hopped on his Norton motorcycle and drove two hundred miles in a south-westerly direction to find out what Mr Blake's inten-tions were.

It turned out there was not just one Mr Blake. Stanley had a brother, Ernest, with whom he was not on speaking terms, though as my father reported to my mother they not only shared the old partly medieval farmhouse, and worked the farm together; they even shared the same bed.

There was also a Miss Blake, sister of Stanley and Ernest, who did the housekeeping and who acted as an intermediary in the event that Stanley had, absolutely, to communicate with Ernest or vice versa.

My father always maintained that he knew from the first moment he turned off the Winsford–Exford road to follow the River Exe for two miles up the bumpy, potholed track to Nethercote that this was the place for him. I know how he must have felt. Even though I have now lived there for fifty-seven years, I can still sense the magic every time I drive across the little bridge over the river to enter what for me is the most special valley in England, if not the world.

My parents must have made a second, unscheduled, visit to Ravenswood later on in the course of the summer term of 1951, because I remember being allowed out one Sunday to accompany them on a visit to the farm. Contracts had already been exchanged though we would not take possession until November.

I remember the day vividly. Since my father was on this occasion accompanied by my mother, he had eschewed the motorcycle and had driven down in the open Lancia instead. This was a low-slung vehicle, which made heavy weather of the ruts and hollows in the long farm track. By then my brother Peter had gone on to Sherborne, so I had the back seat of the car all to myself, except for the two family dogs, Leader, a yellow Labrador, and Minki, a black one.

For me, a ten-year-old, it was sheer heaven. The River Exe, only a dozen miles or so from its source high up on Exmoor, sparkled brightly to our right. At the height of summer it was more of a stream than a river, though it could turn overnight into a raging torrent as we would discover a year later at the time of the famous Lynmouth Flood Disaster. On our left, new bracken had pushed through the old, swathing the hillside – known as Bye Common – in green. Halfway up the drive we rattled across a cattle grid and drove through a field full of cows.

'These will be Victor Stevens' cows,' my father shouted to my mother above the snarl of the engine. 'The Stevens have the place next door, East Nethercote. We're West Nethercote.'

Minutes later we crossed another bridge, drove up a short hill, passed through the first farmyard without stopping, dipped down to cross a stream, then climbed again into West Nethercote's farmyard.

Nowadays, West Nethercote has seen a certain amount of gentrification. Though we still take our water off the hill, towards the end of the 1990s we had mains electricity installed, replacing the diesel generators. More recently, we have put in a second bathroom. The farmyard is no longer used primarily as a place to herd sheep and cattle. The mud has grassed over and, if you take a mower to it from time to time, it has the makings of a lawn.

But that day in the summer of 1951 we were looking at a time capsule. The Blakes, Stanley and Ernest, thin and wiry and wearing leggings and cloth caps, were there to greet us, the new purchasers. They were only too pleased to show us round the place they had lived in all their lives.

The west end of the farmhouse was a byre, occupied by cows.

My father nodded approvingly. 'Very good place to have them. Keeps the heat in the house. You store the hay above, I imagine?'

As he spoke, I was busy climbing up the wooden ladder into the loft, which was indeed, as my father had surmised, full of hay.

I could see that tossing the hay down from the loft into the manger in the byre below had much to commend it in terms of efficiency, but I don't think my mother was totally convinced. She had her eyes on the loft as a place for a proper bathroom and lavatory instead of having to make do with the fly-infested bucket in the outhouse. And she was ready to turf the cows out if it meant she could have a decent kitchen.

We walked along a long stone passage from the byre into the farmhouse's central hall.

'The kitchen's here, m'am,' Stanley Blake said.

When we looked all we could see was a huge open fireplace with implements of various kinds slung over the hearth. A large blackened kettle was steaming gently over the fire.

'We do all our cooking here,' Stanley Blake explained. 'All the cooking we need to do anyway. This room is called the Middle Kitchen.'

When – in November 1951 – we finally moved in, we brought some builders from Surrey and my mother got both a new kitchen, where the cows had been, as well as a bathroom in the old hay loft, but on the whole the changes we made were minimal.

The one I most regret is the loss of the bake oven in the Blakes' Middle Kitchen, which was demolished in order to make room for a window, the room otherwise being rather sombre.

Happily there is a second bake oven in the room at the east end of the house known as the Back Kitchen. This is the room where I (occasionally) work and where we have, miraculously, installed a broadband connection for the computer. I wonder what the Blakes would have made of that. Maybe they would have taken it in their stride. After all, even in those days West Nethercote had a telephone, on a line which we shared with neighbouring Staddon Farm. If you picked up the phone to find the other party already engaged in conversation, you might exchange pleasantries before replacing the receiver to try again later.

The Back Kitchen also had – and still has – a stone staircase leading to the upper floor of the house. When we first came, this was the only way of going upstairs, but our clever builders from Surrey made a decent job of putting an extra staircase in the centre of the house. Having that second staircase made all the difference if you were playing sardines or murder in the dark.

The dairy, which we inspected next, was sandwiched between the Middle Kitchen and the Back Kitchen. A small stream ran through it.

'Keeps it cool, mind,' Stanley Blake explained.

On heavy slabs of slate a couple of pans of milk were cooling. Later, my mother would herself learn how to make clotted cream by skimming the thick crust from the surface after the milk had been brought almost to the boil. But this was never a major enterprise. Though, when my mother was still alive, and some of my own children mischievously hand-painted a sign which said *'Granny's Cream Teas!'* and placed it in a position where it would attract the attention of dedicated hikers, the reality was different. We were not in the dairy business.

We took over a couple of milking cows from the Blakes but I doubt if we would have kept them on if it hadn't been for Arthur who, with much cussing and swearing, could usually manage to fill a frothing pail or two, though I suspect the hygiene inspector, if he had ever chosen to visit, might have had a thing or two to say about the facilities.

Arthur was the gardener, or handyman, whom we had brought with us from Surrey to Somerset. Even then he was well into his seventies. He had fought with the Royal Warwickshire Fusiliers in the First World War and still wore the regimental beret with a cap badge, which he polished weekly. Quite why Arthur agreed to make the move from the Home Counties to Somerset I never understood. He had a 'lady friend' who, he told me, had not been at all keen to lose him to the wilds of Exmoor. Nor, to tell the truth, were his living circumstances on the farm particularly luxurious.

We converted a nearby outbuilding for him and christened it 'Arthur's house'. It didn't have a bath or a shower, though we managed to install a WC in the cubbyhole, which had previously housed the communal latrine.

Arthur came to the kitchen door to collect his meals on a tray, his faithful dog, Shep, at his heel. Since he always knocked to announce his arrival, our own dogs would bark wildly at the intruders until my father shouted at them to keep quiet. This little ritual was repeated three times a day, except on Sundays, when my father would take Arthur down to the Royal Oak in the village around noon and then bring him back home to have lunch with us in the kitchen.

Arthur also came into the house on Tuesday evening to have his weekly bath.

One day, after he had been with us on Exmoor for about five years, Arthur told my father that his 'old lady' was 'being rather pressing' and that he had decided to go back to Surrey. He must have been nearing eighty by then, so we could all understand that if he and the old lady were going to make a go of it in the end, it wouldn't do to wait too long.

I don't think my parents heard from him after he left, though my father, visiting Surrey one day, made some enquiries as to his whereabouts. Nor am I sure what happened to Shep.

As to the outbuilding where Arthur lived, it has finally received an upgrade. We have installed a shower, rebuilt the walls and the roof and it is now totally presentable. There are even a couple of storage heaters. We still call it 'Arthur's house'. If I want to be somewhere where I can't be interrupted – no email, no telephone – that is where I go.

Arthur had brought his twelve-bore with him when we moved from Surrey to Somerset. My father, soon after we took over the farm, bought me a .410. On summer evenings during the school holidays when his chores were over, Arthur and I would walk up the farm, looking for rabbits. In those pre-myxomatosis days, it is amazing how many rabbits there were. You'd round a corner, peek across a hedge and see literally hundreds of white tails running for cover. You couldn't miss even with a .410. Fried rabbit and onions made a frequent appearance at high tea.

I say 'high tea' deliberately. We didn't do dinner, unless, as was the custom in the country, by dinner you meant lunch. High tea was at six o'clock. The theory was that by getting the last meal of the day under your belt early, you could profit from the long hours of daylight (in summer at least) to get on with farm jobs of various kinds, like turning the hay in the meadows or mending gaps in the fences.

In practice, I couldn't help observing as a child that having high tea as opposed to supper or dinner simply meant that my father had more time to go to the pub.

I once made a remark to this effect to my mother as she cleared up the kitchen one evening, my father having long since departed to some nearby hostelry.

'The men have to go to the pub,' she told me. 'That's where you meet people if you want to get something done on the farm or if you need to find out what's going on in the sheep or cattle markets.'

'What about the telephone?' I asked. 'Can't Daddy use the phone?'

My mother shook her head. 'Daddy doesn't like using the phone. He'd much prefer to go to the pub.'

It seemed rather hit and miss to me but I could see that, from my father's point of view, it was a system which worked. When you are a farmer you are in the nature of things on hand all day, so you have to be able to get out of the house in the evening, particularly if there's a risk you might be called on to join in a family game of Scrabble, Monopoly or Cluedo.

I have no doubt that my father was a serious drinker. He would reach the pub by, say, 7.00 or 7.30 and stay there well past closing time. On Exmoor, closing time was notional anyway. Those who remained in the bar after the landlord had called time knew the form. You could stay into the small hours and my father very often did. The only difference was that once the shutters had come down and you were snug around the fire, you tended to order whisky rather than beer for the next round.

My father once explained it to me. 'After eight or ten pints, a chap has probably had enough beer for the evening, so he may want to move on to something stronger. Besides, there's more in it for the landlord.'

The landlords of the Royal Oak, Winsford, or the similarly named establishment in Withypool, or the Crown or White Horse in Exford, or the Sportsman's Inn at Sandyway (all places which my father frequented when he needed to 'talk to a man about a dog' or whatever) in practice ran very little risk of falling foul of the law even if they stayed open all night. There were very few policemen around on Exmoor and those that were around turned a resolutely blind eye.

The situation, I am glad to say, doesn't seem to have changed much even with the introduction of the drink-driving laws. The chances of being breathalysed by a police patrol on the short stretch of road between Winsford and the beginning of our drive when you turn over the bridge to follow the track up to Nethercote must be next to zero.

Admittedly, my father did once drive off the bridge into the river at Christmas one year after a longish evening in the pub.

Jenny and I were by then living in the farmhouse and my parents had moved into the cottage, Nethercote Cottage, which is now occupied by my sister Birdie. Well after midnight, we heard a Land Rover drive into the yard. The blazing headlights lit up the landing where, in days gone by, we used to store the fleeces after shearing.

'Your father's gone in the river,' Mike Winzer, son of a neighbouring farmer, shouted as we opened the upstairs window and leaned out to see what was going on. 'We've pulled him out all right though. We were worried the police would see the tail-lights of his car sticking out of the water!'

Later, Mike described the episode to me in greater detail.

'I 'appened to drive up behind Father as 'ee was getting ready to cross the bridge. I could see 'im hesitating, lining 'imself up, like, if you follow me. So I jumped out and walked over and asked 'im, "Are you sure you're all right?"'

'Father took one look at me,' Mike continued. '"I'm quite all right, thank you", he said. 'Then he drove straight off the side of the bridge into the river. The water was flowing fast that night and father got his foot stuck under the pedal. Might 'ave drowned. We had the devil of a job getting him out.'

My father had a different take on that particular event. 'I would have been quite okay if Mike Winzer hadn't driven up behind me like that and put me off my stroke!'

THREE

Early Days at Nethercote

That summer afternoon in early July 1951 when I first saw West Nethercote was the beginning of a lifetime of memories. Sometimes, when I look at the house, I can see it as it was then. We have, I am afraid, converted the dairy into a downstairs lavatory-cum-laundry room. The pans of milk no longer sit on the great slate slabs and the stream which used to keep the little room cool has been diverted elsewhere. But even now I can see my mother, skimmer in hand, coaxing the thick crust of cream into a jug. She never expected to be a farmer's wife but, with typical gusto, she turned her hand to whatever was needed.

When we converted the dairy, we rescued one of the slate slabs where the milk used to cool. Chris How, the builder from the village who has known our house almost as long as I have, suggested we use it as a hearth stone in the Middle Kitchen. It fits perfectly. One day I want to have it inscribed with the words *BENEDICITE OMNIA OPERA*, which could be roughly translated as '*Let all of creation bless the Lord!*' That is the way I feel about Nethercote.

As a matter of fact my mother's sister, Den, who often came to stay with us during those early years at Nethercote, used precisely those words for the great kneeler which she wove for the Church of St Bartholomew-the-Great at Smithfield in London. Den was a loyal member of the congregation there for many years and, being a considerable artist, was only too happy to contribute in this way when the call went up for the old kneeler to be renewed.

It is a long time since I have been to St Barts, but the last time I was there Den's kneeler was still in place. As I remember, Den wove a pattern of birds, beasts and flowers to exemplify the Benedicite's injunction. At the very centre of the kneeler, which I suppose must be forty or fifty feet long, she placed a painstakingly embroidered picture of West Nethercote farmhouse. I wonder how many communicants, as they kneel before the altar, hands outstretched to 'receive these Thy creatures of bread and wine', have asked themselves why a traditional Somerset longhouse should be thus represented in a famous London church.

Den also painted a wonderful picture of the 'front' of the house, in other words the side which looks out at the River Exe across a small field known as The Splat. (For us children, learning the many centuries-old field names of our new property was a pleasure in store, one made easier by the large-scale 1905 Ordnance Survey map of the farm which the Blakes handed over.) Den's painting of Nethercote from the front must date from our first few months there because the Middle Kitchen's huge chimneybreast that my parents pierced to add a window is at that moment still intact.

Den painted other pictures of Nethercote over the years, including a fetching study of Birdie reading in the garden. She also painted a less successful study of the track leading up to some of our rough ground 'on top'. She always maintained that, while working on this picture, she was threatened by our huge Red Devon bull and in the end had to abandon the task before she had properly finished it.

My mother was Den's older sister. A couple of years separated them. They both went to Cheltenham Ladies' College but Den, by her own admission, hated her time there, whereas my mother thrived. When my mother went on to Oxford, Den went to art school. In later years, when the pressures of farming had eased, my mother and Den twice went to the West Indies for extended periods where Den would paint while my mother worked on a memoir about life on Exmoor. Over the years, the manuscript was submitted to various publishers but it never attracted an offer. It had various titles. Off-hand I can remember three of them: *From Ladies' College to Exmoor Farm*; *Pitch-forked into Deep Litter*; *Alas, Poor Johnny!* There might have been others. My mother was an incurable optimist. She might have invented the saying 'If at first you don't succeed, try, try and try again'. More than once she submitted her manuscript under a different title to a publisher who had already rejected it.

'You never know your luck, darling,' she would say.

I can see her now, rifling through the mail to see if an acceptance letter had arrived, hoping all the while that her luck had turned. In truth, her book deserved to be published. It was funny, informative and well written.

In our first years on the farm, the Exford postman actually came in person to the kitchen door, walking miles to deliver what might turn out to be a pools coupon from Littlewoods. Later, Walter Barwick, who lived in Winsford, took on the job and chugged up the track on a motorcycle in the course of his rounds. There is a splendid photo of Walter, as well as a thumbnail sketch, in the book about Exmoor that my sister Birdie has recently published called *Reflections*. For the last twenty years we haven't seen a postman of any sort. The Royal Mail has simply refused to go those extra miles. Instead the postman parks at the bridge and leaves our letters in a box at the end of the track.

The box is easy to open. It is a convenient place for storing your wellington boots when you leave the farm and want to wear something smarter in, say, Taunton or Exeter. If we are not on Exmoor for any length of time, the mail can mount up in the box. I sometimes wish passers-by would help themselves to the juicier items, such as communications from the Inland Revenue.

I haven't spoken of the land that went with the house. Actually, I've got that wrong. On Exmoor in those days land didn't go with the house. The house went with the land. The land was what counted. The house was thrown in. A farm had to have a house, otherwise where would the farmer live? But when you were sizing up a place, wondering how much to offer, or how much to bid at auction, if it came to that, the state of the house was fairly low on your list of priorities.

West Nethercote, with its 250 acres of hill land (including 100 acres of rough grazing known as 'the brakes'), cost my parents £4500 in 1951, a few hundred pounds more than the sum they received when they sold their house in Surrey. I don't have the particulars of the sale. I'm not sure the place was ever advertised. I think my father's sudden dash into west Somerset on his motorcycle meant that he got his bid in before others got wind of the opportunity. But I am certain, even if the place had been advertised, that in those days the farmhouse itself would have barely rated a small paragraph.

Ernest Blake took over from his brother Stanley for our tour of the land that day. He set off at a cracking pace up the steep lane known as Fuzzball (or Furzeball, an accepted variant). The path was rocky and heavily overhung with gorse. It was also steep.

'The farmhouse is at around nine hundred and sixty feet,' Ernest told us, as we panted after him. 'But the land rises to almost twelve hundred feet.'

To a ten-year-old like me the hills we climbed that afternoon seemed more like mountains. We wound our way up Fuzzball, then headed straight up – or so it seemed – on what was called the Staddon side of the farm to the top land from which you could see Dunkery Beacon, the highest point on Exmoor, and the Bristol Channel beyond. Once we reached the top, we paused.

'What's the name of this field?' My father gestured at the long rectangular expanse, newly mown, in which we found ourselves.

'This 'un's called Staddon Nine Acres,' Ernest Blake replied.

My father looked left and right. The ground was almost flat.

'You could land a plane here,' he said.

It wasn't the only time he talked about landing a plane on the farm. I think he saw it, one day, as a serious possibility, though that day never arrived. If you had asked him to describe the happiest days of his life, I'm fairly sure he would have put his years with the RAF high on the list.

That afternoon, of course, everything was much more down to earth. We were due to move in only a few months later. It was all very well to have pipe dreams about building an airstrip in one of the top fields. In reality, there were a large number of important practical decisions to be taken. How many sheep and cattle would we buy from the Blakes? Would the ewes all be in lamb when we took over? What was the water situation? The River Exe ran through the valley, but what about the high ground?

The 250-acre farm we bought in 1951 was oddly configured. The Staddon side, which we had reached by climbing up Fuzzball, was separated from the Nethercote side by a tongue of land, belonging to East Nethercote, the neighbouring farm. East Nethercote also owned some rough land on the other side of the river known as the Warren, as well as some pasture along the farm track leading in from the Winsford–Exford road. And it had grazing rights on Bye Common, lying south of the river.

When we reached a suitable vantage point, about halfway to the top, Ernest Blake pointed out the lie of the land.

'We're on West Nethercote land now, but the fields in the middle there' – he waved his hand in a westerly direction – 'belong to East Nethercote. They're known as The Slades. They'm Victor Stevens'. But if you go beyond 'em, there's West Nethercote land again.'

I'm not sure I absorbed all the topographical details that first afternoon, but it didn't take long to work out who owned what. When we moved in a few months later, we got to know Victor Stevens well. Unmarried, he lived with his widowed mother. In 1956, my parents bought East Nethercote from them, thereby adding another 120 acres to our land and acquiring a second farmhouse and outbuildings. In fact, Victor Stevens and his mother didn't move far. They bought a house at Larcombe Foot, on the Exford–Winsford road, which is where the Exe finally emerges from the Nethercote valley. For years, the Stevens very kindly allowed Dulverton laundry to use their garage as a storage place for their deliveries to Nethercote.

Now both Victor Stevens and his mother have died and the house at Larcombe Foot has changed hands a number of times. The new owners are not keen to take in our dirty laundry, if only in transit as it were, so we take it to the village shop instead, where it waits for collection.

Around the time we bought East Nethercote we also bought from the Ministry of Agriculture 128 acres of rough land known as Room Hill, bringing our total holding on Exmoor to around 500 acres. This latter acquisition resulted from a confused situation in which the Ministry of Agriculture sought to dispose of land which it had gained through compulsory purchase a few years earlier.

Nethercote, owing to the proximity of our land to Room Hill, had a good claim to be considered as a serious purchaser, but the case had to be made. I remember that my father complained vigorously about having to dig his suit out of mothballs and go to London to talk to the man from the ministry in Whitehall, but he obviously made a splendid job of it since we acquired the Room Hill land for the staggeringly low figure, as it seems today, of £250.

Having Room Hill as part of our Exmoor holding brought us then, as it still does today, enormous joy. To get to Room Hill you go through the meadows along the river in the direction of 'the brakes'. You cross the river at the ford, to see a long, looming crag on your left. In the autumn, when the bracken has turned and the rowan trees in all their rumbustious orange-scarlet glory are crowding the slopes beneath the jagged line of rocks which leads up to the summit, Room Hill can be astonishingly beautiful. Its north slope is almost sheer. Long Combe, the western boundary, is the limit of our land on the south side of the river, a favourite haunt of red deer. As children we called it 'Deer Valley'.

From the flat land at the top of Room Hill you can look north and see the whole of Nethercote and, beyond Nethercote, the moors around Dunkery. Winsford Hill lies behind you and, deep in the valley of the Barle, a mile or so away, lies the picturesque village of Withypool. In the Royal Oak, the Withypool pub, a framed letter of thanks behind the bar records the visit of General Dwight D. Eisenhower, when he was Supreme Allied Commander during the Second World War.

My father always maintained that if he went to the pub in Withypool on his horse, Ranger, a 17.1-hand chestnut, no matter how much he (my father) drank and no matter how dark the night was, Ranger could find his own way back, down Room Hill's rough track, to ford the river and finally head home through the meadows.

To me, a somewhat stocky if not chubby ten-year-old, Ranger did indeed seem enormous. One hand, I knew, was four inches wide, so 17 x 4 made 68 plus one made 69, divided by 12 made five foot nine! And that was just at the withers. When Ranger lifted his huge head into the air at the end of his unconscionably long neck, he loomed above you like a colossal dinosaur, frighteningly large. You needed a stepladder to climb on board.

Talking of horses, one of the first things my parents did when we finally took possession of Nethercote that autumn of 1951 was to buy ponies for those of us children who wanted one. My brother, Peter, declined (he was happier with a chess set), but my sister Hilary and I acquired Chips and Bracken respectively. Birdie had a small Dartmoor pony known as Muffet.

Apart from Ranger, we also had Peter, a large cob, whom we used for the heavy work, such as pulling the farm cart or the hay wagon.

Peter's back was so broad that when, as a child, I rode him I had the sensation of doing the splits.

There was also Kismet, a magnificent Arab, which belonged to B. B. (her full name was Beatrice) had joined us almost as soon as we moved in that first November to help on the farm. I stress the words 'on the farm'. Her family had lived in the country quite near us in Surrey. B. herself, an outdoors enthusiast, had set her heart on a career involving animals, preferably horses. The opportunity to help out at Nethercote was from her point of view too good to miss.

I was eleven when I first met B. and she is still a friend today. She has known Nethercote as long as I have and she knew both my parents over several decades. Her husband-to-be, John, came to Nethercote our first summer there and persuaded her to marry him.

I remember my mother telling us at breakfast one morning that she had been kept awake half the night because B. and John, sitting and talking till the small hours in their car, somehow managed to sound the horn from time to time.

As a result of John Paine's successful suit, B. stayed with us on that first occasion less than a year, before leaving to be married, though both she and her family have been regular visitors since then.

A few years ago B.'s life took a tragic turn when one of her sons shot his father, John, and then turned the gun on himself. I attended John Paine's funeral in Lydd, during which B. showed immense grace under pressure (she had lost a son as well as a husband) and Michael Howard, a friend of the family and local MP, gave a moving address to a packed congregation.

Soon after the funeral, B. came down to Nethercote for a couple of days.

'You see, Stan,' she told me as I drove her around the farm. 'This place is so tremendously special and it means so much to me.'

As we drove up through the fields where she had once herded sheep, she reminded me of the manner in which she had first reached Nethercote.

'I put Kismet on the train. I stayed with him in his compartment all through the night to make sure he kept calm until we reached Dulverton around seven o'clock the next morning. Then we rode out onto the platform, through Dulverton and up over Winsford Hill. Kismet went straight as an arrow over the moor, then down over Bye Common into Nethercote and that, of course, was the first time I saw the place.'

I'm not sure if First Great Western allows you to put horses on the train any longer; it's difficult enough loading a bicycle. And, following the review of the structure of British Railways which Dr Richard Beeching carried out for the government in 1963, the Taunton–Dulverton–Barnstaple line has been closed, as has the Exe Valley line which used to follow the course of the River Exe downstream from Dulverton to Exeter. Dulverton station has been turned into second homes.

The full Johnson posse, as such, did not have many outings. As far as I can recall, the last time we all rode out together was on Christmas Day 1951.

It was a brilliant sunny day. After Christmas lunch, my father suggested that as many of us as had mounts should go for a ride. A French girl, called Minouche, was living with us as an au pair at the time. She was confident that she could handle Ranger, large as he was, so my father let her borrow his horse. Hilary rode her pony, Chips, and I rode Bracken, while Birdie (still not seven years old – she was born on 27 December 1944) was helped onto the little Dartmoor, Muffet. My father saddled up the cob, Peter, who, though not the most comfortable of rides, was certainly well up to his weight. B., as was to be expected, rode Kismet, who danced and pranced and looked altogether magnificent.

'Keep an eye out for Birdie, B., won't you?' my father called as we headed off along the meadows, splashed through the ford, then up Room Hill, before cutting back towards Bye Common along a tract of land known as Norway, which lies more or less directly opposite Nethercote, on the other side of the valley.

You know how it is when you're riding. Your horse, which may have been fairly sluggish at the start, looking grumpy with ears laid back, seems to pick up a bit of speed when he thinks you're heading for home. You start to trot, then trot turns into a canter and before you know it you're out of control.

That, at any rate, is my analysis of what happened. Once we turned onto Norway, Muffet decided that the stable at Nethercote where, she hoped, a bucket of oats awaited would be her next stop. Birdie yanked at the bit to no avail. As the saying goes, Muffet had the bit between her teeth. She knew what she wanted and she was going to get it.

Muffet went faster and faster and we could all of us see it was only a matter of time before Birdie fell off. In the meantime, B. was thundering up on Kismet and might, just conceivably, have grabbed Muffet's reins, if Minouche on Ranger hadn't just at that moment barged by at speed.

I could hear my father shouting, 'Look out, you silly French cow!'

Actually, I'm not sure whether the word he used was 'cow' but it definitely began with a 'c'.

He was too late. Birdie fell off Muffet right into Ranger's path. Ranger crashed on, Minouche still aboard. She may or may not have heard my father's insults. Meanwhile, Birdie lay curled up motionless on the track.

It was certainly a bad moment. B., agile as a circus acrobat, leapt from Kismet's back. She cradled Birdie's head while my father pounded up on the cob. Hilary and I did our best to bring our own mounts to order. Minouche was nowhere to be seen.

As it turned out, Birdie was winded but not concussed. Miraculously, Ranger's flailing hoofs had totally missed her.

When we got home, my mother took Minouche's side. Hearing my father's account of the day's drama and sensing his determination to send Minouche back home to France then and there, she urged caution.

'Why on earth did you let her ride Ranger in the first place?' she said.

At which point my father muttered something under his breath. My mother wasn't as deaf then as she later became.

'There's no point calling her a silly f***ing French bitch, Johnny. That doesn't help!' And then she added, pointedly, 'If some of you had stayed behind to help me with the washing-up after Christmas lunch, maybe this wouldn't have happened.'

So Minouche stayed, though she never rode Ranger again. Birdie kept Muffet for a few years but, after a while, gave up riding. I am sure that Christmas Day experience had something to do with this.

FOUR

'Come and see me in my study after prayers'

I first arrived at Ravenswood School in the winter term of 1948, when I was just eight. I stayed there until the end of 1953, when I went on to Sherborne at the age of thirteen.

I know that boarding prep schools nowadays have a bad press. There is a school of thought that believes it is harsh, even cruel, to send children away for two-thirds of the year, with only letters and the occasional visit to substitute for the tender loving care a parent can provide.

Personally, I don't remember being miserable at the prospect of leaving home. On the contrary, I was intrigued by the preparations being made. My mother received the school uniform list from the outfitters in Exeter and seemed to spend much of that last summer holiday sewing nametapes even on minor items, like socks and garters. Not being much of a seamstress, she complained quite loudly at the work involved. I suspect she was not alone in this.

My father was responsible for producing a tuck box. The joining instructions specified that every boy had to have such an item. In my case, it was an old toolbox, whose contents my father had transferred elsewhere. On the outside he attached a metal plate and banged out my name (S. P. JOHNSON), using a hammer and heavy-duty nail. This is not as easy as it sounds and the typography left something to be desired.

Sixty years later, I still have that tuck box. I keep it in the Back Kitchen at Nethercote, on top of another larger tuck box, which is full of papers my elder sister, Hilary, left behind when she emigrated to Australia in 1969 and which she has promised to sort out one day.

Quite recently, I had reason to lift the lid, literally, on the past.

I was invited in May 2004 to appear on the TV programme *Have I Got News for You?* The chairman that particular evening was William

Hague, former leader of the Conservative Party, and Ian Hislop and Paul Merton were there as the regular stars of the show. My fellow guest was an attractive young woman called Claudia Winkleman.

On the whole, it seemed to me, the event passed off quite well. Claudia managed, hilariously, to describe the finer points of fellatio during her first intervention. My own performance also had its moments. At one stage William Hague asked if any of us knew how many houses the (then) Deputy Prime Minister, John Prescott, was planning to build in the South-East. I'd seen a story about that when I read the newspaper on the train coming up to London, so I pressed my buzzer and shot up my hand as well and said, 'Four hundred thousand!'

'Stanley, you're brilliant!' Hague commented. After that I decided I was quite enjoying the evening.

Exactly a week after the show, I received a letter forwarded to me from Boris's office in the House of Commons. (I should explain that Alexander Boris, my oldest son, in later life became an MP. Most recently, in 2008, he was elected Mayor of London, defeating the incumbent, Ken Livingstone, after a hard-fought campaign.)

The letter I received out of the blue in the early summer of 2004 read as follows: 'Dear Boris, is the Stanley Johnson who recently appeared on *Have I Got News for You*? by any chance your father? If so, is he the same Stanley Johnson who wrote to Winston Churchill when he won the 1951 election? That Stanley Johnson got a letter back which he proudly showed around the school!'

The letter was signed 'Philip Cooke'.

I vaguely remembered Philip Cooke as one of my prep school contemporaries. And I definitely remembered the thrill of listening to the general election results in October 1951 as they came in. The head-master brought a wireless and the whole school assembled in the panelled hall, where we normally had prayers or played basketball and ran inter-house relay races when it was too wet to go outside. The four houses were named after Britain's imperial heroes: Rhodes, Rodney, Gordon, Nelson. I was in Rhodes house.

There was no doubting our political affiliation. We all whooped with excitement as the '*Conservative Gains!*' were announced.

It wasn't an overwhelming Conservative victory but, following the inroads the Conservatives had made in the previous year's election, it was enough to ensure that Winston Churchill, at the ripe old age of seventy-five, once more received the seals of office.

Next day, as Winston moved in to No. 10 Downing Street, whence he had been summarily ejected by an ungrateful nation in 1945 at the end of the Second World War, I decided to write him a letter of support and encouragement.

'Dear Mr Churchill,' I began, 'I would like to offer you my sincerest congratulations on your recent election victory ...'

When I had finished I walked down to the end of the drive and posted the letter in the box located halfway down the road, which led from the school gates into Stoodleigh village.

Looking back, I realize that this was possibly the first time I formally identified myself with the Conservatives. In later life I have met people who say they sometimes think before voting. They say they like to know what the different parties have to offer, so that they can make their own considered judgement before they exercise their democratic rights in the voting booth. That is not my way. Ever since Churchill won that autumn election in 1951, I have been a Conservative. My reasoning was simple: Churchill saved the country and probably the world. He was a mega-hero. That was enough for me. It still is. I find it hard to imagine the circumstances in which I would change the habit of a lifetime. For me, there is something deep down, instinctive, almost atavistic about this. It's like supporting Oxford, rather than Cambridge, in the Boat Race.

One day, about a fortnight after I had written my letter to the new Prime Minister, Mr Schuster, Ravenswood's headmaster, made an announcement at assembly: 'Would Johnson minor come and see me in my study after prayers?'

Such a summons usually meant trouble. The headmaster's study was an oak-panelled room, leading off the assembly hall. The main feature of the room was a large desk. Two heavily bound volumes were placed at the front corners of the desk as it faced into the room. One volume was entitled *The Glory That Was Greece*. The other was called *The Grandeur That Was Rome*. I can't remember the author's name, but I do remember the springy, willowy cane which spanned the two volumes in much the same way as the Verrazano Bridge guards the entrance to New York Harbour.

'Come in, Johnson,' Schuster called, when I knocked at the door.

As I entered, I could see that he had a thick white envelope in his hand. I could make out the words '10 Downing Street' in heavily embossed black type on the back of the envelope.

'I see you've been writing to the Prime Minister,' Schuster said. 'I don't remember giving you permission. And how did you send it? I've checked with Miss Nicholson. She says she never mailed a letter to Downing Street when she collected up all the letters on Sunday for posting.'

Miss Nicholson was the school secretary who also taught French to the upper forms. I knew she was a trusted ally of the headmaster and there was no point in pretending she had dispatched my letter unwittingly.

Eyes fixed on the cane in front of me, I confessed: 'I walked into the village, sir, to post it.'

'You know that's out of bounds,' Schuster hissed. He paused. I could see him weighing matters up.

'I'll let you off this time,' he said finally. 'But don't make a habit of writing to Mr Churchill. The country will grind to a halt if the Prime Minister has to spend all his time answering letters from boys like you.'

'Thank you, sir!' I grabbed the letter from the headmaster's outstretched hand and made a quick exit.

Thinking about that little episode fifty-three years later brought a blush to my cheeks. It wasn't much fun being beaten by Schuster. Why on earth had I run the risk?

I put Philip Cooke's letter down, walked across the room, cleared some debris off the top of my old prep school tuck box and opened the lid. If Churchill's letter was going to be anywhere, this was the place.

Over the years I have tossed a lot of documents into that tuck box. Finding things in it is a bit like the great Schliemann's excavation of Troy. You have to lift off layer after layer. Each discovery may be more precious than the last.

The Churchill letter was right at the bottom. It was still in its envelope. I had remembered the heavy Downing Street crest on the reverse side, but I had forgotten the stamp on the front of the envelope, which said 'First Lord of the Treasury'.

I pulled out the letter. 'The Prime Minister', I read, 'has asked me to send you his warm thanks for your good wishes.'

The letter, from the Prime Minister's Private Secretary, was dated 9 November 1951. The election had been held less than two weeks earlier. The communication might not, strictly speaking, have been from Winston Churchill himself but I had absolutely no doubt that he had personally authorized the reply.

Well, I thought, if Philip Cooke recalled that I had gone around the school boasting about my coup, he no doubt remembered things correctly.

By some strange irony, it turned out that Philip Cooke lived in Newton Abbot. Soon after I received his letter, I found myself in the running as a possible Conservative candidate for the Teignbridge constituency, a Devon seat whose main population centre was Newton Abbot.

My attempt to win the Conservative nomination was successful, though I subsequently failed to capture the seat from its Liberal Democrat incumbent in the May 2005 general election. At this point all I need to say is that when the chairman of the selection committee asked me how long I had been a supporter of the Conservative Party I was able to give the precise answer.

'Since October 1951,' I said, 'and I have a letter from Winston Churchill himself to prove it!'

Later, during the course of the election campaign, when I was being driven in my 'Battle Bus' around Newton Abbot, I called on Philip Cooke. He lived high up on a hill in the middle of town, with a wonderful view over Newton Abbot Racecourse.

'I'm so glad you reminded me about that Churchill letter,' I told him. 'Gave me a great line for the selection committee.'

'Any time, old boy. We old Ravenswoodians must stick together.'

FIVE

My Mother Didn't Often Wear a Hat

I should like to be able to report that Ravenswood is still going strong, but that is not the case.

As the years have rolled on, life has not been kind to boarding prep schools located more than two hundred miles from London. Parents seem ever less inclined to send their children long distances from home with only occasional visits being practicable. They are also perhaps more sceptical of the merits of boarding prep schools, no matter where they are located, and possibly more confident of their own parenting skills.

The last time I visited Ravenswood was when I had to call on a local osteopath who, as it happened, had his surgery in his own house in Stoodleigh, a stone's throw from the school gates. I had put my back out leaning awkwardly across the newly laid slate hearthstone to lift a large log onto the open fire in the Middle Kitchen. The osteopath worked his magic and with time to spare I decided to visit the old school.

I parked the car by the gates and walked down the drive. The house, formally known as Stoodleigh Court, was a huge mock-Elizabethan construction, built in the 1920s, with tall windows giving out onto a rose garden on one side and a Devon panorama on the other. Scrunching across the gravel, I peered in through a window to see whether the oak-panelled hall was still there. It was. I could imagine the eighty or ninety boys lined up in front of the dais, waiting for the headmaster to welcome them back at the beginning of the new term. *Lord, behold us with thy blessing, once again assembled here!*

I examined the panels at long range. In my days they had been inscribed with the Ravenswood 'Roll of Honour', captains of the school, winners of scholarships, star athletes – that kind of thing. High up above the panels, I remembered, the hall had been circled by a line of armorial crests, which Miss Nicholson, a jill of all trades, had painstakingly painted on a series of miniature heraldic shields.

During school prayers, or on other occasions when we were gathered in the hall, I used to study those crests closely for want of anything better to do. Each one depicted the armorial bearings of one of Britain's leading public, i.e. private, schools (there were around fifty of them). Miss Nicholson had even added the relevant school motto. Even now, when I meet an alumnus of one of those schools, I am often able – to his evident surprise – to give a description of his school's coat of arms and an accurate rendering of the school's motto.

I myself was destined for Sherborne, so my eye would stray to the place, high above the huge fireplace, where Sherborne's coat of arms was emblazoned. You could clearly read the words '*Dieu et mon droit*' on the gilded scroll.

Miss Nicholson had a habit of speaking quietly, almost in a whisper. 'Sherborne has the royal coat of arms and motto because Edward VI founded the school – in 1550. He also founded Shrewsbury, which is why Sherborne and Shrewsbury have identical coats of arms. So I had to paint that one twice.'

Sometimes in his address to leavers Mr Schuster would refer to the great transition they would be making as they left Ravenswood for the world of the public school.

'Tett will be leaving for Oundle,' he would say, gesturing in the direction of Miss Nicholson's heraldic frieze, 'Hopkins will be going on to Canford.' Another wave at the wall of honour. 'Smith, Jones and Batten will all be going on to Blundell's ...'

Since Blundell's was just down the road in Tiverton the fact that several boys would be heading there made sense but I had the feeling that Mr Schuster yearned, one day, to be able to announce that a boy from Ravenswood had won a scholarship to Eton.

That particular triumph didn't happen in my time. I'm not sure it ever happened. The reality was that Ravenswood was a good prep school, at least from my point of view. But it wasn't in the same league as, say, the Dragon School in Oxford.

Standing there on the gravel, I peered through the glass darkly. The Roll of Honour had been obliterated. Though the oak panels were still there, the gold lettering had been removed. And there was absolutely no sign of the heraldic crests.

What a shame! I thought. What a crying shame! Miss Nicholson had put so much effort into getting each and every last detail right. Then someone comes along and rips it all down!

'Bloody hell!' I muttered to myself, only to feel a hand on my shoulder.

'Can I help you, sir? I'm the caretaker. The place is closed at the moment.'

When I explained what I was doing, the man was perfectly friendly. 'The school closed down years ago,' he said. 'It's a conference centre now.'

We talked for a while and I calmed down. As I walked back up the drive, I reflected on the fact that altogether I had passed five years at Ravenswood. Even with the increases in longevity that recent generations have witnessed, five years is still a significant proportion of the (average) life span. Were those years well spent?

Academically, I would say that Ravenswood did me proud. Though I took the Sherborne Scholarship Exam without success during my last year at prep school, I made up for that by winning an Open Scholarship at Sherborne in the summer term of 1954, soon after I had arrived, and I am sure that this success had to be ascribed at least in part to the sound preparation Ravenswood had provided.

Much of the credit must, I believe, go to R. L. Schuster himself. He carried a heavy teaching load because he took most of the classes in both Latin and Greek. And it wasn't just a question of teaching the sixth form in those subjects. I began Latin during my first term at prep school and Greek shortly afterwards. In fact, if I look back at my school days, both prep and public school, it seems to me that a very large proportion of my time was spent on Latin and Greek.

I calculated when I went up to Oxford that something like 80 per cent of all the tuition I had received at school over the years had been in Greek and Latin and a large proportion of the rest had been spent on Ancient History or Divinity. It didn't seem particularly odd at the time – I stayed with the Classics for almost half my Oxford career, which included taking Classical Honour Moderations, or Mods, still – I believe – the longest exam (with sixteen three-hour papers) ever set, except possibly for the tests given to mandarins wanting to join the Chinese civil service in the days of the Qing emperors.

34

That said, it does in retrospect seem a trifle bizarre that I was not at any point asked to demonstrate any proficiency in a scientific subject – Physics, Chemistry, Biology or whatever. I didn't sit any O levels in these subjects. I certainly didn't sit any science A levels. Since much of my subsequent career as an environmentalist has involved dealing with scientific issues, I have learned to see the oddities in what seemed to me at the time a wholly normal approach to education.

The Glory That Was Greece! The Grandeur That Was Rome! Mr Schuster, I have to say, laid the foundations of my love of the Classics. As a ten-year-old I learned about the tyrannicides Harmodios and Aristogeiton. I heard about Cimon and Solon, Xerxes and Darius. He didn't skimp on the grammar either. I could recognize the aorist tense at twenty paces as well as a past participle passive.

His great achievement was to make the Classics come alive and he did so without any of the props of the modern classroom. There were no PowerPoint presentations of life in ancient Rome. The nearest we got to a mechanical aid to learning was the production, in Latin, of a newspaper. It was called *Acta Diurna* – Daily Deeds. One issue, I remember, recorded Caesar's arrival in Britain in 55 BC as seen by Joe Bloggs – Josephus Bloggus. We drew diagrams showing how far a centurion could march in a day, the armour he wore and the enormous load he had to carry (it included picks, shovels and bundles of stakes – *sudes* – to make defensive palisades at night).

I ask myself today, as I write this, where Schuster's own love of the Classics came from. I don't know the answer. I know he was a soldier, had fought in North Africa and had been taken prisoner at the fall of Tobruk. Had he taught himself Greek and Latin in prison? Had he graduated before the war with a degree in Classics or at least a classical background enough to tell a gerund from a gerundive? I have no idea and it is too late to ask.

Schuster's co-headmaster, Major Hunter, was a rather different kettle of fish. I don't believe he took any classes, though he coached us at cricket. Like Mr Schuster, he had fought in the North African campaign and had been wounded, with the result that he had a metal plate in his head. His forte, I remember, was describing the Battle of El Alamein, in which he had participated, in great detail. He drew elaborate diagrams on the blackboard, using different coloured chalk to denote General Montgomery's 8th Army on one side and Rommel's desert troops on the other.

'And over here,' Major Hunter would bark, indicating a great expanse of territory to the south, 'is the Qattara Depression. Rommel never anticipated that Monty would swing a long left hook through the Depression. But he did. As Monty himself said, he hit Rommel for six!'

Major Hunter took the same approach, *mutatis mutandis*, to the annual Oxford and Cambridge Boat Race. Once again plentifully supplied with coloured chalk, he would outline the positions of the opposing forces on the blackboard: 'Cambridge has the Surrey Station; Oxford is on the Middlesex side. Provided Oxford can hold off Cambridge's early challenge, they'll have the advantage of the bend as they come down to Barnes Bridge ...'

In much the same way as we had gathered to listen to the results of the general election, we assembled to hear John Snagge reporting breathlessly for the BBC from his unique vantage point just behind the umpire's boat.

'One – Out, Two – Out, Three – Out. My word, Oxford are putting on a spurt now ...'

In those pre-TV days, the radio was the eyes as well as the ears of the nation. Once, famously, Snagge had kept his audience on the edges of their seats by announcing: 'I can't see who's in the lead but it's either Oxford or Cambridge ...!'

As I have already indicated, my letters home from school, whether from Ravenswood or, later, from Sherborne, were never particularly illuminating. They were in fact archetypically Molesworthian. 'Dear Mummy and Daddy, my marks this week were 230, I came 3rd. We played St Aubyns and beat them by six wickets ...'

Sometimes, there were special events, like listening to the Boat Race, which begged for inclusion in the weekly missive. Another such event was the annual meet of the Tiverton foxhounds.

At the beginning of each hunting season, the local hunt met at the school. Boys were recruited to offer sherry to the master, huntsmen and mounted followers. Once hounds had moved off to draw the thickly wooded coverts leading down to the Exe, we were allowed to run after them.

If you stayed with the pack and were lucky and/or persistent enough to be in at the kill, you might be blooded by the huntsman, who would take the fox's severed pad and wipe it across your cheek. On such occasions Matron gave a special dispensation. As we were tucking into our evening meal with the extra enthusiasm that a long and vigorous day in the fresh air can generate, she would announce: 'Boys who have been blooded need not wash their faces before they go to bed.'

One boy, I remember, managed to keep the blood on his face for almost a week. He was a local Devon boy, a farmer's son.

''Tis the way it has to be in the country,' he told me. 'If you wipe t' blood off, it don't work.'

As I look back, it is the sheer ruralness of life at Ravenswood that I remember. All the sounds you heard were country sounds. You would wake up early on a summer morning, even before the bell, and listen to the cooing of wood pigeons. Even now, when I hear the sound of wood pigeons in the morning, I find myself back in the school dorm.

If you were in one of the upper dorms, say Ivanhoe or Talisman (all the school dormitories were named after Walter Scott's novels), and you snuck out of bed and looked out of the window while your schoolmates were still asleep, you could look down on this vast sweep of the Devon countryside. I can see it now. The squat tower of Stoodleigh church in the foreground, the stooks of wheat in the surrounding fields waiting to be gathered in by horse and cart or the occasional tractor and then, in the distance far below, a hint of mist (or was it smoke?) over Tiverton, all of eight miles off.

Each Sunday during term time the school would attend morning service at Stoodleigh church. The vicar would mount the pulpit in his billowing cassock and deliver the traditional sermon. I search my memory and I cannot find any trace of the homilies that I am sure I must have absorbed over the years. What I do find is an abiding sense of peace, the sense of walking through the lychgate, finding a pew, listening to the words of the Book of Common Prayer, singing the hymns from the Ancient and Modern Hymn book.

Harvest Festival was an especially joyous occasion, the little church being decorated with all manner of flowers, fruit and vegetables. The staff of the school helped but this was above all a time when the locals – the farmers and villagers, who were usually heavily outnumbered by the staff and pupils of the school – came into their own. They brought the potatoes, the tomatoes, the giant marrows, which seemed almost to dwarf the altar itself, the sheaves of wheat and oats and barley.

If the school occupied the centre aisle, the village sat over to the left below the pulpit. They received, with quiet nods of the head, the vicar's praise at the gifts brought at harvest time and when it was time to sing the harvest hymns they joined in with gusto.

> Fair waved the golden corn
> In Canaan's pleasant land
> When full of joy one shining morn
> Went forth the reaper band.

Sometimes, in our enthusiasm, we would run ahead of the organ. There was an organ rota each week and, if it was your turn, you climbed into a small cupboard behind the instrument, perched on a chair and pedalled away at the foot pump, which was what kept the air flowing in the pipes. If, absent-mindedly or out of sheer exhaustion, you stopped pedalling, the organist would bang sharply on the wall. One boy called Norris (he had strange sticking-out ears) once simply stopped pedalling altogether in the middle of a hymn. Chaos ensued, even though the vicar gamely tried to keep us all going.

Norris was quite the hero, though he was caned later that day.

'How many did you get, Norris?' we asked him, as he came out of the headmaster's study.

'Six.' Norris winced. I think he wondered at that moment whether the game had been worth the candle.

'What did Schuster say?'

'He said: "This is going to hurt you, Norris, more than it's going to hurt me!"'

I don't want to give the impression that Schuster was a sadist. He certainly wasn't. Yes, he used the cane, but he used it sparingly. I don't suppose I was beaten more than half a dozen times and I am sure that on all those occasions the punishment was richly deserved.

I certainly wasn't unhappy at Ravenswood. I can remember my very first night away from home for the first time listening to a boy in the next bed snivelling.

It was after lights out so I asked him, in a whisper, what the problem was.

'I miss my mummy,' he whimpered.

Well, I'm sure I missed my mummy too, but that didn't seem to be the point. As a matter of fact, I remember my main preoccupation that first night was how to mask the fact that I had gone to bed without untying my shoelaces. I could see my shoes on the floor at the bottom of the bed, laces firmly knotted. Could I manage to ease myself over to them without actually getting out of bed? I attempted the manoeuvre but ended up on the floor with an audible thump.

Matron must have been listening outside the door, because she was there in a trice.

'Why are you out of bed, Johnson?' Amazingly, she knew the names of all the new boys already.

I picked myself up. 'I'm afraid I didn't undo my shoelaces, Matron.'

'Well, do it now and get back into bed. No more talking.'

I wanted to say to the boy in the bed next to me, 'No more snivelling, either', but I didn't. We each of us have our own way of dealing with life's little emergencies.

Quite recently, I have discovered that some of the boys who were at prep school with me in the late forties and early fifties didn't just snivel from time to time; they were actively unhappy.

Paul Johnson, the former editor of the New Statesman, and his wife Marigold have a house on the Quantocks, about forty minutes' drive from Nethercote, where they give an annual New Year's Day lunch whose feature is Marigold's supremely subtle kedgeree. I was in the queue for a second helping a couple of years ago when I felt a light tap on my shoulder.

I turned to see a sandy-haired man about my own age.

'Are you Johnson?' he asked.

'Yes. Who are you?'

And then it came to me. I hadn't seen him for more than fifty years but, as Wordsworth put it, the child is father to the man. Though time had inevitably wrought some changes, the distinguishing features of a face I remembered could still be discerned.

'You're Anderson, aren't you?'

Nicholas Anderson and I had been contemporaries at Ravenswood so quite naturally we took our food into a quiet corner and started talking about the old school.

I don't think I actually used the phrase 'fit for purpose' but that was certainly the gist of my comment. Ravenswood might not have been in the top drawer of prep schools but, as far as I was concerned at least, it had done the job it was intended to do. It had given me grounding in the basics and sent me on to the next stage, viz. public school, without mishap.

Anderson could not have disagreed more. 'I hated it,' he said. 'I've never been so unhappy.'

I had a feeling that he took some comfort in the very fact of being able to make such a statement to someone who would understand the circumstances. It was as though a burden had been lifted from his shoulders and as he continued I began to understand why.

'We none of us dared tell on him.'

'Tell on whom?'

'Major Hunter, of course. He had his circle of favourites. There seemed to be nothing we could do. Eventually, during one of the school holidays, one of the boys at last plucked up enough courage to tell his parents. They got hold of Schuster and said, "Our boy is not coming back next term if Major Hunter is still there." Schuster got the message and Hunter left. Heavens knows what happened to him. I sometimes wonder how many of us there are out there carrying scars from that time. I certainly do. It has taken me a long time to come to terms with it, if I really have.'

It is strange how a casual, unanticipated conversation with someone you haven't seen for more than five decades can force you into a re-evaluation of an establishment about which you used to have a high opinion.

Of course, as a boy at the school I had been aware that Major Hunter, the co-headmaster, had suddenly disappeared from the scene. But whatever announcements had been made as to the reasons for his disappearance hadn't elicited any dire suspicions on my part. But now, with the New Year's sun streaming in to Paul and Marigold's living room, I had to confront the nasty reality. Why had Major Hunter not included me in his circle of favourites?

'He never made a pass at me!' I protested.

I meant it as a joke but Anderson took it seriously. 'Then you were one of the lucky ones. That man came close to ruining my life.'

What is intriguing to me, looking back, is my inability to recognize the pressures some of my contemporaries at Ravenswood were under. On the surface they could be clean-limbed, fresh-faced young boys, playing cricket for the First XI and winning a new bat if they scored fifty in an inter-school match, or a new ball if they took four wickets or more. But these apparently sunny lives could be overshadowed by a dark secret. When stumps were drawn, there might be meetings with Major Hunter behind the pavilion or wherever he worked his evil ways. Yet, of such goings-on I knew at the time precisely nothing.

The fact that it all came to an end when it did (if it did) owed nothing to the school, but simply to the courage of one small boy in bringing the matter to the attention of his parents and to the determination of those parents to do something about it.

I don't want to over-egg this Major Hunter business. On the whole, I still take a positive view of my time at Ravenswood.

There are some aspects of prep-school life that have stayed with me forever. A drizzly Sunday afternoon brings back images of long school walks. Sometimes we would even walk, two abreast, all the way from Stoodleigh to the 'Iron Bridge' across the Exe on the Tiverton–Bampton road. Going down was easy but it was a long haul back up.

Sports Days were always particularly memorable. There was the usual cocktail of events on the school playing fields, which covered several acres in total (one of the advantages of Ravenswood's rural situation). The First XI played the Fathers and my own father, when it was his turn, always put up a more than passable performance.

I have already mentioned that he was an immensely strong man. He had very broad shoulders and could heft a cricket ball a great distance if he caught it in the middle of the bat. There was often a delay while the ball was retrieved from amid the stooks of the neighbouring farmer's fields. He also earned the admiration of the boys by allowing them to pile onto the back of the open Lancia while we drove at speed up the school drive.

One such episode was recorded at the time in a black and white cine film taken by the father of one of the boys and subsequently shown to the school on one of those wet autumn Sundays when there was not much else to do. I can see myself now, sitting in the back surrounded by a gaggle of schoolmates and the two Labradors. Most of the boys are half in, half out of the car, and, of course, none are wearing seat belts because no one had heard of seat belts in those days.

My father has a pipe in his mouth as he drives. My mother is wearing a hat. She didn't often wear a hat, but she made an exception for Sports Day.

SIX

'Hard Wood Grows Slowly'

For reasons I have forgotten – if I ever knew them – I didn't go on to Sherborne in September 1953, at the normal beginning of the school year. Instead, I waited for the beginning of the following Easter term, January 1954. My brother, Peter, was already at Sherborne, in School House. I was to go to Lyon House, less centrally located.

By the beginning of 1954 we had been farming at Nethercote for more than two years. Our old Lancia had finally succumbed to the potholes on our long drive and had been replaced by an ex-US Army Jeep. Exceptionally, on my first day at Sherborne, my father offered to drive us (my brother and me) to the school.

I say 'exceptionally' because going to Sherborne and back from the heart of Exmoor from my father's point of view occupied a huge chunk of the working day, the journey taking more than four hours there and back. This was a serious matter. My father wasn't a 'gentleman' farmer. The farm wasn't a hobby. On the contrary, it was our livelihood. I'm fairly sure that part of him felt we shouldn't be going off to boarding school at all when we could be at home helping on the land. Truth to tell, our first two years had not been easy. We had a terrible lambing the first year and the second had not been much better. Our third lambing was only a few weeks off (we lamb late on Exmoor) and there was much to get ready.

'I'm not going to do this every term,' my father warned us and we clambered into the Jeep where a bale of straw served as a seat in the back.

My father dropped Peter off at School House first, and then found his way to Lyon House, a 1920s red-brick building down a cul-de-sac on the edge of town.

As we drew up outside, he didn't turn the Jeep's engine off. But he took the pipe out of his mouth long enough to say a brief 'Good luck, old boy', as I climbed out of the back, and then he was gone, the Jeep backfiring as it went down the hill.

Moments later, I found myself in the day room. This was the communal room where the thirty or so junior boys who did not yet have studies stowed their tuck boxes and generally congregated when they weren't attending classes, on the games fields or tucked up in bed.

I noticed, as I unpacked my things, that every few minutes an electric bell or buzzer would sound above the door. This would be one of the prefects calling for a fag. As soon as you heard the bell, you were meant to put down whatever you were doing and sprint to the end of the corridor where the prefects had their rooms. The boy who arrived last was the one who had to do the 'fag'.

Being a new boy, and possibly not as quick off the mark as some of the older hands, I found I did a lot of fagging that first term at Sherborne. Most often the tasks were menial. Cleaning the prefect's rugger boots, making him toast or a cup of tea, pumping up bicycle tyres, even warming up the loo seat in advance of the great man's arrival!

Sometimes, the assignment could be so trivial as to be laughable.

Buzzer from Fitzmaurice's study. General rush of fags from the day room.

Fitzmaurice: Are you last, Johnson?

Johnson: I think so, Fitzmaurice.

Fitzmaurice: Very well. I just dropped my pencil. Pick it up, would you?

Johnson: Of course, Fitzmaurice. Certainly, Fitzmaurice.

Fitzmaurice was Captain of the House when I arrived. He was also a school prefect and a 'Blood'. Bloods were the demi-gods of our day, boys who had above all demonstrated their sporting prowess on the rugby or cricket field. They had special privileges, such as wearing a fez with a gold tassel if they been awarded their First XV colours. When they passed, you stood to attention with your arms pressed firmly to your side.

It was 'Fitz', as House Captain, who gave me my first beating. Being beaten at Lyon House was something of a ritual. You walked across the yard to a building we knew as the 'Sweat-House'. If you looked up, you could see faces lining the windows. Word would have got around that there was fun to be had after house prayers. Inside the Sweat-House you bent over and touched your toes while Fitzmaurice swished the air a couple of times before letting loose. If you were lucky, and Fitz had his eye in, the weals and welts would all be on the fleshy part of the buttocks. If you were unlucky, you would end up with raw red marks halfway down your leg.

When it was over, you straightened up painfully, gritted your teeth, fought back the tears, and said: 'Thank you, Fitzmaurice.'

Of course, your schoolmates crowding the windows around the Sweat-House Yard couldn't see what went on inside the building. You were at least spared that indignity. But they could hear the swoosh and the thwack as the blows struck home. Fifty pairs of eyes would wait for the doors to open. The trick was to keep a straight face as you walked back. Not to blub. Not even to pucker the lips. Your backside might sting like hell but you held yourself stiff as a ramrod.

Moments later, the great Fitz himself would emerge, cane in hand. As you stiff-legged it back to the day room, he would re-enter his House Captain's study. Seconds later, the buzzer in the day room would sound and normal service would resume. *Fag! FAG!* On such occasions, the boy who had just been beaten would, by convention, be exempted from running to answer the summons. There had to be some compensation somewhere.

Fifty years on, many people may find it surprising that discipline at establishments like Sherborne was largely maintained, not by the masters, but by the boys. It wasn't just the Captain of the House who was allowed to beat. As far as I can remember, all house prefects had that privilege. Did the system work? I think it did. If you left your socks on the changing-room floor, you knew you were in for a beating. After you had been beaten once or twice, you took more care about picking things up and putting them away.

Was the system abused? Did the House Captain or house prefects ever go overboard? Did they victimize some poor snivelling sod, reduce him to a quivering jelly?

Frankly, I doubt it. In a house like Lyon House, though the prefects were in charge, the housemaster was always there in the background. If the housemaster was on top of things and knew what was going on, things wouldn't get out of hand.

My first encounter with Col. H. F. W. ('Hughie') Holmes, who was to be my housemaster during my five years at Sherborne, took place under somewhat bizarre circumstances.

Because I had entered Sherborne, as I have explained, in the Easter rather than Michaelmas term, there was only one other new boy in Lyon House. He was called Peter Patrick, came from Harrogate and had a strong Yorkshire accent. We had both been allocated beds in the same dormitory and we found ourselves, that first evening at Lyon House, getting ready for lights out. When we had brushed our teeth and run a flannel over our faces, Peter Patrick and I wondered what to do next. We noticed that all the other boys were waiting in their pyjamas at the foot of their beds.

'Looks like some kind of drill,' I muttered to Patrick.

'Aye, it does that.'

Seconds later, we understood the reason. 'TC inspection!' the dormitory prefect shouted.

Outside the dormitory we heard some deliberate throat-clearing, Hughie Holmes's way of warning us of his imminent arrival.

'What does TC mean?' I whispered to my fellow new boy.

'Damned if I know,' Peter Patrick replied.

Well, we soon found out that TC stood for Tinea cruris (*tinea=worm*; *crux, cruris=leg*) and that one of the housemaster's tasks at the beginning of every term was to check that no boy had returned with a case of athlete's crotch. When Hughie came into the dorm, the drill was you dropped your pyjama bottoms to the floor, and cupped your privates in one hand, so that Hughie could peer into the recesses of your groin for tell-tale sores or pustules.

Usually, Hughie would take a quick look, grunt and move on. At which point you would retrieve your pyjamas from the floor and, relieved, hop into bed. If you were unlucky, and Hughie spotted some suspicious symptom, you would be off to the school sanatorium, or 'san', in short order.

'Only thing to do with TC,' Hughie harrumphed, 'is stamp it out.'

These words, as I recall, were the very first I ever heard Hughie Holmes utter. At that precise moment, his neck was bent forward and he was inspecting Peter Patrick's private parts. Seconds later, still bent forward to economize on effort, he shuffled sideways to accord me the same treatment.

Satisfied, he straightened up and looked me over.

'Ah, you must be Johnson! Glad you made it. Welcome to Lyon House!'

A few years ago I was invited by Patrick Francis, the then housemaster of Lyon House, to address a black-tie dinner of old Lyon House boys, some of whom had been my contemporaries. I accepted with pleasure. It would be amusing, I thought, to go back to the old place after a gap of so many years. Would it have changed? In my day, for example, none of the cubicles in the ablutions block known for obvious reasons as the White City (WC!) had doors. Would Lyon House have moved with the times and at last achieved closure?

To refresh my memory of what was by then becoming quite a distant past, I once again rummaged around in the tuck box which, having accompanied me from Ravenswood to Sherborne and on to Oxford, now – as I have explained – resides in the Back Kitchen at Nethercote.

To my surprise I found a letter, addressed to me, dated 20 December 1953, and signed H. F. W. Holmes. The purpose of the letter, H. F. W. Holmes said, was to welcome me as a new boy to Lyon House.

It was a thoughtful letter, written in fountain pen in spidery handwriting. My housemaster-to-be had given it his full care and attention, covering both sides of the page. At the end he wrote: 'You will find some things strange. The main thing is: do your best, that's all we ask.'

I flipped the letter over in my hand, trying to remember what I had felt when I first went to Lyon House.

Had I found some things strange? Well, yes, not having doors on the loos had been strange. What else? Not much, actually. I was in a way tailor-made for public school. I enjoyed both work and games and, if you were to make a go of things at a school like Sherborne, this was a pretty essential combination.

Actually, one of the strangest things, it seemed to me as I looked back, was the way the random choice of a house, and therefore, of a housemaster, can influence one's life. Because of the quirks of the system, you probably see more of your housemaster, as you are growing up, than you do of your own parents. He is in a literal sense *in loco parentis*. Like them, he can praise you and he can punish you. If he is going to manage successfully a house of sixty or so adolescent boys, he must above all command your respect.

As far as I was concerned Hughie certainly managed to do that. Like so many schoolmasters of that time, he had interrupted his career to fight in the Second World War. He himself had served with a famous Irish regiment, though unlike Ravenswood's unlamented Major Hunter he tended not to reminisce about battles past. Before the war, he had been at Cambridge (Gonville and Caius), spoke good French and German and taught those subjects in school, though not being a (modern) linguist I never experienced this at first hand. His wife, Daphne, was much younger and exceptionally pretty. She can have been barely in her twenties when they married and she had the hard task not only of looking after her own young family but of the wider family of boys, some of whom (at least the senior ones) were not much younger than she was and not averse, I imagined with hindsight, to eyeing her with interest.

As it happened, the guest of honour that night at the Lyon House Old Boys' Dinner was Daphne herself, now Hughie's widow of several years. During the course of my remarks, I pulled out Hughie's letter from my pocket and read some choice extracts. I had found a second letter from him, too, written almost exactly five years later, after I had left Sherborne and was waiting to go up to Oxford.

Hughie had written that second letter on Christmas Day 1958. Like the first, it was in his own hand, though it covered four sides, rather than two. If the first letter had been a Welcome letter, this one was more of a Farewell. You've had five years at Sherborne, Hughie wrote. You've done well. Now you're heading for the wider world.

Did Hughie have some special words of advice for me?

I paused when I reached this point. Daphne Holmes, grey now but still strikingly handsome, was sitting across the table from me. To my right was Patrick Francis, the current housemaster. To my left was General Sir John Wilsey, former commander of the Devonshire and Dorset Regiment, and Head of House during my third year at Sherborne. (Had Wilsey whacked me? I couldn't remember.) We were dining in the Sweat-House, that scene of so many painful memories. I held Hughie's letter in the air.

'This is a man,' I told the gathering, 'who takes the trouble to write a four-page letter on Christmas Day when most of us are sleeping off the turkey. And what does he say? This is what he says. I'm quoting now. "Above all don't give up the Classics. It will be a slog but it is worth the effort. Remember, hard wood grows slowly".'

I am not on the whole an emotional person. In recent years the only time I have seriously 'teared up', as President George W. Bush used to put it, was when I saw that brilliant film *Chariots of Fire* at the Swiss Cottage Odeon. Yet I have to say, as I read out the words which a former housemaster had written to me forty-five years earlier ('hard wood grows slowly'), I could feel the lump in my throat.

Seeing Daphne opposite made it all the more poignant. I never thought of Holmes as a grumpy old disciplinarian but, even if he had had tendencies in that direction, Daphne would have headed him off. She was always a warm, humanizing influence on the old boy.

That night at dinner I noticed that she had only one arm. The other had been amputated above the elbow. When I first knew her, she had both arms. I asked her about it over the pudding.

'Got an infection a few years back,' Daphne replied. 'Wouldn't go away. Had the arm off. Best way.'

At that moment, she sounded just like Hughie himself. I was almost waiting for her to harrumph.

I have met people over the years who don't have as much time for Hughie Holmes as I have. I have heard former pupils say that Hughie failed to understand that 'the world has moved on', whatever that means. Tim Heald, for example, who was two or three years my junior in Lyon House, started a satirical magazine when he was at Sherborne called *Sixth Form Opinion*, which, by all accounts, caused Hughie Holmes much concern. Some of the boys seemed ready to challenge the very ethos of the place. Soon after I reached Oxford, for example, I heard on the grapevine that a Lyon House boy called Melliar-Smith (one of my contemporaries) had actually taken off his rugger boots in the course of a house match and refused to continue!

Well, I wasn't there at the time and I do not know what efforts at mutual comprehension took place. Knowing Tim Heald well (he has made his name as a writer after leaving Sherborne), and vividly remembering Melliar-Smith (I'm not sure what happened to him), I could imagine they might have been quite exasperating customers.

Had men like Hughie Holmes by then outlived their usefulness? Maybe so, maybe not. From my point of view, he was spot-on. If he were an essay, I would give him ten out of ten.

SEVEN

'There go the pips!'

In my first summer term at Sherborne (my second at the school), being still under fourteen – the upper age limit – I sat for a scholarship and was lucky enough to win one worth £150 a year, a large sum in those days. My grandfather, Stanley Williams, who – as I have already mentioned – was paying the fees, sportingly let me keep the money myself on the grounds that I had earned it.

My father, when he heard of the riches which were now flowing my way, cannily persuaded me to invest the money in livestock.

'Say you give me £50 per cow,' my father calculated. 'That means every year you own three of the cows. When they calve, we'll work out a profit-sharing scheme.'

The idea seemed simple enough. In practice, it was never clear to me which cows I owned. No profit was ever shared. Occasionally, I would receive a report that an animal had become bogged on some of our marshy ground on Room Hill and unfortunately could not be saved in spite of best efforts with ropes and tractor.

In such circumstances, the poor beast would have to be written out of the farm accounts. 'One of yours, I'm afraid,' my father would inform me when I returned to the farm at the end of term.

Having been assigned to the Fourth Form (IV Alpha, to be precise) on my arrival at Sherborne, I also found myself during the summer term of 1954 taking five O levels: Latin, Greek, French, English and Maths.

It was the Maths that caused the problem. I had a very brilliant Maths teacher called Dr Martin Cundy. He had written a classic textbook about the properties of the dodecahedron. He found it very difficult to disguise his disappointment at my failure to understand the most elementary principles of his subject.

At the end of the summer term he wrote in my report: 'This unfortunate boy will be exceptionally lucky to gain a pass in Maths O level.'

The phrase 'this unfortunate boy' caused much merriment at home. Though my parents did not on the whole spend much time scrutinizing my school reports, Dr Cundy's characterization of my mathematical abilities was never forgotten. It entered into the Nethercote lexicon.

'Ha ha!' laughed my father.

'Ho ho!' chortled my mother.

Even though, in the event, I scraped over the bar with a couple of inches to spare, thereby gaining that vital Maths O level (you couldn't go on to university without it), the psychological damage was done. If the world was to be divided into those who are literate and those who are numerate, I never had any doubt as to which side I would be on.

Actually, I don't remember any discussion about my post-O-level future. When I was just fourteen, I entered the Classical Vth, to concentrate on Greek and Latin. A year later, when I was just fifteen, I entered the Classical VIth and, a month or two before my sixteenth birthday, took and passed Greek and Latin A levels.

Nowadays, people tend to express surprise at the idea of taking A levels before one's sixteenth birthday. All I can say is that it didn't seem strange to me at the time. If you could get the exams out of the way, you could concentrate on other things.

The same applied to university entrance. In December 1956, with two A levels already in the bag, I went up to Lincoln College, Oxford, to be interviewed for a place.

The Rector of Lincoln, Walter Oakeshott, interrogated me gently. 'Why do you want to come up to Lincoln?'

'My grandfather was at Lincoln.'

'What did he read?'

'Actually, he concentrated on rowing, sir. He was stroke for the Lincoln VIII when the college made four bumps in three days in Torpids. We still have his oar at home.'

It was the truth. On his death, my mother had inherited my grandfather's college oar and had hung it on the landing of West Nethercote farmhouse above the billiard table where we used to stack the wool after shearing. (Until the lorry came to cart the fleeces away – backing up under the landing window so we could chuck them straight into the vehicle – the whole upper floor of the house would smell of lanolin mixed with sheep dung, since even the most skilful shearers found it difficult to deliver a totally clean fleece).

Grandpa's oar is still in exactly the same place today as it was when I had that interview at Lincoln. If you get on a stepladder, unhook the oar from the clasps which hold it to the wall and examine the blade, you can still read the gold-engraved details of the extraordinary achievement of the 1901 Lincoln College Torpids VIII.

The chief objective of this annual inter-college contest is to 'bump' the boat ahead of you without being bumped by the one behind. A crew that bumps one boat every day without being bumped itself or that finishes at the Head of the River is awarded 'blades' – the right to get trophy oars painted up in their college colours with the names and weights of the successful crew emblazoned on them.

Grandpa's oar, as presented to him over a century ago, records the names of the eight colleges that Lincoln 'bumped' that year: Trinity II, Oriel, Christ Church II, Queen's, Exeter, Worcester, BNC II and University. And below that you can read the weights of the team. Bow: H. D. Swinstead … 10 st. 11 lbs; 2. E. H. Cobb … 10 st. 9 lbs, etc.

My grandfather, S. F. Williams, as number 6, clocked in at 13 stone 2.

Precisely how long the Rector of Lincoln and I talked about rowing, I don't remember, but it certainly did the trick.

At the end, he positively beamed. 'Thank you so much for coming up to Oxford to see us.'

I barely had time to return to Sherborne before the Rector's letter arrived at Lyon House, offering me a place to read Classics at Lincoln. There was no suggestion that I should sit any more exams. The deed was done. The die was cast. *Iacta est alia.*

In practice, getting a place at Oxford while I was still sixteen was a terrific relief in the sense that it took all the strain out of my last three years at Sherborne. With my main A level subjects out of the way, there was time to broaden one's perspective. Before I left, I had added A levels in Ancient History, Divinity and English.

Throughout my time at Sherborne, R. W. Powell was headmaster. The boys called him 'Chief'. I came to know him well since he took the Classical VI in some of my main subjects. One of the set books the year

I took Greek A level was Sophocles' *Oedipus Tyrannus*, the tragic story of the King of Thebes. Powell brought it to life brilliantly. We used Jebb's edition which was copiously annotated. Early in the play, there is a passage describing how Oedipus has encountered and unwittingly killed his father high up in the mountains at a place 'where three roads meet' (*en triplais hamaxitois*). When we reached this point, Powell would pause to draw our attention to the detailed footnote, in which Professor Jebb attempts to retrace the precise routes the protagonists would have taken on their way to that fateful encounter.

'Ah, Jebb!' he would say appreciatively, 'how much we owe him!'

I think Bob Powell was right about that. Few plays are as gripping as *Oedipus Tyrannus*, who, besides killing his father, manages to marry his own mother as well. But Jebb's exegesis, complemented by Powell's own insights, as far as I was concerned really brought it to life.

The other A level Greek set book that year – 1956 – was Plato's *Republic*, Book I.

Powell would read out the opening line in Greek, of course. 'I went down to the Piraeus yesterday with Glaucon.' *Kateben xthes meta tou Glaukonos eis ton Peiraeon.*

'Do you know,' Powell told us, 'that Plato wrote that opening phrase in twenty-seven different ways before he finally settled on the one we have in front of us?'

Today, whenever I find myself in Piraeus waiting to catch a ferry, I think of Bob Powell introducing us to Plato and taking us through that first book of the *Republic* step by step.

Do I remember the actual text? Could I still translate it today without a crib? I'm not sure. But some bits of it stick in my mind.

'Justice is the interest of the stronger', Thrasymachus argues. But Socrates soon sets him straight. 'Surely not, O Thrasymachus! If justice was the interest of the stronger, then might not right would prevail.'

Socrates, it still seems to me, had a point. Today's political leaders, notably former President George W. Bush and former Prime Minister Tony Blair, seem to tend more towards Thrasymachus's point of view, even if they have had to tear up the United Nations rule book along the way.

Bob Powell didn't just take us for Greek. He took us for Latin too. The set book for Latin A level that year was the first book of Horace's

Odes and here again Powell was in his element. I can see him now, reciting the familiar verses without bothering to glance at the text in front of him.

> 'Vides ut alta stet nive candidum
> Soracte, nec iam sustineant onus
> Silvae laborantes …'
> *See, how it stands, one pile of snow,*
> *Soracte! 'neath the pressure yield*
> *Its groaning woods …*

As he spoke, one could feel the mountain groaning with snow.

Or else he would lithely change tone and pitch. '*Quis multa gracilis te puer in rosa perfusus liquidis urget odoribus …?*' What slender youth, besprinkled with perfume, Courts you on roses in some grotto's shade?

For me, it was a mind-blowing experience. Never mind that old Horatius Flaccus was writing in Latin. This was poetry of a high order and Powell made sure we understood that.

Of course, Powell could overdo it. If an aeroplane flew overhead, interrupting our work, he would sigh melodramatically: 'Let us pause awhile as progress passes.' But he was always self-aware.

Once, towards the end of my time at Sherborne, Powell took a holiday in the West Country (term had already ended and I was back on the farm). Powell enjoyed fishing and he had arranged for a few days on the Barle, a river that rises on Exmoor and joins the Exe at Dulverton. He telephoned to say he was in the area with his friend, the school doctor, and my mother, who was a naturally hospitable person, invited them for tea.

This turned out to be a tremendous performance. As a family, we didn't do tea. Tea was not part of the farmer's day.

My father exploded when he heard the news: 'Good God, you haven't invited them for tea, have you? What on earth for?'

My mother stood her ground. There were not so many occasions in her long married life when she dug her feet in but this was one of them.

'We shall get out the Louis Philippe silver,' she insisted, 'and have a proper tea in the garden.'

I should explain about the Louis Philippe silver. This was a comprehensive set of silver, including cutlery, salvers and teapots, each engraved with the Pfeffel arms. The set resided in a special oak casket, which was kept in the sitting room of our Exmoor farmhouse, known, as I have explained, as the Middle Kitchen. Being about the size of a large pouf, the casket was quite handy for sitting on if other seats were taken.

On the day of the headmaster's anticipated visit, I spent an hour or two extracting the silver from the casket and polishing it to perfection before laying it out on the tablecloth which had been spread on the table in the garden.

At one stage my father, covered in engine oil (he was fitting a new sump to our pickup, a vehicle that had replaced the Jeep), poked his head round the garden gate.

'What in heaven's name is all this for? We're not having the Queen of England to stay, are we?'

My mother once again stood her ground. Bob Powell and the doctor arrived in due course. Tea was taken. My father made a brief appearance and even volunteered to take our guests round the farm in the pickup.

I was editor of *The Shirburnian*, the school magazine, at the time and in the next issue I included a photograph of the headmaster sitting in the back of our farm pickup in his country tweeds.

It was a good photograph. The headmaster is clearly in a genial mood. He is wearing country tweeds and a cloth cap. If you look closely, you can see that he is chewing a long piece of straw.

As I say, Powell was always self-aware. He probably knew I would print a picture of the visit in the magazine. This was the image (straw included) he chose to project.

Some years later, Anthony (Tony) Howard, whose role in launching my career as an environmentalist (such as it has been) I will describe later, invited me to write Robert Powell's obituary for *The Times*. Powell was not yet dead but Tony, who was then the Obituaries editor, was keen to get a piece on file.

'I'd go down and see him, if I were you,' Tony advised. 'Mind you, don't tell him you're writing his obituary.'

'No, of course not.'

After retiring from Sherborne, Powell and his wife, Charity, had retired to the nearby village of Child Okeford. Powell must have been in his late seventies by then and it was decades since I had seen him.

He welcomed me warmly. While we talked in his study, Charity prepared lunch.

'You're writing an article, are you?'

'That kind of thing,' I parried, remembering Tony Howard's warning. 'Looking back, how do you see your time at Sherborne?'

It was a strange moment. Powell used to write reports about me. The Headmaster's Report was always the last one in the little booklet of reports that would be mailed out to parents at the end of each term. My mother collected these assiduously. Some time after she died (in 1987) my sister Birdie found a packet of papers labelled 'Stan's School Reports', which she handed over to me.

Powell's last report on me (December 1958) had been lethal as far as I was concerned. 'No boy in my experience has made a larger or more vigorous contribution to the life of the school.'

That's the problem with the public school system. Because you're Head of School or Captain of Games or whatever, and not a total dunce where academic work is concerned, you start thinking you're a big shot and that you really count in the world. I know as I left Sherborne that I had tendencies in that direction. Powell's final report only served to consolidate them. It took me quite some time to recover from a swollen head.

Well, it was my turn now to write the report.

What struck me, as we talked that morning in that sleepy Dorset village, was – yet again – Powell's self-awareness. He had stayed on as headmaster of Sherborne for almost a decade after I left. As the years passed, he had seen deference replaced by irreverence. The gown and mortar board which he wore both in the chapel and in the classroom had ceased to be the potent symbols of authority that they once were.

All this he spoke about with insight and not a little passion.

'"*Tempora mutant et nos mutamur in illis*",' he murmured, offering me another glass of pre-lunch sherry. 'I could probably have done more to adapt to the new situation. I certainly tried.'

Over lunch, I posed the inevitable *Desert Island Discs* question, as perfected by Sue Lawley during her time as host of that programme.

'Do you have any regrets?' I asked. 'Would you have done anything differently?'

He thought about that one for a while. 'I would have liked to have edited the *Agamemnon*,' he said at last. 'Of course, Frankel's edition is superb. He was probably the best Aeschylus scholar in the world. But it would have been good to have another shot at it.'

That was the last time I saw Bob Powell. He died a year or two later. *The Times* duly printed the obituary I had written, together with a picture of Powell in full academic regalia.

One of the most vivid memories I have of Bob Powell is from the last day of my last term.

Traditionally, the whole school would gather in the Big Schoolroom for the end-of-term concert. The final item on the programme that day was a '*piano duet played by R. W. Powell and S. P. Johnson*'.

I should explain that, with time on my hands that last term at Sherborne, I had decided to take up the piano. Two or three times a week an elderly teacher gave me piano lessons in the Music School. By the end of term, she reckoned I was ready for my first public performance.

That night Bob Powell and I performed two works in front of a packed house. The first was the cheerful little piece called *Gossip Joan*, which received a rousing reception. The second – the *pièce de resistance* – was Sir Hubert Parry's rendering of *Three Blind Mice*. Powell took the bass part which depicts the general scurrying of mice hither and yon. My task was to capture the essential melody. *Tum, tum, tum. Tum, tum-ti, tum.* I am no expert, but I think I performed quite competently.

The assembled audience certainly thought so. I sometimes meet old Shirburnians of my vintage who say they remember the moment when 'Chief' and I took a bow together in front of a wildly cheering crowd.

I stayed on at Sherborne, beyond the end of the normal school year, so as to be Head Boy for the autumn term of 1958.

Being Head of School was quite a big deal in those days. Your name went up in gold letters on a board in the Big Schoolroom. You could put it on your curriculum vitae.

Not long ago my elder daughter, Rachel, wrote an article in the *Spectator* about 'head boys and head girls' she had known. On the whole, she didn't rate them highly. She maintains she forgot – if, indeed, she had ever known – that I was once head boy of Sherborne.

Looking back at my term in the top job, I think Rachel was right. I don't think I made much of a mark as Head of School. I don't think I left much of a 'legacy', to use that Blairite term. My only lasting contribution, as I remember, was to reorganize the collection during Sunday morning chapel.

I had noticed as I progressed up the school that there was often an embarrassing hiatus during the final 'Offertory' hymn. The school prefects would still be parading up and down the aisle with their little bags into which the boys would drop their usually modest contributions, long after the actual singing itself was over. The organist could, of course, try to cover the clink of coins and the clatter of shoes by some judicious improvisation, but on the whole it was an unsatisfactory situation. Even if the Offertory hymn was a long one, such as '*The Church's one foundation*', and even if the organist took it agonizingly slowly, there were simply too many boys to collect from. (Sunday service was compulsory so, with staff and hangers-on, the congregation probably approached seven hundred at any one time.)

Quite soon after taking office, if that is the right expression, I called a meeting of the school prefects in the medieval cloisters. The school prefects that term were an impressive bunch. They included, for example, Colin (C. R.) Lucas, who would go on to become Master of Balliol and Vice-Chancellor of the University.

'Look, chaps,' I said. 'We have a real problem here. Does anyone know how to solve it?'

Fortunately one of the prefects was an immensely clever boy called Hardwick who had already gained a scholarship in Mathematics to Cambridge. Hardwick took out pen and paper and drew a plan of the School Chapel.

'You have to split the prefects into three groups, do the transepts before the aisle and leave the choir to last,' he said authoritatively. 'I can express the formula algebraically if you like.'

We took Hardwick's word for it and, after that, those awkward clinks and pauses were eliminated from Sunday service.

The second, and more important, reason I stayed on for the autumn term of 1958 was to have another full season with the school's rugby XV.

In my day Sherborne was one of the top rugby schools in the west of England and probably in the country as a whole.

We didn't always win, of course.

The very first time I turned out for the school First XV was in November 1956. I was thrilled to be selected, being only in my third year at school. The match was an away game against Blundell's, the school in Tiverton which I already knew something about, since, as I have mentioned, Ravenswood tended to look on Blundell's as the 'local' school to which Devonians certainly, but also others, might naturally aspire.

It was a windy, blustery day. I kept yanking on my socks, trying to keep them up. On the touchline I could see my father and mother, who had driven over from Exmoor. My father was a very serious rugby player in his time, having captained a London side in the pre-war years. I couldn't help hoping that Sherborne was going to put up a decent show. I couldn't help hoping that *I* was going to put up a decent show.

In the event, Sherborne suffered one of the most humiliating defeats in its history. Our nemesis was the brilliant Blundell's fly-half, Richard Sharp, who single-handedly scored all the points against us (the final score was Blundell's 22 Sherborne 0).

I can see Sharp now, weaving and jinking, sometimes wafting a drop kick over the crossbar, sometimes darting through an impossibly narrow gap to touch the ball down with the most graceful of gestures (*quis puer gracilis ...?*) and a look of disdain on his face. In due course, Sharp went on to play for both Oxford and England. He became a schoolmaster after leaving university and, by some strange irony, came to Sherborne, where he was an inspiring rugby coach.

I don't think I touched the ball throughout the match that day at Blundell's. When the final whistle went, I looked at the touchline to see my parents had already gone home. There were no songs in the bus on the way back. It is not often that Sherborne crashes so comprehensively, but we certainly crashed that day.

The coach wisely dropped me for the rest of that season, but I played for the XV in 1957 and 1958, both successful years. Long after I stopped playing, I would dream of catching the ball from the kick-off, then crashing through the opposition to score beneath the posts. I think I saw rugby as a metaphor for life.

In my time at Sherborne, when the XV was playing at home, the whole school had to turn out to watch. I can still hear the roar of seven hundred voices as the team ran out onto the pitch. They didn't shout Sherborne … they shouted, 'School! SCHOOL!' It was an extraordinary sensation.

When you gained your colours you were allowed to wear pale blue games socks and a collar on your rugby shirt. It may all seem silly now, but it didn't seem silly then.

In the end I didn't go up to Lincoln College, Oxford, at all because Lincoln was 'trumped' by Exeter where, in March 1958, I won a classical scholarship. So I spent four years at Lincoln's neighbour in the Turl, rather than at Lincoln itself.

I don't want to give the impression that I was an outstanding academic achiever at Sherborne. There were others of my vintage far cleverer than I was and some of them took much 'better' scholarships (the grand total in my year was a record twenty-one Oxbridge awards). Let's be frank about this. I tried and missed an award at Balliol in December 1957. I tried and missed again at Lincoln in January 1958 (I already had a place there, of course, but the glory lay in getting the scholarship). The Exeter group of colleges, which held exams in March 1958, was very much in the long-stop position, there to catch those who had otherwise fallen through the net.

Truth to tell, I almost blew it at Exeter too. I had done well, I suspected, at the Greek and Latin proses. I had made a reasonable job of the Unseens and had even made a good fist of the verse papers, though I found it easier to write Latin hexameters than Greek iambics.

We also had three hours to write an English essay on a set topic. I can't remember now what the subject was but I do recall that as I considered what to say I had a rush of blood to the head. Instead of delivering what the examiners were looking for, namely a closely reasoned case for and against, with satisfactorily balanced conclusions, I decided I would write a short story.

I can't remember now what my short story was about, except that it was set in the Alps and involved fishing.

The reason I know it involved fishing is that soon after I heard officially from Exeter that I had been awarded the Stapeldon Scholarship in Classics, I received a letter from Exeter's Senior Tutor, J. P. V. D. Balsdon, more usually known as 'Dacre'.

Dear Johnson,

I am delighted that you have won the Stapeldon and much look forward to taking you in Greats in due course.

Yours sincerely,

J. P. V. D. Balsdon

PS I shall be interested to know where in the Alps you can get fresh trout in winter.

As I recall this letter, I find myself blushing. How on earth did I think I could get away with *not* writing an essay when that was what was required? How could I have been so totally inconsiderate of those who over the years had put such an effort into teaching me? In short, what on earth had possessed me, except possibly some kind of adolescent arrogance that had led me to think it was all right to break the rules as long as you did so in style?

When word of what had happened got back to my teachers at Sherborne, there was some raising of eyebrows. Of course they were pleased that I had at last won an award at the third time of asking, but they were frankly surprised at my egregious lapse of concentration. Rushes of blood to the head are precisely not what are needed when you are sitting a competitive exam. They expected better of me.

The headmaster caught me in the quad after morning chapel. He peered at me with a beady eye from beneath his mortar board.

'I hear you wrote a short story instead of an essay ...' His voice trailed off. Some rebukes are more stinging when not actually voiced.

My parents, to be fair, felt no such reservations about my achievement. We didn't have mobile telephones in those days, of course. We didn't ring home at all. In fact, the only time I can remember telephoning home during my five years at Sherborne was that day when I received the news from Exeter College, Oxford, that I had won the Stapeldon Scholarship in Classics.

Though K. C. Wheare's letter (Wheare was Rector of Exeter) had come with the morning post, I dutifully waited until after 6 p.m. (cheap rates) before walking from Lyon House to the public telephone box outside the Plume of Feathers Hotel.

'Hello, is that you, Mummy? This is Stan.'

My mother was already quite deaf by then. She relied to a large extent on lip-reading and found it difficult to distinguish consonants. Talking on the telephone was particularly hard for her. But she was nothing if not game and would always try her best.

'Did you say van? Which van?'

'No, *Stan*! I've won the top award!'

Fortunately I had found that narrow window of opportunity between the end of high tea and the moment my father took off for the pub.

Clearly heading for the door, he came on the line. 'Good show! Well done, old boy.'

He was pleased. I knew that. And I was pleased he was pleased. Not long before he died, he told Jenny how much he missed not having been able to continue his own education after the age of thirteen (I shall explain the reasons for this later). I'm not sure he saw the Classics as the root of all civilization in the way I did. He had never done Latin or Greek as far as I knew. But he recognized that, since I had come thus far along the road, it made sense to take the next step, even though that meant the chances of my taking over the farm in due course as my full-time occupation were that much slimmer.

'Yes, jolly well done! Good show!' he repeated. 'I'll tell Ma. There go the pips!'

I put the receiver down and walked out into the street. Across the way, the great flying buttresses of Sherborne Abbey, one of England's finest churches, soared into the air. I was lucky in so many ways, I thought. For five years, I had received a supremely good education in a supremely beautiful environment. The school's honey-coloured hamstone blends perfectly with the exquisite medieval town that surrounds it, the whole being set off by that magic rolling Dorset countryside which, by some quirk of fate, remains largely unspoiled even today. Could a man ask for more?

EIGHT

Strictly Speaking, I Ought to Be a Turk

Like so many others of my generation, after I left school I enjoyed a gap year, defined as the period when, having finished your studies at secondary level, you are waiting to go on to university.

Nowadays, of course, the gap year can extend to eighteen months, if you leave school in June one year and don't start at university until October of the following year. In my case, I had only nine months, since I left Sherborne at Christmas 1958 and was to go up to Oxford at the start of the next academic year, October 1959.

Truncated though the gap year might be, I was determined to make the most of it. I decided, in the first instance, to visit my Turkish relatives.

Let me explain.

Strictly speaking, I ought to be a Turk. My father's father – Ali Kemal – was Turkish, though his wife, Winifred, was half English (on her mother's side) and half Swiss (on her father's).

Ali Kemal, born in 1867, was variously a journalist, editor of a newspaper and a politician. The first decade of the twentieth century was a turbulent time for Turkey. The Ottoman Empire was in its death throes and the Great Powers were all clustering round, waiting to scavenge from the corpse. Ali Kemal and Winifred had already had one child, my aunt Celma. When Winifred was pregnant with my father, Ali Kemal decided that, given the hazards of life in Constantinople (as Istanbul was then known), it would be wiser for her to have her baby in England. Though I do not know the exact date of her departure from Constantinople, in my mind's eye I can see an elegant, visibly pregnant lady boarding ship in the Golden Horn with three-year-old Celma at her side.

I never met my paternal grandmother Winifred, though I know what she looked like. Winifred had a sister, Viva, who married a Swiss businessman, Ernest Tremblay, and who lived to a ripe old age in Geneva. A couple of summers ago, one of my Swiss cousins, touring the West Country, spent the night on our Exmoor farm and brought with her a portrait of Winifred. She seems to have been quite a beauty. Her carefully coiffed dark hair has a surprising stripe of white through it. She is wearing a high collar and a pearl necklace.

We have hung the picture in the Middle Kitchen. From time to time I study it with interest and not a little regret. As I have explained, I have only the haziest recollections of Marie-Louise, my grandmother on my mother's side, and, for reasons which will become obvious in a moment, none at all of Winifred.

In the seventies, when I was working in Brussels for the European Commission, I would sometimes have to go to Geneva on business. I would call on Aunt Viva, as my father called her, first in the rather large house in Chêne-Bougeries which she continued to live in after the death of her husband, then later in the old people's home where she spent her last years (she was almost a hundred when she died). Once I picked her up and we went to the Beau Rivage hotel for lunch beside the lake.

Though her sister Winifred had by then been dead for more than sixty years, I could see how close they had been. She remembered Ali Kemal's courtship of Winifred.

'We were living in Lucerne,' she told me, 'when Ali Kemal first met Winifred. They spent as much time as they could together and were clearly very keen on each other. When it was time for him to go back to Turkey, he said to her: "I have to go now. You will not hear from me nor must you try to communicate with me, but at this exact time, exactly a year from today, I will be at this bridge in Lucerne. If I find you here, then we will be married."'

It was a deeply romantic tale. In May 2006, I happened to go to Lucerne for business reasons. One afternoon, I escaped from the meeting to walk along the shore of the lake. I stood at one end of the famous covered bridge and tried to imagine what it must have been like for Winifred to have been in this same place, almost exactly a century earlier.

For a whole year there has been radio silence from Ali Kemal. Not a letter, not a telegram. No communication at all. Just a few articles in the press about the growing turmoil in Turkey as the Young Turks begin to shake the foundations of the Sultan's throne, a process which will not be completed until Atatürk himself takes over.

I look across the lake and, putting myself in Winifred's place, seem to see, as the clock strikes noon, a distant figure at the far end of the bridge, walking towards me. He is not a tall man, but he is very solid. He wears a high-collared coat and a pair of pince-nez spectacles.

Aunt Viva was definitely able to understand the attraction Winifred must have felt for Ali Kemal: a strong, mysterious figure deeply involved in the affairs of a country of which she could have known little.

But I also sensed a twinge of hostility. It was as though she felt that Ali Kemal had in some way let his wife down. If Ali Kemal hadn't packed Winifred off to England to have the baby (my father), would the ensuing tragedy have occurred?

I have no way of knowing whether Winifred's accouchement would have gone better if she had stayed in Constantinople, rather than travelling to England. Aunt Viva seemed to believe that the stress of the journey might have contributed to the unhappy circumstances of Winifred's confinement. Be that as it may, Winifred gave birth to my father in Bournemouth on 4 September 1909. Some days later she died from puerperal fever, her beloved sister Viva having reached her bedside just before she expired, though Ali Kemal himself never had a chance to say goodbye to his wife.

So I never knew my maternal grandmother and my father, born that September day in England, never knew his mother. He was effectively an orphan from birth, since Ali Kemal's two children with Winifred (my father and his sister, Celma) stayed in England in the care of Winifred's own mother, Margaret.

My father did not often speak about his childhood. He was not on the whole a talkative man. He preferred to keep his jaws clamped on the stem of a pipe. He never gave any indication that he had any memories of his father, nor any knowledge of the fact that – as I have recently discovered – Ali Kemal came to England to visit his 'English' family, by then residing in Wimbledon, before the outbreak of the First World War in 1914.

I do, however, remember my father referring to his own grandmother, Margaret (who for all practical purposes became a substitute mother from his earliest days), as 'Gran' in a tone which was certainly positive.

It must have been Gran who called him Wilfred in tribute, I imagine, to the late Winifred.

On one of my visits to Geneva, in the seventies, I asked Aunt Viva what her view of the matter was. Had Ali Kemal ever seen his children, Celma (my aunt) and Wilfred (my father), after Winifred succumbed to puerperal fever in Bournemouth?

'Ali Kemal certainly found time to go to Paris,' she said, pushing aside uneaten the best *bœuf en croûte* which the Beau Rivage could supply.

I had the distinct sense that Aunt Viva thought that Ali Kemal, having travelled as far as Paris, might have slipped across the Channel to visit his offspring, as well as his late wife's mother, who was now bringing up their children.

'Of course you have to remember,' Aunt Viva continued, obviously determined to be charitable, 'that the Great War made it impossible for Ali Kemal to come to England. Turkey was on the other side. And your grandfather married again. His wife, Sabiha, gave birth to your uncle Zeki in 1917.'

The other side! Of course! The First World War had begun in August 1914, just before my father's fifth birthday. Turkey had joined the opposition. German generals – like Otto Liman von Sanders – were training Turkish soldiers who would a couple of years later inflict a devastating defeat on the Allies at Gallipoli.

It was at this point, I believe, as the thunder of war rolled across Europe, that my father formally acquired the name Johnson, derived from his maternal grandmother's maiden name. (Before she married the Swiss businessman Herr Brun, Margaret Johnson had lived in Yorkshire.)

My mother once explained the circumstances of the name change to me: 'Pa's grandmother, whom he called "Gran", decided to write to the Home Office to ask whether it was all right for Pa to be called Johnson. She got a letter back saying there were no problems with Johnson. As far as the Home Office was concerned it didn't matter what he was called!'

The letter to the Home Office was not the only piece of correspondence that Gran addressed to UK officialdom on my father's behalf. In
July 2006 the historian David Barchard, who has an astute grasp of
Turkish affairs as well as a more than passing acquaintance with the
story of my Turkish family, invited me to dinner at the Reform Club.
You can't take out papers in the dining room but after dinner we found
a small private conference room in the basement.

'I've been in the Public Record Office [now known as the National
Archives] this afternoon,' David told me somewhat mysteriously. 'I
think you ought to see this.'

He passed over a photocopy of an A3 size sheet of paper, containing
facsimiles of two documents.

The first was a letter from Gran to the Secretary of the British delegation at the Versailles Peace Conference in 1919. As I read it, eighty-
five years after it was written, I couldn't help thinking how dignified,
and yet how poignant, Gran's appeal was. She had obviously learned
from somewhere that Ali Kemal had been a member of the Turkish
delegation to the Conference. This was certainly not a happy position.
Turkey had entered the war on the wrong side and by the end the
Ottoman Empire that had lasted for more than five hundred years had
finally fallen apart. Not the least important business in Paris was
distributing the spoils to the victors (e.g. Iraq to the British, Syria to the
French).

But Gran was less concerned with Ali Kemal's role in the geo-polit-
ical game. What bothered her was that 'since the outbreak of war with
Turkey' he hadn't, so she averred, provided her with any help as she
brought up his two children.

'I am very anxious to see him,' she wrote, 'if possible in order to get
money from him towards the support of his two children.'

The letter is well composed and well typed. It was posted on 27 June
1919. It arrived in Paris, according to the official stamp, on 2 July.

The fact that the Post Office appears to have worked then with
amazing efficiency does not seem to have done Gran any good. Swift
though the delivery had been, it was not swift enough.

The second letter, which is a copy of the official reply made by the
Foreign Office, is dated 5 July and informs Gran that the bird has
flown.

There is no attempt to deny that Ali Kemal has been in Paris as a member of the Turkish delegation to the Peace Conferences: merely the laconic statement that the 'delegate in question' has now left Paris to return to Turkey and that further enquiries should properly be addressed to HM Ambassador in Constantinople.

Receiving this deadening official response must have been a cosh blow for Gran. By now Celma was twelve and Wilfred nine. Though she would have understood the circumstances which obtained during the war, she might well have expected that when peace – or at least the armistice – was declared, some substantial help might have been forthcoming from Ali Kemal.

It was not to be, for Ali Kemal himself only lived another three years, being murdered under tragic circumstances which I shall shortly describe. My Turkish grandfather seems, at the beginning of the 1920s, to have been in the thick of Turkish politics. The great Turkish nationalist movement led by Mustafa Kemal, the hero of Gallipoli, was gathering force. Mustafa Kemal, later to be known as Kemal Atatürk, was determined that the Ottoman Empire should not be dismembered without at least leaving behind a residual independent and, hopefully, modern Turkish nation. When the Greeks, aided and abetted by the French, invaded Turkey in 1922 intent on expanding their hegemony in the eastern Aegean, Atatürk with his colleague Ismet Inönü fought them off. Mehmet VI Vahidettin still reigned as Sultan in Constantinople but it was only a question of time before he would be toppled. Who would give him his final push?

Looked at in a historical context, my Turkish grandfather, Ali Kemal, was clearly on the wrong side. As far as I can tell, he believed that the Great Powers, particularly the British, should have an enduring role in Turkey's future. He was not a nationalist, but that did not mean he was not a patriot.

There is a very touching passage in the short memoir which my uncle Zeki Kuneralp published about his own life entitled *Just a Diplomat*. (Zeki – half-brother to my father through Ali Kemal's second marriage to Sabiha Hanim, daughter of Zeki Pasha, Marshal of the Ottoman Army – was, as I shall explain later, a Turkish diplomat of distinction, serving twice as Ambassador to the Court of St James's, as well as Turkey's envoy to Switzerland and Spain.) Zeki describes how –

as an eight-year-old – he is at his father's side in Constantinople (Istanbul) when news reaches the capital of Mustafa Kemal's great victory over the Greeks at Smyrna, now Ismir. Zeki excitedly tells his father: '*Papa, les Grecs sont battus!*'

And Ali Kemal joyfully replies, '*Mais oui, mon petit, ils sont battus à plates coutures.*' They'd been beaten hands down.

I was tremendously moved when I first read this passage in Zeki's memoir. Zeki had grown up knowing that his own father was a controversial character, to say the least. Ali Kemal had been serving as the Sultan's Minister of the Interior when he had effectively 'outlawed' Mustafa Kemal in the sense that he had advised all official government posts throughout the country that no aid or comfort was to be offered to Kemal. There were many in Turkey who believed, with hindsight, that this was the act of a traitor. The snatch of remembered dialogue in Zeki's memoir tends to argue precisely the opposite.

I remember being fascinated, too, by the fact that father and son in this little cameo exchange addressed each other not in Turkish but in French. French was not just the language of diplomatic discourse; it was the language of choice if you were a civilized Turk living in Constantinople in the early part of the last century. I have copies of letters Winifred received from Ali Kemal over the years of their marriage. They are all in French. Classy, perfectly idiomatic French. The kind of French you don't even know you are writing since you've been brought up with it.

I came to know Zeki well over the years, having encountered him both in London and Switzerland as well as on several occasions in Turkey. I would say that his memories of his father Ali Kemal, and his awareness of Ali Kemal's ambiguous position in the history of the modern Turkish nation, were dominant influences in his life.

In 1990 Jenny and I visited Zeki in his flat in Fernabahçe on the Asiatic side of the Bosphorus. Zeki by then had retired from the diplomatic service and was crippled by multiple sclerosis. He talked to us with passion about Ali Kemal. A large oil painting of Ali Kemal, finished – I imagine – only a few months before his death, dominated the room.

'My own view', Zeki told us, 'is that Atatürk had nothing to do with my father's death. The responsibility lies with the officials at Izmit.'

That particular occasion was the first time Zeki spoke to me directly about Ali Kemal's murder. I knew in broad terms what had happened. Though, as I have already mentioned, my own father never spoke about Ali Kemal, I remember my mother when I was still at prep school outlining the macabre circumstances of his death.

'Ali Kemal, Daddy's father, was murdered,' she told me one day at the end of the holidays as she was getting my school trunk ready. 'They kidnapped him when he was having his morning shave in Istanbul, which was then called Constantinople. They carried him off across the Bosphorus and stoned him to death.'

Since then, two massive biographies of Kemal Atatürk have been published in English (one by Lord Kinross, the other by Andrew Mango), which explain the circumstances of my Turkish grandfather's death in some detail.

Ali Kemal was indeed having his daily shave at his favourite barber's shop on Istiklal Caddesi (now Independence Avenue) when he was abducted, apparently by Atatürk's agents. He was carried by boat across the Sea of Marmara to be put on a train bound for Ankara, Atatürk's newly established headquarters. However, so the story goes, he was forcibly taken off the train at Izmit (about sixty miles east of Istanbul), to be handed over to the garrison commander.

It is at this point that the story becomes rather murky. In theory the garrison commander should have sought instructions from Atatürk, or at least from his headquarters at Samsoun in eastern Turkey. There is no evidence that he did so or, if he did seek instructions, that any precise advice was received. There is no evidence that Atatürk himself expressed the wish, as Henry II did in the case of Thomas à Becket, that someone should 'rid me of this turbulent priest'. As I have indicated, Zeki never held Atatürk personally responsible for his father's death. In his own memoirs Zeki recounts how, on his induction to the Turkish foreign office as a junior diplomat, the then President of the Turkish Republic – Ismet Inönü – had expressed his pleasure and had indicated that Zeki's ancestry would in no way prove a bar to his progress in a diplomatic career.

That said, the absence of any clear signal from the Nationalist HQ seems to have been taken as a mandate by the garrison commander at Izmit to wash his hands of the problem posed by the sudden arrival of the prisoner. By all accounts, Ali Kemal was turned over to the tender mercies of the crowd.

Was he actually stoned to death? Was he beaten? Was he – as I have heard – slashed in pieces with his body parts stuffed into a nearby tree? As a child I confess I did not press hard to know more.

I have often wondered what impact Ali Kemal's death must have had on my own father. Ali Kemal died in November 1922. By then my father was thirteen years old. We have a photograph of him taken around that age, in cricket gear and carrying a bat. He looks very much like the English schoolboy. You can imagine him taking guard at the crease ('*Middle and leg, please. Thanks*'), or you can visualize him, when it is the turn of his side to field, being given the ball for an over or two. You can almost hear him calling out 'how's that?' to the umpire. A discreet, restrained appeal, of course. That was how you did it in those days. None of those dramatic Freddie Flintoff gestures, when the bowler spins on his heel, flings both his arms wide and tries virtually to intimidate the umpire into raising his index finger to the sky.

I try now to put myself in my father's position. There he is, a thirteen-year-old schoolboy who has never known either of his parents. His mother has died giving birth to him. In these more sensitive times psychologists could have some fun with that. Did my father, whose arrival on this earth was the proximate cause of his mother's demise, actually blame himself for that event? I don't know, but I doubt it. I don't think he was a man to wallow in introspection. That said, you would be hard pressed as a schoolboy playing for the First XI and hoping to win your colours before the end of the season not to notice that your father never showed up at cricket matches.

'*I say, Johnson, where's your old man, then?*'

I can hear the changing-room banter down the years. I wonder what my father would have replied. In later years he elevated mumbling into an art form. Step One, put the pipe in your mouth and grip the stem firmly between your teeth. Step Two, slide a hand across your face. Step Three, speak in the lowest possible voice without removing the hand, thus ensuring that your wife (my mother), who is seriously deaf, (a) can't hear and (b) has no chance of lip-reading.

Even as a schoolboy I believe my father would quickly have developed the technique of the inaudible response.

'Come on, Johnson, where's your old man?'

'Well, actually, Carruthers, my old man's stuck in Turkey. Fighting on the wrong side, I'm afraid.'

'But the war's over, Johnson. It's been over for three years. They patched things up at Versailles. We're all friends now. Couldn't your old man at least have made it over for the Fathers' match?'

My father died in 1992 so it's too late to ask him now, but sometimes I find myself wishing I had broken through those walls of reserve (on my side, probably, as much as on his) to ask him the obvious question. I could have picked a good moment, say at the end of a long day's dipping or shearing, when the sheep have been turned out and there is a sense of a job well done. We could have had a man-to-man talk.

'I say, Pa,' I could have begun, as he tamped tobacco into the bowl of his pipe. 'You were already thirteen years on this earth. Your father was alive all that time. And yet, as far as you know, you never saw him, or he you. The other boys' parents came down for Speech Day. But you just had Gran. Did you mind?'

As I sit here writing these words on the Exmoor farm where he lived for over forty years, I try to continue this imaginary conversation. What might my father have replied if I had asked him straight out what it felt to be in practice fatherless when his father was very much alive and at times no further away than Paris?

I suspect that even under the favourable circumstances I have posited his response would not have been very forthcoming. He would, I suspect, have turned the question, muttering something like 'tricky times, after the war'. Or else he would have ignored it altogether to concentrate instead on bagging some loose fleeces or sluicing the slats of the sheep dip.

What I am absolutely convinced about is that my father would never have said: 'Actually, I missed my father terribly. All the other boys had parents, I didn't. I minded that.'

This probably says as much about the relationship between my father and me as it does about the relationship between my father and his father. The truth is: when I grew up, asking the sort of question I outlined above wasn't really on the cards. One operated on the 'need to know' principle. If Daddy wanted to talk to you about his childhood, he would. But if he didn't want to talk about this or any other matter, you didn't press him. In these touchy-feely days, one tends to forget how much relationships were founded on reserve.

I sometimes say jokingly that the closest I ever got to my father was one day when I was about fifteen and he helped me put on my black tie for some Pony Club dance. The evening is still seared in my memory. First, there was the tremendous hassle of trying to tie the knot correctly. My father stood in front of me trying to guide my fingers. When that didn't work, he stood behind me and tied it himself.

When, finally, I was properly kitted out with pumps on my feet and silk handkerchief peeping from the breast pocket of my newly acquired dinner jacket, he drove me with my sister Hilary to the dance, dropping us off before repairing to a nearby pub, promising to return later.

It was, as I recall, on the second or third dance of the evening that the disaster happened. My partner at the time was a spirited young girl who, I believe, went on to become High Sheriff of Somersetshire. We were doing the Gay Gordons. (Is the dance still called the 'Gay Gordons', I wonder, in these politically correct days?) As I ducked my head to avoid an oncoming cummerbunded Etonian, both my feet in their shiny new leather shoes slipped from under me and I hit the parquet floor of Morebath Manor with a thundering crash.

Such was the noise that the band stopped playing at that instant.

Later when my father came back to pick us up and we had put on our ex-RAF bomber jackets for the cold ride home in the Jeep, he asked us how we got on.

'Had a good time, then?'

My sister Hilary, fifteen months older than I am, let the cat out of the bag.

'Stan fell over with a tremendous crash. The band stopped playing.'

Perched on my bail of straw in the back of the car, I didn't actually hear my father's comment above the noise of the engine. But I'm pretty sure he chuckled.

Reverting for a moment to Ali Kemal, I suspect without knowing for certain that another reason my father didn't talk much about his father was the Turkish thing. When I was at my prep school in the late forties, there was a boy who used to go round saying, 'Wogs begin at Calais and I strongly distrust the men of Kent.'

This may have been an extremist stance. The point I want to make is that racism was fairly rife not only when I was at school but, *a fortiori*, when my father was at school too. If you were a Turk, or the son of a Turk, you had two strikes against you. First, Turkey had been our enemy in the Great War and, second, the Turks were basically wogs so if you were the son of a Turk you were the son of a wog. *QED*.

I don't think my father ever looked very Turkish. Ali Kemal himself, judging from the portraits, seems to have had brown rather than black hair. I asked Zeki where the blond gene came from. Most of the Johnsons seem to be blond.

'We're called the blond Turks!' I said.

Zeki had explained that his own grandfather, Ahmet Hamdi, Ali Kemal's father, had come to Constantinople from a small village called Kalfat in Anatolia where even today you can see blond Turkish children running around.

'The blond Turk,' Zeki said, 'is not a totally unknown phenomenon even in Turkey.'

That said, looks are one thing; paternity is another. I remember my mother saying to me once, 'Pa had to be careful at school. People might say he had a touch of the tarbrush.'

A touch of the tarbrush! There's a phrase which has receded with the mists of time. Nowadays, with multi-culturalism all the vogue, to suggest that someone might have a hint of the Orient in his background is definitely not the conversation stopper it might have been two or three generations ago. Dorset, when my father grew up there, was a deeply rural county. If you talked of immigrants in Piddletrenthide, you probably meant people who had come from two or three villages away, like Tolpuddle or Sturminster Newton. This was Thomas Hardy country, with haywains and stooks of corn and dairy maids thwacking pats of butter on wooden boards. If you were a young man of unusual background, living in straitened circumstances, it would have been odd to have stressed one's exotic origins. Better to let sleeping dogs lie.

As I see it now, it wasn't just his Turkish origins which might have caused a problem. It was also the fact that Turks were Muslims. There probably wasn't, in the first part of the last century, the paranoia over Islam which we see today, but if you were heading for one of the great

English public schools, there wasn't much mileage in stressing your family's connections with Saladin and Mehmet.

In the event, my father's hopes of playing cricket for Charterhouse or even Harrow went up in smoke with Ali Kemal's death. Notwithstanding her plaintive letter to the leader of the British delegation at the Versailles Peace Conference, I suspect that Gran had indeed received some support from Ali Kemal during his lifetime towards the care and maintenance of his two children with Winifred. And on his death, Gran received some funds from the sale of Ali Kemal's collection of oriental manuscripts (now in the British Library). But these funds, such as they were, were certainly not enough to pay for my father's continued education, least of all at one of the great English public schools.

The harsh truth is that my father was forced to leave school at the age of thirteen and make his own way in the world.

I know he worked on a farm in Dorset, before going to Canada. I remember him talking about travelling around on trains in the Rockies. (Was he a hobo?) I know he went to Egypt in the thirties where Aunt Viva's husband, Ernest, had business interests and where he met my mother. It was in Egypt, as I have already related, that my mother wooed and won my father over the shove-halfpenny board.

I know that, though older than he should have been, he managed to join the RAF as a pilot at the beginning of the war and was still serving in that capacity when, towards the war's end, he had that unfortunate prang on the runway at Chivenor.

But this, pretty much, is all I know about the first forty years of my father's life.

NINE

Gap Year Travels: Istanbul and Anatolia

With my father unwilling to enlighten us much about his early years, I decided that, when I myself left school, I would try as hard as I could to find out for myself about his Turkish ancestry. As I set out on my gap year travels, Turkey was to be one of my first ports of call.

After staying with my godmother, Dolly Rau, in Paris (her husband was an antiquarian book dealer and they lived on the Boulevard Haussmann), and with my aunt in Rome (my mother had twin sisters, one of whom – Monique, known as Minki – had married a Russian and they had a flat near the Piazza Mazzini, not far from the Vatican), I moved on to Florence and Venice. A week later, having absorbed as many churches and museums as my system could digest at one sitting, I caught a train from Trieste, heading for Athens.

If you are, as I was, a classicist, there is something quite unforgettable about waking up around 6 a.m. after an uncomfortable overnight train journey through the Balkans to see the snow-clad summit of Mount Olympus, the highest mountain in Greece, on the starboard bow. Nowadays, of course, I see Mount Olympus quite often because Jenny and I have built a house in the Southern Pelion and if you fly to Thessaloniki (as we often do), then drive south, you skirt the base of the mountain.

But in February 1959 I was seeing Olympus for the first time in my life. It was a mind-blowing experience. Olympus was the home of the gods! You weren't just sitting in the Upper VIth form room reading about all the celestial goings-on on those mountain peaks. If you pushed up the blind, pulled down the window and stuck your head out and gazed up at the snowy slopes, you could almost see the gods at play.

Incredible as it may seem to our well-travelled younger generations nowadays, apart from one holiday visit to Norway I had never before been out of England. Truth to tell, I had hardly been to London. Once we had moved from Surrey to Exmoor, as we did in 1951, my life tended to focus around the Dulverton–Sherborne axis.

Seen in this perspective, it is probably not difficult to understand that the first few months of 1959 are etched indelibly in my mind. In the space of a few weeks I had visited the very wellsprings of European culture (Paris and Rome, Florence and Venice). I had continued the Grand Tour by stopping for a few days in Athens and had then spent the next two weeks travelling, by local bus, around the Peloponnese.

One day I ran on a mat of spring flowers around the stadium at Olympia, imagining I was competing in the first Olympic Games. On another occasion I stood centre stage in an empty theatre at Epidauros chanting the choruses from the *Agamemnon*. On yet another occasion, I crawled on all fours – like the great Heinrich Schliemann – through the Lion Gate at Mycenae. 'I have gazed on the face of Agamemnon', Schliemann exclaimed when he came upon the famous gold mask which now resides in the Kunstmuseum in Berlin. Could such a revelation, I wondered as I continued my journey, be vouchsafed to any of my generation? If I didn't become a farmer, might I become an archaeologist? Archaeology seemed then, as indeed it still seems to me now, a high calling.

After about a fortnight in Greece, I headed for Piraeus (like Plato and his friend Glaucon at the beginning of the *Republic*) and boarded a ferry for Istanbul.

Actually, I didn't make it all in one go. I disembarked at Mykonos, halfway across the Aegean, and spent two or three nights there, walking round the island, visiting the churches, sitting in the bars and chatting to the locals. Mykonos in 1959 was far from attaining the peak of celebrity which it has today. It was just another sun-drenched Cycladic island. I hired a donkey one day and rode inland to visit some of the churches, as well as the famous windmills. I even wrote a mawkishly sentimental poem called 'Isle of the Sunset'!

I don't remember whether I slept on deck during the journey from Mykonos to Istanbul. I suspect I did. I certainly could not have afforded a cabin. At all events, I remember standing at the port rail soon after dawn as we steamed past Gallipoli. What carnage those cliffs had seen! And, yes, what a tremendous performance the Turks had put up! Gallipoli had been the making of Atatürk, then a young colonel in the Turkish armed forces. In many ways, it had been the making of modern Turkey as well.

A few hours later, as we swung round to enter the Golden Horn, I had my first glimpse of one of the most extraordinary cities in the world. Call it Byzantium, call it Constantinople, call it Istanbul – until you have seen it, nothing prepares you for that stupendous array of domes, minarets and ancient battlements, silhouetted against the morning sky.

I grabbed my bag and headed down the gangway to be engulfed immediately by scores of importunate hands. I had sent a cable from Mykonos to my step-grandmother, Sabiha, whom Ali Kemal had married several years after my grandmother, Winifred's, untimely death, giving an indication of my arrival time, so now I cast my eye around hoping to see her. I didn't know what she looked like, since none of my family had ever met her.

'Don't worry, darling, if they don't come to meet you by the dock,' my mother had cheerfully reassured me. 'I have Sabiha's address. It's 3 Beyoglu-Yeniçarsi.'

'How do I say three in Turkish?'

Miraculously, my mother had found out. 'Just say Beyoglu-Yeniçarsi *Ootch*. *Ootch* is the Turkish for three.'

My step-grandmother Sabiha's abode was an old house, built on a steep and narrow cobbled street in the heart of the city which, as it turned out, was inaccessible to vehicles. I had to get out of the battered taxi and haul my bag the last few hundred yards, all the while mouthing the magic password 'Beyoglu-Yeniçarsi *Ootch!*' at passers-by.

By coincidence, I arrived at Sabiha's door at precisely the moment she herself returned home from a fruitless quest to find me at the ferry terminal. We had managed to miss each other in the general hubbub.

She was amazed to see me. '*Tiens, tu es déjà arrivé, mon petit.*'

I rather enjoyed being addressed as 'mon petit' by Sabiha even though I was considerably taller than she was. I can see her now, peering at me through thick lenses as we stood together on the step in front of the house. She already suffered from cataracts and subsequently lost much of her vision, though late in life an operation restored her sight.

I stayed five days with Sabiha in Istanbul on that first visit and I came to appreciate her enormously. Though her own father, Zeki Pasha, had been one of the Sultan's key officials with a famous *yali* on the Bosphorus, her life had not been easy. After Ali Kemal's death in 1922, Sabiha had deemed it safer to take their son to Switzerland. There had been little money and it must have been a strain in every sense bringing the child up single-handed and putting him through school and then university in a foreign land. The compensation, if such it can be called, came later after their return to Turkey as she was able to observe Zeki's rapid progress in the Turkish diplomatic service.

Sabiha's brother, Sedat, was staying with her when I arrived. He was a delightful old gentleman who told me he had once been governor of one of the provinces of the Ottoman Empire. I could envisage him as a powerful pro-consul ruling some desert outpost. One such pro-consul, I recalled from having read *The Seven Pillars of Wisdom*, had traumatized T. E. Lawrence during his stay in Dera'a. I didn't think Uncle Sedat, as I quickly came to know him, was that way inclined.

His chief pleasure was not small boys but the airmail edition of the *Daily Telegraph*. He would send me off to Taksim Square in the afternoon to buy a copy at one of the news-stands. Sedat explained that he made a profit on every newspaper. After perusing it thoroughly he would pass it on to his tobacconist who in turn had a network of customers eager to use this thin but tough paper to roll their own cigarettes.

I still have a carpet which I bought in the bazaar during that first stay in Istanbul. I also have the Guide Bleu to the city which I used then. Almost all the distances you needed to cover you could manage on foot. I would walk down the cobbled steps from Sabiha's house to the Golden Horn, cross it by the Galata Bridge, then climb on up to the bazaar, the Blue Mosque or St Sophia. I spent several mornings in Topkapu and several afternoons visiting the little villages along the Bosphorus, the wooden houses still overhanging the water as they had done for centuries.

One day, wishing to venture further afield, I caught a bus up the Turkish side of the Bosphorus towards the Black Sea. I got out at the last stop and went on walking, determined to glimpse this famous body of water which Sherborne's headmaster, R. W. Powell, always referred to as the Euxine, or Hospitable Sea.

The Euxine was not very hospitable to me that afternoon. I had passed a couple of signs ignoring whatever message they bore since I couldn't understand Turkish. I had walked on to enjoy a first tantalizing glimpse of sea when suddenly a squad of soldiers started to chase me, rifles at the ready. The soldiers were clearly conscripts, swarthy, almost Mongol in appearance. One or two had taken off their round helmets as they ran so I could see their thick black hair.

What puzzled me most of all were the hand gestures. When Turks want you to 'come here', the sign they make with their hands is 'go away'.

The more they gesticulated, the faster I headed in the wrong direction. When I saw one of them raising his rifle, I decided that the safest course was to sit down on the ground and wait for them to come to get me.

It took an hour to sort things out. The problem was that I had inadvertently strayed into a military area. The Turks are very sensitive about such things. With minimal Turkish I had to explain that my intentions were wholly benign. I had just been hoping to see the sea.

When at last they let me go, I was effusive in my thanks. '*Teshekur ederim*,' I said. '*Chok teshekur*.' Thank you very much.

We shook hands all round. They could not have been friendlier. As conscripts they were probably not much older than I was. I could have been carrying a rifle myself, I reflected, if the British government hadn't decided to end national service a few months earlier.

The next day I left Istanbul for Ankara. The bus station was by Galata Bridge. The noise was deafening as the different travel companies cried their wares. 'Ismir! Bursa! Ankara! Ankara!'

I found the right bus in the end, hoisted my luggage onto the roof along with sacks of potatoes, motorcycle tyres and a pair of hens tethered to the railings. For the next twelve hours we bumped our way across the Anatolian Plateau.

Near Bolu, high up on the plateau, we broke down comprehensively. An axle had collapsed under the strain. We clustered round a roadside canteen and had endless glasses of clear sweet tea while repairs were made.

We finally arrived in Ankara in the evening of the following day. It was too late for me to try to find my Turkish family, so I checked into a hotel for the night.

Next day was Saturday. The Turkish Foreign Ministry was closed but I made my way there anyway.

'Take a taxi,' Sabiha had advised. 'Ask for Hariçe Vekaleti. That's Turkish for Foreign Office.'

Around 11 a.m. I found myself in front of a modern concrete building flying the Turkish flag. A soldier with round helmet and rifle stood guard. Remembering my recent experience by the Black Sea, I approached nervously.

What was I to say to him? I wondered. I didn't speak Turkish and I felt sure he didn't speak English.

I stood there for a minute or two, undecided. Then inspiration dawned.

In my last term at Sherborne, with time on my hands, I had read a brilliant book on the subject of lyric poetry by Maurice Bowra, the Warden of Wadham College, Oxford. He had included in his eclectic collection a short Turkish poem.

'*Two red-legged partridges sat piping on a hillock. Partridges, pipe no more! The world is sorry enough!*'

By some fluke, I more or less remembered the Turkish original which Bowra had printed alongside the English translation.

'*Iki kiklik bir tepende otiyor,*' I spouted. '*Otme de, kiklik, benim dertim yetiyor, aman! aman!*'

Amazingly, my impromptu recital did the trick, thereby confirming me in my long-held belief that it's not so much what you say that matters, it's how you say it. The soldier lowered his rifle; he smiled a gap-toothed smile; he made urgent motions with his hand as though telling me to go and field at long leg.

But this time I didn't make a mistake. I knew he was beckoning me forward. And when he shook his head, I knew that meant 'yes' too. When a Turk says 'yes', he shakes his head as though he's saying 'no'.

And when he says 'no', he nods as though he's saying 'yes'. You get the hang of these things in the end.

Half an hour later, I found myself being ushered into a huge oblong room with a vast carpet on the floor, a large desk at the far end and a large portrait of Kemal Atatürk, first President of the Turkish Republic, behind it.

My uncle Zeki Kuneralp, then Political Director of the Turkish Foreign Ministry, was sitting behind the desk as I entered. He rose to his feet and walked towards me. I could see that even then he had a slight limp. In later years, as multiple sclerosis took hold, he started to use a stick and for the last part of his life, after he had retired from the Turkish diplomatic service, he was confined to a wheelchair.

'Ah, Stanley! I am so glad you are here. Did you have trouble finding me? They telephoned me at home to say you had arrived.'

Zeki embraced me warmly with a kiss on both cheeks, as is the Turkish way between friends and family. I was momentarily taken aback (when I was growing up even a handshake was regarded as excessive) but I rallied quickly. When in Ankara …

I spent two weeks in the Turkish capital that spring, getting to know my Turkish family. Zeki's wife, Neçla, could not have been kinder. Her English was not as good as Zeki's so we spoke mainly in French. Quite what she made of the sudden appearance of an English nephew, the son of a man she had never met, I don't know, but I never felt the slightest bit awkward in her house. The Kuneralps had two boys, Sinan, around eight years old then, and Selim, around five. We all got on well and I have stayed in touch with them over the years. Sinan became a leading publisher of historical research in Istanbul, while Selim followed his father into the Turkish diplomatic service and served as Ambassador to Sweden and South Korea before returning to Ankara to a high position in the Foreign Ministry where, at the time of writing, he is responsible for negotiating Turkey's entry into the European Union. At the current rate of progress this will probably keep him busy until he retires.

The Kuneralps lived at the top of one of Ankara's many hills. Quite soon, I mastered Ankara's public transport system – the ramshackle buses or the shared taxis, known as *dolmu* – and I was able to come and go at will. Ankara then was quite a small town, far different from the throbbing, noisy metropolis that it was to become in later years. I visited the huge Atatürk Mausoleum, climbed up to the old citadel, and even went to a performance – in English – of *The Importance of Being Earnest*, organized by the British Council. Zeki introduced me on that occasion to the British Ambassador, Sir Bernard Burrows, a tall man with craggy eyebrows. Sir Bernard in due course retired to the village of Steep, near Petersfield in Hampshire, and when I was campaigning to be elected as an MEP there in 1979 kindly attended one of my meetings. I recognized him at once in the audience. There was no mistaking those splendidly beetling brows.

One day during that first visit to Ankara I asked Zeki where the name 'Kuneralp' came from.

'Before the Republic was established, we didn't have surnames,' he explained. 'If your father was Mehmet Ali, you could be Ali Mustafa, and then your son could be Mustafa …'

He paused. 'Mustafa … er …'

'Mustafa-cup-of-tea?' I suggested.

'Why not?' Zeki laughed. 'Anyway, all that was over. In 1934, Atatürk decreed that all Turks were to have proper family names. There was an official list of names to choose from. One of the names was Koneralp, but we decided on 'Kuneralp' instead, which had more of a Swiss sound about it and fitted in with our Swiss background. Anyway, Ali Kemal's father, Ahmet Hamdi, came to Constantinople and made his fortune selling candles. He is also thought to have taken a Circassian slave girl as his wife!'

I rather liked the idea of having a Circassian slave girl as a great-grandmother.

'Sounds rather romantic,' I said.

'Maybe it was.'

Looking back, it seems ironic that I came to know Zeki Kuneralp and his family quite well long before Zeki and my father, his half-brother, ever met. In the 1960s Zeki came to London as Turkish Ambassador to the Court of St James's. My parents invited the Kuneralps to my sister Hilary's wedding, which was held in Winsford church. Hilary had met her future husband, Peter Heanly, on board a P & O liner, where they were both serving as pursers. Soon after their marriage, they emigrated to Australia with their young family. They are still there almost forty years later. At the last count, I had thirteen Australian great-nephews and great-nieces. There are, therefore, lots of good reasons to arrange regular trips Down Under and I make the most of them.

I wish I had been there in Winsford, Somerset, to witness that first encounter between my father and his half-brother Zeki. By then my father was almost fifty-five and Zeki himself must have been nearing fifty. Unfortunately, I couldn't make it. I was living in New York at the time where my first wife, Charlotte, was about to give birth to our eldest son, Alexander Boris, and it simply wasn't possible to make the journey.

But my mother, always a first-rate correspondent, kept us in the picture. 'Daddy and Zeki got on like a house on fire!' she wrote. 'Unfortunately, the Kuneralps weren't able to come back to Nethercote for the reception. Zeki was very busy with the Cyprus crisis and some Turkish Minister was arriving in London.'

There's always a Cyprus crisis, I thought, when I received the letter. I felt it was a great pity the two brothers had not had more time together but at least they had met each other at last.

I don't think Zeki and my father saw each again during Zeki's first London posting. I say 'first' because, some years later, Zeki was handed an unprecedented second diplomatic assignment as Turkish Ambassador in London. Even in the course of that second five-year stint, I am not aware that there was any further encounter between the diplomat and the farmer. Certainly, Zeki never made a repeat visit to Winsford and to the best of my knowledge my father never visited his half-brother in London.

What, with hindsight, do I make of this?

Well, deep down, I think it's a bit odd. If I had been in my father's situation, I would have made more of an effort. I think my mother felt it was odd too. Paradoxically, she was more interested in establishing the Turkish connection than my father was. I suspect he was only too happy to let sleeping dogs lie.

It was my mother, for example, not my father, who wrote to Sabiha when I went to Istanbul and who somehow sent Zeki an early warning that I was later heading for Ankara.

At all events, looked at in a longer perspective, her efforts were not wasted. The Johnson–Kuneralp link has endured, a fact which is largely due – I suspect – to the friendships I was able to form during that first visit to Turkey in the spring of 1959.

When the time came for me to leave Ankara, I took the train across country to Ismir. I made my way by various means up Turkey's Aegean coast, visiting some of antiquity's greatest ruins: Ephesus, Pergamon and Troy itself.

It's hard to describe, almost fifty years later, the sheer excitement I felt climbing up the ramparts of Troy and looking out over the plains to the sea. As I stood there, I could imagine Achilles dragging Hector's battered and bloodstained body around the walls. I could imagine the Greek fleet, standing offshore, waiting for a favourable wind to bring them home after years of conflict. In my mind's eye I saw Agamemnon, preening himself in victory, little knowing the gory fate that lay in store for him.

Walking round the ruins late one night, I had an eerie sensation of having somehow journeyed backwards in time. For me, as a classicist, the Homeric World was where it all began. I hadn't been brought up on the *Epic of Gilgamesh* and other gems of Sumerian literature. These works might pre-date the *Odyssey* and the *Iliad* but I didn't know enough about them. I certainly hadn't read them in the original.

But Homer I *had* read in the original. Not yet the whole of the *Odyssey* or the whole of the *Iliad* but large chunks of them anyway. And with Classical Honour Moderations lying ahead of me as soon as my gap year was over, one thing was sure. Whatever books of Homer I hadn't already read would have to be studied line by line over the next few months. That was one of the irreducible requirements of Classical Honour Moderations, the public examination I would be taking halfway through my second year at Oxford.

So as I paraded around the ramparts, trying to work out precisely where the Greeks had entered with their Wooden Horse, or where Priam had held court, I found myself looking forward as well as back.

Over the years I have visited many of the world's great monuments. Many are far more spectacular than the ruins of ancient Troy. But as far as I am concerned, none of them send a shiver up my spine the way Troy did.

Helen and Menelaus, Priam and Aeneas, Achilles, Patrocles, Paris and Cassandra – the legends of Troy have endured down the ages. There was absolutely no one else around that night, not even a night watchman. But as I stood there I could hear the voices of the past loud and clear.

TEN

Brazil: In the Heart of Mato Grosso

I travelled back from Istanbul on the Orient Express. 'Express' was a misnomer. As we passed through the Balkans, we seemed to stop at every wayside 'Halt' to let off or pick up passengers. My third-class compartment was crowded with Yugoslav peasants and their livestock. I spent at least one of the three nights that it took us to cross Europe wedged in the luggage rack. I remember waking up at one point from a fitful sleep to hear some newly boarded passenger enter our crowded compartment and exclaim: '*Voilà, il est dans le filet!*'

I stayed in London with my mother's sister, Den, on my way back to Exmoor. Den had a small house in Kensington where she pursued her artistic career.

She seemed glad to see me. 'Ah, the wanderer returns!' she exclaimed, as she opened the door.

'Not for long,' I replied. It was still only April. The Oxford term didn't begin till October. There was still plenty of time to cover some more ground. The question was: where to go?

Towards the end of my last term of Sherborne, the headmaster, Bob Powell, had received an enquiry from Alec Dickson, the man who founded the organization called Voluntary Service Overseas, or VSO. It was the British equivalent of the US Peace Corps and already had a high reputation. Powell very kindly put my name forward as a possible candidate.

In my subsequent correspondence with Mr Dickson, it emerged that since I only had a 'gap' of nine months I didn't qualify for VSO. Dickson was kind enough to suggest instead that I might have a word with Alexander Glen, the Managing Director of H. Clarkson, the shipping company.

My mother feeding tame lambs
at Nethercote, c.1952. When
newborn, orphans such as these
were popped in the kitchen oven
to warm them up.

My father at Nethercote,
c.1952. His pipe was his
inseparable companion.

ABOVE: Latin lesson at Ravenswood school, c.1952. I am in the front row, looking disgustingly keen.

BELOW: My mother at the wheel of the Lancia, Carbis Bay, c.1944. It was a great car, but too low-slung to survive Nethercote's long bumpy track.

ABOVE: My parents in the summer of 1954. My older brother, Peter, is on the left, my older sister, Hilary, on the right and my younger sister, Gillian (Birdie), is patting our yellow Labrador, Leader.

BELOW: My father at Nethercote, c.1951.

ABOVE: My mother in the garden of East Nethercote, c.1980. She was always young at heart and acted the part.

ABOVE: My father and I at Nethercote, March 1980. As I grew older, I came to know him better.

BELOW: Nethercote Valley seen from Bye Common, 1951. This photograph was taken by 'B' Paine, who arrived on her horse to work on the farm at Nethercote just a few days after we did.

ABOVE: My Turkish grandfather, Ali Kemal, and my grandmother, Winifred Brun, on their wedding day in London, 11 September, 1903. My great-grandmother, Margaret Brun, née Johnson, is on the left. Winifred's sister, Viva, is on the right.

BELOW: My English grandfather, Stanley Williams, and my French grandmother, Marie-Louise de Pfeffel. The photo was taken around 1905.

ABOVE: My mother as a girl. She acquired the nickname 'Buster' when she went to Cheltenham Ladies College.

ABOVE: My mother with shrimping-net, Carbis Bay, Cornwall, around 1922.

BELOW: The Pavillion du Barry in the Avenue de Paris, Versailles, is now the seat of the Chambre de Commerce, Versailles. This magnificent house, presented by Louis XV to his mistress, was owned by my French great-grandfather, Baron Hubert de Pfeffel. My mother was born there on 7 May, 1907.

ABOVE LEFT: Sir George Williams (1821–1905), my mother's great-grandfather, founder of the Young Men's Christian Association (YMCA). ABOVE MIDDLE: Carlo Pocci, Rome 1904, one of my Italian relatives. ABOVE RIGHT: My great-grandfather, Baron Hubert de Pfeffel, in 1867.

BELOW LEFT: Franz Pocci Bavaria, 1905, one of my German relatives.
BELOW RIGHT: Franz Pocci, and Hans Friedrich, Bavaria, 1930.

Oxford, 1961. Tim Severin and I plan the Marco Polo Route Project in my room at Exeter College. Heading across Asia on motorcycles was a great way of spending the Long Vacation.

After a crash near Tabriz, Iran, we have to manhandle one of our motorcycles onto a passing lorry.

'Glen may be able to help,' Dickson wrote.

It seemed a fairly slender reed but it was all I had. Around eleven o'clock on the morning after I returned from Turkey I found myself in front of a bronze plaque mounted in the wall outside a building in Bishopsgate, in the City of London. The plaque read: 'H. Clarkson Shipping (Brazil) Ltd'.

It was the word in brackets that particularly drew my attention. Brazil! Now that was an idea! An image of Rio's famous Copacabana Beach, populated by lithe bathing beauties, came to mind. Exmoor was rather short of bikini-clad beauties. And though there were plenty of girls at Sherborne Girls' School, some of them quite attractive, the opportunities for fraternization were limited.

I took the lift up to the fourth floor and bandied Alec Dickson's name about.

'Could I possibly see the Managing Director, Mr A. R. Glen?'

I made it as far as Mr Glen's outer office.

'I'm afraid he's in a meeting,' a well-spoken middle-aged lady told me.

'Don't worry. I can wait. As a matter of fact, I can probably wait till next October.'

The prospect obviously alarmed her because quite soon Mr Glen himself appeared. He was not particularly pleased to see me. He knew when a buck was being passed.

'Really,' he tut-tutted, 'Dickson shouldn't have done this.'

He looked me up and down. I think I was perfectly presentable. I had washed my hair at Den's that morning and put on a clean shirt and tie. It might even have been an old school tie, since I was now entitled to wear one.

Glen sighed. 'Why don't you write down precisely what you are looking for and leave it with Mrs Coombes?'

When he had gone, I asked Mrs Coombes if she could kindly lend me a pen and paper. She duly obliged.

'Dear Mr Glen,' I wrote. 'Thank you so much for sparing the time to see me this morning. I am keen to go to Brazil sometime between now and October. I am, of course, ready to work my passage on one of your boats.'

I handed it over. 'Do you think this might do?'

Mrs Coombes examined it critically. 'I shouldn't say "boats" if I were you. We prefer to call them "ships".'

I spent the next week on the farm, anxiously waiting for some communication from Clarkson. Lambing had already begun and there was much to do. Each morning my sister Hilary and I would ride round the sheep, checking which ewes had had lambs overnight and whether all was well. It was always good to find twins. By then our breeding flock probably numbered over two hundred ewes. Since some lambs inevitably died in the first days of their life, through exposure to the elements, being taken by a fox or accidentally mislaying their mum, having twins kept the batting average up. If by the end of lambing we had as many newborn lambs as we had ewes, we considered this a successful outcome.

Nowadays, of course, most farmers on Exmoor lamb 'in' as opposed to 'out'. They have built lambing sheds and colour-code the rams so they know precisely which ewes have been served when and, therefore, when they are going to lamb. They bring the ewes in, watch over them in the pens, feed them pellets as well as hay and thereby avoid the high wastage rates, both of ewe and lamb, which characterized Exmoor farming as we practised it.

Of course, we tended to the weakest lambs if we found them in time, most likely huddled beneath a hedge somewhere. If the mother had died, we would bring in the surviving lamb and pop it in the bottom oven of the Rayburn in the kitchen. As it recovered, it would give the occasional plaintive bleat, a signal to warm up a bottle of milk.

Ideally, you tried to find a foster-mother for it. This could often involve a degree of deception. For example, if you found a recently dead lamb and a clearly bereaved mother, you could skin the corpse and drape the jacket over the live lamb you wanted to foster. For a moment, the ewe might be puzzled. The bleat of the new lamb wouldn't sound the same as the bleat of the old lamb. But by the time she had sniffed the jacket draped around the new arrival she would decide that her nose was more reliable than her ears.

For me, it was always a magic moment when you put the two of them in a pen together. You go away for a few minutes so as not to interfere with the bonding process. When you get back, you see the lamb with its head under the ewe's udder and its tail wagging furiously.

Of course, it didn't always work. We were usually left with some 'tamies' at the end of the lambing season. These would hang around the kitchen door and my mother would feed them until they were old enough to fend for themselves.

Some of our 'tamies' decided they preferred living with us than with the flock. They made their way back to the farmhouse even if you turned them out with the rest of the sheep and packed them off up Room Hill. You had to be really persistent to get rid of them.

One such lamb was called Blindie because he was blind. As I remember it, the crows had pecked his eyes out soon after he was born, his mother having deserted him, but unusually he had survived. Blindie stayed with us for years. You could often find him lying against the meadow gate and you had to push him out of the way if you wanted to go through.

Blindie was a peaceful soul. One day my father's horse, Ranger – that friendly giant – leaned his long neck over the gate and, literally, chewed Blindie's ears off. He didn't seem to mind.

In the end, we ate him for Sunday lunch. It was a strange feeling. My father, who for once had come back from the pub reasonably promptly, seemed rather subdued as he sharpened the knife before carving. We had all known Blindie a long time.

From the financial point of view, having a good lambing was a vital consideration. That particular year, I recall, the accountant wrote to us to indicate that we had at last made a profit. A small profit. To be accurate it was £13. 'I think the corner has been turned', wrote Mr Shapland of Amherst and Shapland, Minehead.

That phrase 'the corner has been turned' entered into Nethercote folklore. We had visions of sunlit uplands, populated by healthy bank balances. Alas, those sunlit uplands always remained a distant prospect. When my father finally retired from active farming, in 1969, he had – from his point of view at least – had some of the most enjoyable years of his life. But he had not put a lot of money in the bank.

Talking of money, my father asked me one morning at breakfast after I had come back from my sheep round and fed and watered my horse, how I proposed to finance my trip to South America.

'I expect to work my passage,' I replied.

'And when you're there?'

'I'm going to take some money out of my savings book before I go.'

I still have that savings book, though there are no longer any funds in it. But there were then. Over the years, my grandfather, Stanley, would slip his grandchildren a fiver while encouraging them to invest it wisely. In due course, I opened a Post Office savings account in St Ives, the nearest town to Carbis Bay where Grandpa lived, and deposited these occasional donations. Amazingly, by the time of my Brazil trip, they added up to almost £100 sterling.

'I've got almost £100,' I added confidently. 'That will make several million Brazilian cruzeiros. I'm sure I'll be able to go a long way on that.'

As it turned out, I didn't have to work my passage at all.

About ten days after I arrived home from Turkey, Mr Barwick, the postman, put-putted into our yard on his little BSA Bantam motorcycle. We were all in the kitchen having elevenses at the time at the long rectangular table, which took up most of the room.

Barwick banged on the door. Two little lambs warming up in the bottom oven bleated. The dogs barked madly and rushed to go out into the yard. As far as I remember, we had about six dogs at that point. Our Labradors, Leader and Minki, were still alive, and we had acquired various sheepdogs as well. I don't remember the order in which they arrived but the names – Kylie, Misty, Lassie, Rogue – stick in my mind.

'Come in, Mr Barwick,' my mother called. 'Would you like a cup of coffee?'

'That's very kind of you, Mrs Johnson.'

Barwick produced a letter from his regulation Royal Mail satchel.

'Letter for you, Stanley.'

I could see from the address on the envelope that it was from H. Clarkson. The family was agog. They all knew I was waiting to hear about Brazil.

'Dear Mr Johnson,' I read aloud, 'I am glad to say that though there is no Clarkson vessel travelling to Brazil in the immediate future, we have made arrangements with a sister company and are able to offer you the Owner's Cabin on the *Louis Dreyfus* which will be leaving Workington in Cumberland bound for the port of Vitoria in Brazil on 20 April. Since the *Louis Dreyfus* is not a Clarkson vessel, I am afraid they will have to charge you a nominal victualling charge of £1 (one pound) a day.

'We shall of course arrange for a ship to bring you back from Brazil in time for the beginning of the Oxford term.

'Please confirm by return whether you would like to take up this offer.'

The letter was signed by the Company Secretary, Mr Bell.

'Hang on a moment, please, Mr Barwick,' I said, as I saw the postman about to take his leave. 'Have another cup of coffee. I've got a letter for you to put in the afternoon mail when you get back to the village ...'

My mother always told me I was born lucky. She said it was something to do with having a double crown. I do indeed have a double crown so maybe she was right. Be that as it may, I see the moment when Walter Barwick came into the kitchen at Nethercote, bringing the good news from H. Clarkson Shipping (Brazil) Ltd, as one of the most fortunate moments of an otherwise most fortunate life.

'The Owner's Cabin!' I exclaimed. 'I never expected that. At the very least, I thought I was going to have to work my passage.'

'I'm glad you got back for lambing. Some of it, anyway,' my father commented, pipe in mouth.

He sounded a bit grudging, I thought, but I brushed it aside.

'Anyone know where Workington is?' I asked.

Ten days later, some time after dinner, my train drew into Workington, Cumberland. It was already dark and the glow of the furnaces lit up the sky. Workington was still a steel town then and the task of ships like the iron-ore carrier *Louis Dreyfus* was to bring back the raw material to the foundries.

I went on board next morning and a few hours later we set sail. We were going out empty. As we steamed south, the sea grew calmer and the crew set up a ping-pong table in the forward hold.

When I wasn't playing ping-pong, I sat at a huge walnut desk in the Owner's Cabin just below the bridge, with a superb panoramic view of the surrounding ocean, reading the *Iliad* (in the original). There were twenty-four books in the *Iliad* and we would probably take about twenty-four days to reach Brazil. So if I read one book of the *Iliad* a day, I felt I could crack it. I could read the *Odyssey* on the way home.

One morning, about five days out from Workington, there was a knock at my door. The captain poked his head inside. He addressed me in French.

'The crew is going to be cleaning the holds this morning. Would you like to lend a hand?'

I looked up from the text in front of me. Achilles was still sulking in his tent. I hadn't got very far. I wasn't sulking. Far from it. But I needed to press on.

'*Pas tellement, mon capitain*,' I replied. 'Tremendously kind of you to ask, but I'm all right for the time being.'

The captain took it in good part. Both he and the officers of the *Louis Dreyfus* were a spirited bunch. There was a copious supply of *vin ordinaire* on board. Indeed, I suspected they carried tankfuls of it or even used it for ballast. There would often be a sing-song after dinner.

> 'Buvez un coup,' *they would chant,*
> 'Buvez en deux,
> A la santé des amoureux
> Et merde au roi d'Angleterre
> Qui nous a declaré la guerre!'

I wasn't sure which King of England they were referring to but I raised my glass anyway.

As we neared Las Palmas in the Canary Islands, our first port of call, the first mate informed me that there had been a change of plan. Instead of going to Brazil, the *Louis Dreyfus* had been instructed to head for Sierra Leone, in West Africa.

'No idea why.' The man shook his head. 'Probably something to do with the price of the mineral. Anyway, you've got two choices. You can either come to Sierra Leone with us or we can put you down in the Canaries. They'll pay for a hotel, of course, while you're waiting for onward transport. *Vous avez de la chance, n'est-ce pas?*'

I had to hand it to H. Clarkson Shipping (Brazil) Ltd. Once they had made a commitment, they stuck to it. After three days on the beach in Las Palmas, I received a message saying that the *Clarkeden*, bound for Vitoria in Brazil (my original destination), would be stopping next day

in Las Palmas to pick me up. Since this was a Clarkson vessel, no victualling charge would be payable.

I spent the next fifteen days in the lap of luxury. The Owner's Cabin
turned out to be an Owner's Suite. The food was good (though not quite
as good as what we had had on the *Louis Dreyfus* – the French had a
reputation to keep up). And no one for a moment suggested that I might
have better things to do than chunter on through my Greek set books.

We crossed the equator and, since it was the first time I had done so,
I was dutifully dunked in the canvas pool they had rigged up. As we
headed into the tropics and the weather got warmer, I spent more time
on deck, sitting at the stern in a deck chair. The steward would bring
me a cold beer from time to time. When I had finished, I would toss the
can into the foam and watch it bob out of sight.

The future seemed full of promise. Given a bit of luck, a chap might
do something with his life.

All good things come to an end. One morning I woke up, looked out
of my window and saw that we had at last arrived. We were moored at
a quay. Cranes and derricks hovered overhead. Thickly forested hills
surrounded the harbour.

Clarkson's local agent had come to the dockside to greet me. 'Try to
let me know in advance when you need to go back,' he said. 'I'm not
sure what the shipping schedule is at the moment. I'm sure we'll find
something.'

'I hope so.' I didn't want to be late for my first term at Oxford. Not
too late anyway.

I handed him my Homer, as well as my Liddell and Scott, the huge
Greek–English lexicon. 'I'd be awfully grateful if you could hang on to
these for me until I get back.'

Vitoria is the capital of the state of Espírito Santo, almost 350 miles
north of Rio de Janeiro. That night I caught the long-distance bus
south, the first step in a journey which occupied the next several
months and which took me across the whole of the South American
continent, from Atlantic to Pacific.

Nowadays, given the rapid strides Brazil has made economically
over recent years, many of the long-distance buses are air-conditioned.
Some even have television and on-board toilets. There is usually a
reasonable amount of leg room.

That wasn't the case in 1959. For seventeen hours, I sat with my knees jammed to my chest, wiping the sweat from my brow. Every three hours or so we stopped at some wayside halt. The bus would quickly be surrounded. Long brown arms would thrust small cups of strong, sweet coffee through the open windows.

By the time we reached Rio, towards evening the next day, I felt I had drunk enough coffee to last a lifetime.

I found a small hotel just off Copacabana. In those days, the seafront had not yet been widened. The ocean came right up to the tall buildings, which fronted the beach, and the surge of the sea sometimes broke over the narrow strip of road known as the Avenida Atlantica.

Taking my first dip in the sea that night was a salutary experience. I had had a Cornish childhood and had swum in rough seas before, but nothing prepares you for these Atlantic breakers. I found myself being rolled over and over, the force of the water being such that you had to cling onto your swimming trunks with one hand while trying to regain your balance with the other. It took a couple of caipirinhas in a seafront bar to set me straight.

I did all the things one is meant to do in Rio, such as visiting the Botanical Gardens and the Sugar Loaf Mountain, as well as taking the little funicular railway to see the gigantic statue of Christ which towers over the city on the summit of Corcovado. But I didn't want to stay in Rio long. In the course of that long bus journey down from Vitoria, I had formed a plan. Why didn't I try to get all the way to Machu Picchu, the 'lost' city of the Incas in the heart of Peru?

I didn't, admittedly, know much about Machu Picchu except that it had famously been 'discovered' by the American explorer Hiram Bingham in 1911. But the first few months of my gap year had whetted my appetite for archaeological adventures. I had already done Greece and Rome. I had seen Hittite ruins in Anatolia. I had visited Gordion (site of the famous knot), Pergamon and Troy. Why not add the Incas to the list?

From Rio, I took another bus to São Paulo, Brazil's main industrial city. I went to the railway station. My Portuguese was fairly rudimentary but I had discovered that, with a good grounding in Latin and a willingness to experiment as far as pronunciation was concerned, I could usually get along. They don't call it *Latin* America for nothing.

'*Quando sale el tren per Peru?*' I asked at the ticket office.

The man laughed. He shook his head. '*Não é trem por Peru.*'

Technically speaking, he was right. There was no transcontinental railway. There still isn't today. But by dint of persistence I discovered that there was actually a little train which, once a week, chugged its way across the heart of Mato Grosso, one of the largest states in Brazil, towards the Bolivian border.

I wasn't much of an expert in geography. I hadn't done any since my prep school days. And even then, though the Rockies had featured in our lessons as far as I remembered, as well as the prairies of Manitoba, we certainly hadn't covered South America. But I was pretty sure Bolivia lay in the right direction.

I had by then changed all my pounds sterling into cruzeiros. I stuffed the Brazilian money into a cloth purse, which I hung from my neck under my shirt. It wasn't very practical when all you wanted was to fish out a small denomination note for a quick cup of coffee, but I decided it was the best way of avoiding pickpockets.

'*Un momento!* Hold on a moment!' I fished inside my shirt and yanked out the purse.

'Do you want to go to Corumba?'

'If Corumba is as far as I can go, that's what I'll do.'

I took the ticket and stuffed the purse back in its place. It seemed sadly depleted. At this rate, I thought, I might make it to Peru, but I certainly wouldn't make it back.

Four days later I set off on the journey of a lifetime. In fact, as I look back on years of travel in all five continents, I cannot think of another journey that has marked me so profoundly.

I suspect this has something to do with the fact that I was still young and impressionable. Not yet nineteen, I hadn't seen it all before. The truth was I had hardly seen anything before. But there was more to it than that. South America in those days really was off the beaten track and the particular route I had elected to follow to my chosen destination was eccentric, to say the least.

For three days we chugged across the heart of Brazil. It was a narrow-gauge, one-track railway and we stopped at every station or halt along the way. We were pulled by a wood-fuelled steam engine. At night, you could see the sparks fly from the funnel. The earth was scorched at either side of the track.

I can remember the names of some of those stations now. The first one of any significance was Três Lagoas, which means 'three lagoons' in Portuguese. There was no sign of any lagoons when we were there. The next important station was Campo Grande, the capital of Mato Grosso. Campo Grande nowadays is a big city. There are tall buildings and traffic jams. But Campo Grande then was a place where the ranchers came when they needed a break from ranching. There was a Wild West feel about it. We stopped for a couple of hours. I had time to stretch my legs, buy a beer and eat a steak from one of the local ranches, or *fazendas*.

I wasn't the only person to get off the train in Campo Grande. Most of the other passengers got off and stayed off. One man who returned with me after our break for refreshments shook his head when I told him I was going on to Corumba, a town on the Brazil–Bolivia border.

'*Não!*' he said. The man made swimming motions with his arms. '*Muinto agua!*'

The railway to Corumba had apparently been washed away. Porto Esperança, about fifty miles downstream on the Paraguay River, was as far as we could go. After that we would have to take a boat upriver.

I am ashamed to say that at that moment, as I sat there on the train in Campo Grande station, I didn't know that to the west lay the Pantanal, one of the world's largest and most important wetlands. In fact, I had never heard of the Pantanal.

With hindsight, I wish I had made much more of that magical journey upstream on the riverboat from Porto Esperança to Corumba. In reality, I was just so grateful to have found some means of continuing my journey that I simply stood on deck staring at the vast expanse of water and swamp without appreciating that I was seeing one of the wonders of the natural world.

Forty-two years later, in the late summer of 2001 to be precise, I returned with my (then) sixteen-year-old son, Max, to Campo Grande. We took a small plane into the heart of the Pantanal to land, about an hour later, on an airstrip at the Fazenda Rio Negro, a ranch and conservation centre belonging jointly to Conservation International and Earthwatch. I was at the time a trustee of the latter organization.

We spent our time riding like gauchos around the ranch, or paddling dugouts on the river, enjoying the antics of the giant river otters, fending off the alligators and caimans, and looking out for capy-baras and peccaries on the riverbank. The birdlife was extraordinary. The *fazenda* was, for example, home to an important colony of hyacinth macaw, a beautiful and highly endangered species. Max and I would be woken in the morning by the call of these large birds which had hollowed out their nests in the trees surrounding the ranch house. Sometimes they would spread their wings and circle over us, cawing, as we breakfasted in the open air. The colour of their plumage against the morning sky was spectacular. They are not called hyacinth macaw for nothing.

ELEVEN

Penniless in Machu Picchu

I crossed over the Paraguay River at Corumba into Bolivia and made my way across country. In Santa Cruz, I was lucky enough to be able to hitch a ride on a military plane going to La Paz, Bolivia's capital, high up in the Andes.

On the long journey across Brazil's Mato Grosso I hadn't seen many Indian faces. Brazil's native Indian tribes have had to face centuries of persecution. War, exploitation and white man's diseases have exacted a hideous toll. In the whole of that enormous country, the total number of indigenous people did not then, and still doesn't, exceed a few hundred thousand.

How different it was – and is – in Bolivia, where Indians make up the majority of the population. As I walked the streets of La Paz over the next few days, breathless on account of the altitude, I would find myself surrounded by short, stocky, dark-haired men and women, with brown faces and bright black eyes, wearing ponchos around their shoulders and the distinctive bowler hat on their heads.

Nowadays, of course, the 'Inca Trail' features in many of the tourist brochures, but at the end of the fifties, when I was heading north from La Paz to Machu Picchu, I don't think I saw another white face. When I made my way, this time by bus, from La Paz to the Peruvian border, I would find myself hemmed in by a mass of Indian men, women and children, all of whom looked at me curiously, wondering what on earth I was doing.

Laden to bursting with people and produce from the mountain towns and villages, the vehicle puffed and wheezed its way across the *altiplano*, the high, rocky plain which is the dominant feature of the Andean interior.

I still have the black and white photos I took with an antique camera my father lent me for the duration. Through the window of the bus I snapped huge herds of vicuna (a kind of wild South American camel) and alpaca (which are like small llamas) against a backdrop of mountains. At Tihuanaco, on the shores of Lake Titicaca, the highest navigable lake in the world, I stopped to visit some ancient ruins, dating from the sixth century. Huge geometric stone structures recall what was once a major centre of Andean civilization.

I crossed the lake on the *Coya*, a steamboat built in Britain halfway through the nineteenth century before being exported to South America and carried up piece by piece into the high Andes, to be reassembled on Lake Titicaca. One hundred and fifty years later, the *Coya* was still going strong.

Disembarking at Puno, on the Peruvian side of the lake, I immediately entered into an argument with the authorities, who wished to charge me for a visa. I couldn't afford to pay for a visa, I argued. I truly couldn't. They relented in the end and stamped my passport anyway. I still have that now massively out-of-date document, its corners officiously clipped. As I flip through the pages to locate the Peruvian visa I acquired in 1959, I see that the word GRATIS has been stamped in large letters on the relevant page.

Money, sufficiency of, had by then become something of a preoccupation. Given the cold, I had had to sleep in a hotel during my few days in La Paz. I chose the cheapest place I could find and tried to keep my outlay to less than three shillings a night but still the sums mounted up.

Disaster struck in Cuzco, the (then) small Andean town that is the jumping-off point for Machu Picchu itself. I had found another cheap hotel for the night, a handful of pesos ensuring a flea-infested bed and a rough Indian blanket. To plump up the wholly insubstantial pillow, I removed my moneybag and stuffed it inside.

Next morning, I set off on the little mountain train, which chugs up through the steep-sided terraced valley towards Machu Picchu.

I had already bought the ticket on arrival in Cuzco the previous day so had no need of money when boarding the train. We were halfway to Machu Picchu when a toothless old Indian lady came through the carriage offering cups of *chicha* to the assorted passengers. I should explain about *chicha*. It's made from fermented maize. In the long, dark evenings in Andean villages you will sometimes see Indian families chewing away like football coaches watching the World Cup, then spitting into a communal urn. The brew that results from this process is potent and reasonably palatable. Above all, it is cheap.

I had already given up beer in the interests of economy, but I reckoned I could still afford a *chicha*.

'*Momento*,' I said. I reached for the cloth purse which, for reasons of security, as I have already explained, I always kept beneath my clothes, next to the skin. It wasn't there.

I swore blindly and at length. I knew what I had done with my money. I'd left it stuffed inside the pillow in that fleapit hotel.

I won't say that my trip to Machu Picchu was ruined. I pressed on that day, walked up the mountain, spent hours exploring the ruins and marvelling at the ingenuity of the Incas who had managed to construct this great stone fortress in the middle of a jungle. No, it was not ruined. You can't visit Machu Picchu without being flabbergasted, gobsmacked, totally *bouleversé* or whatever. Almost fifty years later, that spectacular image of the great Inca citadel set against the backdrop of soaring peaks has, justifiably, gained iconic status. I certainly appreciated it at the time.

That said, it was not the most relaxed afternoon I have ever spent. I had a tremendous sense of foreboding. Iago, in *Othello*, might very well say: 'Who steals my purse, steals trash.' But frankly, at this point, that purse was all I had.

Two days, and six bananas later, I came back to Cuzco. I went back to the hotel. I remembered the room I had been in and indicated that I wanted to visit it.

'*Número cuatro, por favor.*'

'*Ocupado*,' the man at the desk said.

I wouldn't take no for an answer. I went ahead anyway and banged on the door.

An old man came to the door in his underpants. I pointed to the bed. 'Just want to check the pillow. So sorry.'

He was puzzled but he let me go ahead anyway.

I lifted the pillow from the bed. It felt lumpy. It *was* lumpy. Miraculously, my cloth purse was still there. I mouthed a silent prayer to the Blessed Virgin Mary, Mother of God.

'*Desculpe me* ... Excuse me,' I said to the old man, slinging the purse round my neck and putting it firmly back where it belonged.

'*De nada.*' He sounded bemused.

I slipped him a couple of pesos anyway. For once, I could afford it.

My journey back from the heart of Peru to Vitoria, where I hoped to find a Clarkson vessel to carry me back to England, took much longer than the journey out. In the first place, I failed to find any convenient planes to cadge a lift on so ended up having to travel on rattle-trap buses the whole length of Bolivia. A journey which had taken me a few hours by air on an old Dakota meant days on the bus.

After a time, you get used to it. A kind of numbness descends. When we arrived in Cochabamba, after another seventeen-hour journey from La Paz, I remember saying to myself: 'What? So soon!'

The technique is always to prepare yourself for the worst, so that when things turn out better than you expected you are agreeably surprised.

The second reason the homeward journey took longer than the outbound was that I stopped off at a cattle ranch in Mato Grosso. It lay to the east of the Pantanal, about a hundred miles from Campo Grande. Called Fazenda de la Reina, it occupied several hundred thousand acres of prime cattle country with its own airstrips and several small single-engined planes.

In return for a plateful of eggs in the morning and some beef steak and rice in the evening, and a hammock beneath the southern stars, I offered my services as a ranch hand.

Being a cowboy in Mato Grosso wasn't like riding on Exmoor. There were no hills to speak of. And when you were rounding up cattle, the clouds of dust were so thick that you could scarcely breathe. All the same, it was great fun.

Over the campfire one evening, my fellow ranch hands started talking about a great project that had been launched several hundred miles to the north. Brazil's newly elected President, Juscelino Kubitschek, had decided that the time had come to 'open up the interior' of the country.

'We need to develop the great expanse of Amazonia', Kubitschek had proclaimed.

The President's basic argument was that the vast Amazon basin with its network of mighty rivers, including the Amazon itself, occupied almost two-thirds of the land area of Brazil and yet only a few hundred thousand people lived there.

Suddenly, Brazil began to be seized with 'development frenzy' as far as the Amazon was concerned. Gold could be panned from the rivers; rubber could be tapped from the trees. Or the trees could be sawn down, acre upon acre, mile upon mile and the logs floated downstream to the Atlantic ports.

Once the trees had gone, the cattle could move in. The land probably didn't belong to anyone. If it belonged to the Indians, that didn't really count. It was okay to go and grab it and if some Indians were killed in the process, well, that was just too bad.

The ranch hands swatted the mosquitoes with their sombreros, spat wads of tobacco into the fire and nodded sagely. They lifted their arms and pointed to the north. 'Brasilia!' That was where the future lay. Rio de Janeiro was fine if you wanted a good time with the girls, they laughed, but it wouldn't do as a gateway to the Amazon. Brasilia was not only going to be the new focal point for the region. It was going to be the capital of the whole country! Even the embassies were going to move! Imagine that! The fat-cat diplomats were going to have to up sticks from their luxurious life in Rio and sweat it out in the interior!

'How do I get to Brasilia?' I asked quietly, when there was a gap in the conversation.

It took me another two days to get by bus to Goias, the capital of the Brazilian state of that name, about halfway to Brasilia. I hitch-hiked on a truck the rest of the way. There was no tarmac, just a dirt road cut through the jungle.

We drove day and night, stopping only for calls of nature and those small, sweet, strong, sticky cups of coffee which by now I had become addicted to. When you saw the headlights of a truck coming from the opposite direction, a game of chicken ensued. Which driver would pull off the road first? If you left it too late, you could be smashed over the edge. Sitting high up in the driver's cab, I counted at least a dozen crashed vehicles. Sometimes, the rear wheels of the abandoned trucks would be sticking crazily up in the air with the mangled forest all around.

I arrived in Brasilia one morning in late August 1959, climbing stiffly down from the cab of the Mercedes truck which had brought me all the way from Goias.

For a while I wandered around fairly aimlessly. I saw what there was to see. By then, the broad outlines of the city, as planned by the brilliant Brazilian architect Oscar Niemeyer, could be discerned. The jungle had been cleared in the shape of a giant crossbow. On either side the red earth had been gouged out. The Congress building, which would house the Brazilian Parliament, was nearly completed. The foundations of the federal ministries had been laid. The lake had not yet been filled with water but the land had already been contoured.

Much of the clearance had been achieved by sheer backbreaking manual labour. There was simply no way huge earth-moving machinery could have had access to the site in those days. Shanty towns of labourers had sprung up in all directions. If you could wield a pick or a shovel, you had a good chance of picking up a job.

Today, I am convinced that moving the nation's capital into the heart of the Amazon region has only served to speed up Brazil's already high deforestation rate. Apart from having a serious impact on the tribal peoples and the local climate, the destruction of the Amazon rainforest has certainly contributed to global warming.

But I wasn't convinced of that at the time. I hadn't even thought about it. I had seen a lot of poor people in my journey across South America. Favelas, or urban slums, climbed the mountains behind Rio's famous beaches. I had seen real poverty in La Paz and some of the other Andean towns and villages I had visited. Insofar as I considered the matter at all, I probably thought building Brasilia was a good thing.

Nowadays, when I go to Brasilia, I like to tell people that I 'helped build' the new capital. Truth to tell, I didn't actually wield a pick or a shovel myself but as funds ran low I thought about it.

I joined a queue of day labourers one morning, waiting to be taken on at some building site. I flexed my muscles and tied a cloth around my head. You don't last long in the sun out there with your head uncovered. I was all set to go when a policeman drove by and asked to see my papers.

He looked at my passport and shook his head. Mine was a tourist visa. He asked me to follow him to his car.

I wondered at this point what was going to happen. Was I going to be beaten up by the police? Was I going to be fined for trying to find work as an alternative to going hungry?

I sat around for a while in the tin-shack police station while they debated my future. At last they told me the verdict.

'You're going to have to leave Brasilia,' the police captain said. 'We're going to fly you down to Rio this afternoon on a military plane.'

'I can't pay for the flight,' I said. 'I don't have enough money.'

'The army will pay,' the police captain said. 'It's their flight.'

It sounded too good to be true.

A week later, having flown down to Rio with the Brazilian military, I arrived back in Vitoria. A Clarkson ship was conveniently already in port. The Owner's Cabin was once again put at my disposal.

Three weeks later I disembarked in Cardiff and headed for the farm. My gap year was over.

TWELVE

'Life's like a tin of sardines'

When I went up to Oxford in October 1959, I found myself from a financial point of view reasonably well off. In fact, more than reasonably well off. *Very* well off.

Exeter College's Stapeldon Scholarship in Classics produced £100 a year. I had a State Scholarship, which also gave me £100 a year, and, as was the practice in those days, the local authority, in my case Somerset County Council, paid the tuition fees.

That wasn't all. I also had a Trevelyan Scholarship, which amounted to the then astronomical sum of £750 a year. The Trevelyan scholarships had been founded in 1958 by Dr Kurt Hahn, the German educationalist who had for years been headmaster of Gordonstoun, the school famously attended by both the Duke of Edinburgh and Prince Charles. The scholarships had been funded by some of the biggest names in British industry, e.g. P & O, British Steel and GKN, with a view to ensuring that up to ten deserving cases each year were financially supported throughout their time at Oxford or Cambridge.

How were these deserving cases to be chosen? The influence of Kurt Hahn was clearly discernible in the official information circulated to schools during my last term at Sherborne. There was to be no examination of any kind, though headmasters might be asked for a report. Basically, the boys who applied for the Trevelyan had to undertake a 'project' which demonstrated in some way the spirit of enterprise and initiative as well as real leadership qualities.

A few weeks after term started I finally met my fellow Trevelyan scholars at a black-tie dinner held in Lincoln College's dining hall. As we sat down at the long candle-lit oak table to be served a four-course meal on glittering silverware, the famous lines from Shakespeare's *Henry V* came to mind: 'We few, we happy few, we band of brothers.'

What had we done to deserve our good fortune? I gently quizzed my fellow diners about the different 'projects' they had put forward before being selected. Most of them, I soon discovered, had shown immense determination and ingenuity. For example, my friend and fellow Shirburnian Colin Lucas had gone to the Near East and had written a brilliant treatise about Crusader castles. Someone else had sailed a coracle across the Irish Sea. A third successful candidate had explored, apparently first hand, the 'myth and reality of flying carpets'.

'What did you do for your project, then?' David Housego, my neighbour at dinner, asked me. (David's project had been about France's Fifth Republic. I would meet him again in the spring of 2006 in Delhi, where – having left the *Financial Times* – he ran an import-export business.)

'I wrote an essay about "The Teddy boy problem in West Ham",' I told him.

'Where's West Ham?'

'In the East End of London.'

'Did you know a lot about the area?'

'Actually, no. But I had an impeccable introduction.'

I went on to explain that during my last year at Sherborne I had been invited by the Rev. David Sheppard, who had once been at Lyon House and who had gone on to play for England at cricket (captaining the team on a couple of occasions), to visit the Mayflower Family Centre in the Docklands where he worked. I had stayed with him and his wife, Grace, at the Mayflower and had observed at close quarters the work they were doing with deprived and difficult teenagers in that part of London. I decided to focus on the life and times of the East End Teddy boy as my Trevelyan 'project'. The term 'Teddy boy' could well have been a misnomer. I wasn't exactly sure what Teddy boys were meant to look like. But I felt it had a ring of authenticity.

David Sheppard was a large man in so many ways. If he had to choose between the sport he loved, and in which he excelled, and his duties as a committed and ordained Christian, he knew where his priorities lay. On more than one occasion he turned down invitations to play for England or for Sussex because of his commitment to his job as a pastor.

This might, I suppose, have had an impact on his performance on the field, because he was often short of practice. Freddie Truman, the England and Yorkshire fast bowler, once commented after David Sheppard had dropped a catch during a test match that he 'wished the Reverend could keep his hands together on as well as off the pitch!'

I spent my time in the East End walking with Sheppard around the Docklands. Canning Town, Plaistow, Barking – I got to know them all. We visited the slums and the working men's clubs, the pubs and church halls. Being famous, as David was, certainly helped. But the light that radiated from him didn't depend on his achievements at the crease, notable though these were. He had tremendous presence, an inner confidence (or so it seemed to me) that resulted from his own convictions and spiritual experience.

When David died in 2005, having been an outstanding Bishop of Liverpool, I was astonished to notice from the obituaries that he was only ten years older than I was. When I first met him he already seemed so solid, so mature, so wise. No wonder the youth of the Docklands came so readily into the Mayflower Family Centre. David and Grace Sheppard offered a viable alternative to life on the street.

After his retirement as Bishop of Liverpool, David Sheppard was made a member of the House of Lords. I met him one day as he was crossing Parliament Square on his way to a debate.

For a moment we stood on the pavement and reminisced. Over the years London's Docklands had changed beyond all recognition. When I first visited Canning Town at the end of the fifties, the sky had been serrated by a hundred cranes, loading and unloading cargo from ships moored by the wharves and quays. All that had gone. The Teddy boys had been replaced by the 'Yuppies'.

'Yuppies have souls too, of course,' David said. And with that he was gone.

It was the last time I saw him, though strangely enough I was reminded of him just the other day as I was writing this book.

I opened my email one morning to find an intriguing message.

'Dear Stanley Johnson', it said. 'I have been meaning to write to you for over forty years but have only just discovered your [email] address. I was at Oriel in 1957–1960. One day in the summer term of 1960 I received a card from David Sheppard inviting me to lunch in Oxford. I am so sorry I didn't send it on to you at the time. It must have been sent to me by mistake.'

The sender of the email gave his name at the end of his message. It was, like mine, Stanley Johnson. No wonder there had been some confusion. David Sheppard's invitation had gone to the wrong Stanley Johnson who, until that moment, I didn't even know existed.

I must say I felt a quick pang of regret. I was sorry to have missed a lunch with David Sheppard at the start of my Oxford career. And how rude David must have thought me not to have answered his invitation!

It was too late now, of course, to make amends, but as I sat over my computer that morning to reply to the 'other' Stanley Johnson, I also composed in my head a brief mental message to a man who had helped me far more than he probably knew. If David's faith was soundly based, he would get the message somehow. Even if it wasn't, it was worth a try.

I still have the essay about Teddy boys in West Ham, which I penned as my Trevelyan project. Written single space and quite legibly in fountain pen, it occupies about twenty foolscap pages. As a composition, I find it now a little too heavy, too earnest for my present taste. I seemed to believe then that the best way to deal with the Teddy boy problem was to get the violence 'off the streets and into the churches'. There is, in other words, a good dose of moralizing.

Had I found out, I wonder, that there were some churchmen on the Trevelyan judging panel? It is not impossible. It is more likely, I suspect, that I was influenced by the whole atmosphere at the Mayflower Family Centre, which, though not preachy, was certainly pious. I also recognize that I was then (in 1959) much more religious than I am today.

I had just had five years at Sherborne. I had attended church or chapel every day and twice on Sunday, to say nothing of house prayers. I had belted out stirring hymns like 'Forth in thy name O Lord I go' or 'I bind unto myself today'. The school chaplains were not figures of fun. Not to me anyway. If they preached that the 'fear of the Lord was the beginning of wisdom', I was ready to concede they might have a point.

One of the school chaplains, the Rev. F. C. 'Freddie' Carpenter, persuaded me to do Divinity S level in my spare time (and, as I have explained, I had a lot of time on my hands, having taken my main A level subjects when I was not yet sixteen). I enjoyed Divinity greatly. I found the notion of 'justification by faith' particularly attractive and wrote a powerful essay on the topic of 'faith, not works'. When the marks came in, I found I had done so well that I had been awarded the Huish Exhibition for Religious Knowledge.

So 'Freddie' Carpenter is someone else I have to thank. The last time I saw Freddie was in 1979 when he was the Very Reverend Dean of the Isle of Wight and I was canvassing for election as the Member of the European Parliament for the Isle of Wight and East Hampshire.

When I knocked on his door with my outsize rosette and candidate's smile, he recognized me at once.

'Good heavens!' he exclaimed. 'God moves in mysterious ways, his wonders to perform!'

Strictly speaking, I should have had an extra £60 a year at Oxford from the Huish, which would have brought the total before tax to £1100. I say 'before tax' because I didn't rule out the possibility that my father would attempt further raids on my income along the lines of the 'cash for cows' arrangement I had agreed to when I won a scholarship to Sherborne.

In the event, my father made no further requests for my help with the farm accounts. On the other hand, the £60 from the Huish didn't materialize either.

I remember reading the headmaster's announcement posted on the notice board in the cloisters. 'The Huish Exhibition for Religious Knowledge has been awarded to S. P. Johnson. The emoluments will go to the runner-up, H. D. Spurr.'

Emoluments! I muttered in disgust. What a word! I have distrusted it ever since.

Even without the cash, there have been some advantages in winning the Huish. Sometimes people ask me if I believe in God and I answer that I have an S level in Divinity. If they persist and say: 'But do you *really* believe in God?' I reply grandly: 'I won the Huish Exhibition for Religious Knowledge.' That shuts them up.

I spent my first year at Exeter in college. Mike Masterson and I had been allocated a set of ground-floor rooms on the staircase in the corner of the main quad, next to the chapel. We each of us had our own bedroom but we shared a sitting room.

Mike was reading PPE. He had attended Sir William Borlase School in Slough and had a beard. I had never met a grammar school boy with a beard before. As a matter of fact I had never met a grammar school boy before. My trajectory had taken me with monotonous regularity from Exmoor to Dorset and back again. Though I had changed trains at Taunton and again in Yeovil (where, lugging your suitcase across town, you actually had to change stations as well as trains), I had not as far as I knew met any grammar school boys.

Early on in our friendship Mike told me how his father had once sought work during the Depression.

'He walked all the way to Scotland and asked for a job on some highland laird's estate, only to be turned away. What really irked him was that, as he left, the gamekeeper aimed his gun at my dad's backside and peppered him. To be fair, the gamekeeper wasn't trying to hurt my dad, just to scare him off.'

'Was he wearing padding?' I asked frivolously.

I'm surprised Mike put up with me, but he did. He got married while he was still in college and invited me to the wedding. The reception was held in the Exeter dining hall, a beautiful room, hung with portraits of the Rectors, past and present. Exeter's founder, Sir Walter de Stapeldon, Bishop of Exeter, had the place of honour above High Table. Sometimes during dinner in hall, I would remember my Stapeldon Scholarship, raise a glass and drink a silent toast to the great man.

As a matter of fact, Mike Masterson not only invited me to his wedding. He asked me to compose and recite a brief epithalamium which I duly did. From a poetic standpoint this effort was more B-minus than B-plus but Mike and his bride, Sylvia, as well as the assembled guests seemed to enjoy it.

Like so many others, when I went up to Oxford (in October 1959), I wanted: (a) to win a blue by playing rugby for the university, (b) to become President of the Oxford Union, and (c) to be awarded a first-class honours degree in Greats, more properly known as Litterae Humaniores.

I'm not saying this was necessarily the order of priorities in which I placed my ambitions but these were definitely the top three.

Let's deal with the rugger first. The nearest I got to a blue was getting a Seniors Trial in my first term. I knew I wasn't fit. For the last several weeks I had been taking it easy in the Owner's Cabin on that Clarkson vessel which brought me back from Brazil. I had played a couple of games for the Exeter College XV but, realistically, the reason I was invited to appear for a 2.30 p.m. kick-off at the Iffley Road ground was more to do with my schoolboy reputation as a tenacious prop forward than to any current evidence of prowess.

I don't think I touched the ball at all that afternoon. My one moment of glory came when I tackled C. M. Payne in front of the grandstand. Colin Payne, who had been at Sherborne two or three years before me, had developed into a tremendously good player. He was six foot four inches in height, which gave him an immense advantage in the lineout. He was also a powerful scrummager and had already won his blue as well as an England cap.

Out of breath and puffing desperately, I found the words of the Sherborne School rugby song chorus ringing in my ears (the First XV used to sing it with gusto at the end-of-term concert): '*Collar him, down with him! Well played all!*'

At some point that afternoon on the Iffley Road I collared Colin Payne all right. I downed him. He fell like a great tree in the forest.

From where I too lay covered in mud I could see the selectors' box. Had I done enough to catch their eye? Would they be impressed, I wondered, these great and good men who wielded such awesome and arbitrary power? They could put a tick against your name, which meant you could get a second Seniors Trial or even be selected on the spot. Or they could put a cross, which meant that your rugby career, at least at university level, was probably over.

I earned the cross, not the tick. In spite of my efforts in bringing down the man who was probably Oxford's best player at the time, no further invitations to appear at the Iffley Road ground came my way.

I don't think that, like Michael Heseltine, I wrote my ambitions down on the back of an envelope but I kept them firmly in my head. Within weeks of the start of my first term at Oxford I recognized that one of them at least would not be realized.

That said, I had two or three years of happy rugby for the college side and was even elected President (i.e. team captain) of the Exeter Rugby Football Club at the end of one summer term, only to decide as the rugby term actually began that I was too busy. As a result of that totally wet and flaccid decision on my part Mike Squire, our scrum half, had to take on the captaincy at the last moment, a task he performed with signal success.

That particular fiasco taught me a lesson. Don't agree to take things on unless you know you can actually do the job. It is a lesson that, in future years, I persistently failed to heed.

Exeter College's 'rugger buggers' were, in my day, a highly visible – and audible – element of college life. In the evening, and particularly after a match, they tended to congregate in the bar at the bottom of Staircase 2 and sing rowdy, vulgar and often obscene songs.

I wasn't one of the hard-core drinkers. Though I might have a pint or two before dinner, I didn't usually make a night of it. When 'hall' was over, I would go back to my room and try to crack on with Homer or whatever. I had finished the *Iliad* on the way out to Brazil, but on the way back had only managed two-thirds of the *Odyssey*. There was a lot of ground to make up if I was to do well in Classical Honour Moderations, 'Mods', which would be held in the Easter term of 1961; in other words in about a year and a half.

Being in the far corner of the quad, Mike Masterson and I were usually fairly well insulated from the raucous noises coming from Staircase 2. But sometimes as the team got into full swing the sounds would penetrate even if you were 'sporting your oak' (most undergraduate rooms in those days had a solid oak external door which you could lock from the inside to indicate that you did not wish to be disturbed).

The Exeter rugger buggers' favourite song, I remember, was called 'Julie'. I can remember the first verse at least but because this aims to be a family-friendly memoir, I won't repeat it here.

The chorus was always sung fortissimo. It was a simple and repetitive refrain. Even the thickest rugger buggers could remember the words.

> 'With a bum titty, bum titty, titty bum
> With a bum titty, bum titty bum,
> With a bum titty, bum titty, titty bum
> And a bum titty, bum titty *BUM!*'

That last 'BUM!' often sounded like a sonic boom. You could hear it in the Turl or even the Broad.

One evening, as the windows in our room began to shake with the noise, I remember Mike Masterson raising his eyes from *Mathematics for Economists* and stroking his beard reflectively.

'The upper classes braying for glass, eh?' he commented.

Mike was a perceptive as well as a genial man. Once I got used to the beard, I learned a lot from him. We took digs in the same house in St John's Street for our third year. He is still married to Sylvia and we still exchange Christmas cards.

Apart from the bar below Staircase 2, the other focus of Exeter College life was the Junior Common Room, or JCR.

I entered the JCR one Sunday evening after dinner to find it already packed with eager undergraduates.

'"*Eyeless in Gaza* ..."' I saw a rumpled fellow in a corduroy jacket peering over his spectacles at the audience. '"*Eyeless in Gaza*", he repeated, paused, looked around, and then added as though that clinched the matter: '"*at the mill ... with slaves.*"'

'Who's that?' I asked the person standing next to me.

'That's Alan Bennett,' the man whispered. 'He's doing postgraduate work but he likes to come in here to practise his sketches.'

As the crowd roared its applause, I started to listen more carefully.

'*Eyeless in Gaza ... at the mill ... with slaves.*'

Once the speaker had come to the end of the line, he turned back and took another run at it, but this time he would vary the pitch, rhythm and intonation.

I started to laugh and, like so many others there, I couldn't stop. How many times in my life so far had I seen the Reverend So and So climb up into the pulpit, cassock billowing, to begin pontificating in the best Alan Bennett style.

'Eyeless' was just the warm-up. By the time we got to 'Sardines' we were rolling in the aisles.

'*Life's like a tin of sardines,*' Alan told us. '*When you roll back the lid, there's always a bit stuck in the corner, isn't there? Is there a little bit stuck in the corner of your lives?*'

I don't think many of us reckoned at the time that Alan's sketches would a few months later be incorporated integrally into *Beyond the Fringe*, which, after opening at the Edinburgh Festival, would go on to take the West End and Broadway by storm. If this was the official birth of 'satire', as many believe, I doubt if we realized the significance of the moment.

In the run-up to Edinburgh, Alan came quite often to the JCR to try out new material. I remember the 'Eyeless in Gaza' opening being replaced by the 'My Brother Esau' variant.

"*My brother Esau is an hairy man, but I am a smooth man*".

I can hear Alan now putting a deliberate stress on the 'n' in 'an'. An hairy man! We whimpered with laughter. As one of the Exeter College rugby songs put it, the tears ran down our trouser legs.

In 1964, when *Beyond the Fringe* was playing in New York, I bumped into Alan in the street. I was living in New York at the time with my first wife, Charlotte. With characteristic kindness, he arranged for us to pick up two complimentary tickets that night at the box office.

Forty years on, we are both residents of London, NW1, and we meet, haphazardly, in Camden Town or on Primrose Hill. *Floreat Exon!*

I wasn't so blinded by my tears of laughter that I forgot about the second item on my wish list: becoming President of the Oxford Union.

How, I wondered, do you set about building a career at the Union? You might make a series of brilliant speeches, but did that deliver the vote?

Philip Whitehead, an Exeter man a year or two ahead of me, had already started on a brilliant Union career. He was Librarian, soon he would be Secretary, before – inevitably, ineluctably, or so it seemed – becoming President.

I watched his progress with awe and admiration. 'How do you do it, Philip?' I asked, as I sat next to him one night at dinner.

'Make sure you line up the OUCA vote,' he replied. 'That's a start. You can become President without the block vote, but it's much more difficult.'

OUCA stood for the Oxford University Conservative Association. At the time, Philip was one of its leading lights though he later became first a Labour MP, then a Labour MEP, as well as being a successful producer of television documentaries.

I followed Philip's advice. I joined OUCA, attended various functions and made one or two speeches from the floor at the Oxford Union. One of them was during Peter Jay's term as President. In the bar after the debate, he was kind enough to describe my interventions as 'remarkably fluent'. Coming from someone who had already been referred to in the popular press as the 'cleverest man of his generation' and who would go on to become Britain's Ambassador to the United States, this was promising, but I failed to carry through with it.

Admittedly, I was elected to the Union's Library Committee, and during my term of office I devised a formula for acquiring books, which involved comparing the weight (avoirdupois) of the book against its price. But this contribution to the Union's affairs didn't by itself get me onto the Standing Committee, the next step up the Union's greasy pole.

My scorecard didn't, at this point in my Oxford career, look very promising.

THIRTEEN

Planning the Marco Polo Route Project

Around the end of November 1960, my fourth term at Oxford, a notice appeared in the Exeter College lodge. It read as follows: '*Gentlemen are reminded that, while the college encourages vacation travel, they should not forget the fact that at least ten weeks of study is expected from them during the Long Vacation.*'

This was an instruction that I was resolutely determined to ignore. At the end of the Easter term in the following year, 1961, I would be taking Mods. There would be seven full terms ahead of me before I would be taking Greats. Surely I could take just one summer off?

A couple of days after that dispiriting notice appeared, there was a knock on my door. I was still living in College, but had moved staircases and was no longer sharing a room.

'Come in!' I shouted.

A slim but rugged looking individual entered.

'My name's Tim Watkins. I heard you're thinking of going to China in the next Long Vac. So am I. Perhaps we should join forces. I'm reading Geography at Keble.'

Nowadays, Tim Watkins is better known as the author and explorer Tim Severin, the name he adopted soon after he came down from Oxford. If you look for his publications on the Amazon website, you will find a list as long as your arm. In his time he has tracked St Brendan, Sinbad and Jason. He has even retraced Ulysses's journey home from Troy to Ithaca, though he wisely left out the visit to the Underworld.

That first afternoon, over tea and toast in my room, we decided that we would try to follow Marco Polo's route from Venice to Peking. We would call our expedition the Marco Polo Route Project. I didn't know much about Marco Polo. My knowledge of history ended with the sack of Rome by Alaric the Hun in AD 479. But Tim seemed to have a lot of information at his fingertips.

'Marco Polo', he told me, 'set out in 1271 from Venice on a three and a half year journey to the court of the Great Khan in Cathay which is modern-day Peking. He reopened the Old Silk Road which for centuries had been closed by the ravaging hordes of Mongols and Tartars. He travelled through Turkey, Iran, Afghanistan, the High Pamir and China on a journey of, at times, incredible hardship and danger.'

Tim made the whole thing sound irresistible.

'Count me in,' I said.

Tim came down to Nethercote during the Christmas vacation for a few days of detailed planning. We established our base of operations in the Back Kitchen. We would appear at mealtimes but otherwise we remained closeted in front of the log fire, with papers spread out on the long oak table which the Blakes had left behind.

My parents were intrigued by our preparations.

'How are you getting on?' my father would ask.

I recalled the famous advice of General Dragomirov: 'My right flank has been turned; my left flank has given way. Everything's fine. I attack!'

'We need transport,' I replied. 'We need money, and we need visas, particularly Chinese visas. Otherwise things are going splendidly.'

'Better get out one of the old Aladdin lamps and rub it!' My father laughed.

By then we had graduated from paraffin-filled Tilley and Aladdin lamps to our own electric generator. It was a four-kilowatt Lister Startamatic. This was something of a misnomer. To start it you had to go out to the engine shed, take the crank handle and whirl away while simultaneously trying to squirt Eezi-Start into the cylinder block. Once it was going it chugged away on the other side of the barn, filling the valley with a low thudding sound which we soon got used to.

My father had worked out a way of turning it off at night without having to go out to the engine shed. He had rigged a wire across the yard into the bathroom. The wire was attached to a stirrup. To shut the engine down, you pulled hard on the stirrup and held on until the lights faded before finally going out altogether. This took quite a time.

Once, when my father was still in the bath, my mother decided to try her hand at turning the engine off.

'Don't jerk on the wire!' my father instructed. 'Give it a long, firm pull.'

Inevitably, my mother yanked too hard on the stirrup. The wire broke and she fell into the bath on top of him. Meanwhile, the engine raced out of control and all the light bulbs exploded one by one. My father had to race naked across the yard and into the engine shed.

My father didn't want a repetition of the disaster. 'Don't bother to turn the engine off,' he would say as he headed for the pub. 'I'll do it when I get back.'

Even though he was seldom home before midnight, Tim and I were often still hard at it, planning the details of the Marco Polo Route Project, as we heard him drive into the yard.

Once he came through into the Back Kitchen to find us poring over maps.

'What are you going to do for a vehicle?' he asked.

We had already worked that one out. 'Marco Polo used camels,' Tim said. 'But he took three and a half years. We've got only four months of the Long Vacation. We're going to go on motorcycles.'

In his youth my father had been a keen motorcyclist. He had come down to Nethercote on his motorcycle on that first tour of inspection. While I was still at school he had bought me a 200cc James scrambler which I used around the farm and for journeys further afield.

'Motorcycles, eh? Actually, that's rather a good idea, actually.'

The only way you could tell my father had been drinking, no matter how long he spent at the pub, was how often he used the word 'actually'. If he both started and ended the sentence with an 'actually', you knew it had been a good evening.

Acquiring transport, the first of the items on our checklist, proved more difficult than we anticipated. Since we didn't have enough money to buy our own vehicles, we knew we had to beg, borrow or steal. We wrote letters, we made visits and telephone calls, without nailing down a serious offer.

One day, early in the summer term with only a few weeks left before our planned departure date, I went to Birmingham where the Motorcycle Show was being held. In the early sixties, British motorcycles still led the world. Triumph, Norton, Enfield and BSA ... these were household names, in the way that BMW, Harley-Davidson and Suzuki are today.

I stood in front of the BSA stand, ogling the huge, gleaming machines. One in particular caught my eye. It was advertised as a 'BSA 500cc twin-cylinder Shooting Star'.

As far as I was concerned it was love at first sight.

A man sat behind a desk.

'My friend and I are planning to ride to China on a motorcycle this summer along Marco Polo's route,' I said. 'Would BSA be ready to let us have a couple of motorcycles? We couldn't pay you anything but it would be good advertisement for BSA.'

The man looked me up and down. The Shooting Star was a big machine.

'Think you can handle it?' he asked.

In the end, after an exchange of letters, BSA gave us one Shooting Star and Costain, the civil engineering firm, provided the second. Because of the amount of equipment we thought we needed, we decided to fit both bikes with sidecars, one a normal passenger sidecar, the other a box-type. We found sponsors for this too.

If the transport question had been solved, funding was still a problem. Though we planned to camp out throughout the journey, there would be fuel and food to buy. It all added up.

But with an advance from the (newly launched) *Sunday Telegraph* of £100 for 'exclusive rights' to our story, and another £200 from a publisher for a book about retracing Marco Polo's footsteps through Asia, we thought we were in business.

But we still hadn't managed to obtain Chinese visas. However often we presented ourselves at the Chinese Embassy in Portland Place, the result was always the same. Like the lady in the song, they wouldn't say yes and they wouldn't say no. They just kept us waiting. I came to know one official in the Visa Section particularly well. His name was Chi.

'Hello, Mr Chi', I would say.

'Please, no "mister". All people equal in Chinese People's Republic. No bourgeois titles. Just Chi, please.'

After half a dozen fruitless journeys to London from Oxford, we were at our wits' end.

Finally, I went to see Sir Cyril Hinshelwood, a Fellow of Exeter College, in his splendid rooms in the front quad. 'Hinsh', as he was widely known, was a scientist of immense distinction, probably the only person ever to have been simultaneously President of the Royal Society and the Classical Association.

He served me China tea in a delicate porcelain teacup.

'How are you planning to enter China?' he asked.

I explained the route as far we knew it.

'We plan to leave Afghanistan, as Marco Polo did, via the Pamir Corridor, that narrow tongue of land that today connects Afghanistan with China. After that, like Marco Polo, we'll have to cross the Gobi Desert.'

Hinsh looked puzzled. 'Is there a road through the Pamirs into China?'

I put my cards on the table. 'Frankly, we don't know for sure. But if the Chinese won't give us a visa, we'll never be able to find out.'

Hinsh took a sip of his tea.

'Have you tried Professor Needham in Cambridge? I'll give him a call.'

Two days later, I was on my way from Oxford to Cambridge in a 1932 Sunbeam Talbot. This was a splendid vehicle, even then a collector's item. It had been used as the 'school car' at Ravenswood during my time there. Later, Miss Nicholson, the school secretary-cum-French teacher whom I have already mentioned, had acquired it. Miss Nicholson had left Ravenswood some years earlier but we had kept in touch sporadically. One day, out of the blue, I received a letter offering me the Sunbeam Talbot.

'There's only one problem,' Miss Nicholson added as a PS; 'it's very difficult to find spare parts, if not impossible.'

I had written back to her. 'Delighted to inherit Sunbeam. As for spare parts, we'll cross that bridge when we come to it.'

This, then, was the lovely classic vehicle which I piloted from Oxford to Cambridge around the middle of June 1961. I parked in front of the Rutherford Science Building, to be told that the professor was probably in the lab.

That made sense. Professor Needham, I had by then established, was the author of the world-renowned publication *The Science and Civilization of Ancient China*. He had already produced twelve volumes and was working on the thirteenth. More were planned.

The professor was also, crucially, the patron of the Anglo-Chinese Friendship Society.

One or two people, when I had made my enquiries, had tapped the sides of their noses meaningfully to indicate the Anglo-Chinese Friendship Society was probably a Communist front and that Needham himself might not be wholly pukka. That was the least of my concerns, I decided. He could be a fully fledged member of the Comintern for all I cared. We just wanted his assistance.

When I eventually found him, wearing a brown beret behind a bank of scientific equipment, Needham was cautiously helpful. We went off to his office, and talked for half an hour about the difficulties we would certainly encounter if we did actually get into China.

'Are you sure you will find petrol for your motorcycles in the Gobi Desert, Mr Johnson?'

'Not one hundred per cent, sir.'

'And what about Lop Nor? They won't want you to go anywhere Lop Nor.'

'No, of course not.'

Tim and I had already found out about the Chinese nuclear testing site in the middle of the Gobi Desert and knew we would have to give it a wide berth.

In the end Professor Needham summoned his secretary, an ancient Chinese lady.

'I'll give you a letter to take to the Chinese Ambassador in London.'

'Dear Ambassador Huang,' he dictated, 'I do hope you will feel able to give Mr Johnson and Mr Watkins every possible assistance. The historical-geographical research which they are expecting to undertake this summer in Asia, including in the People's Republic of China, will – I believe – contribute significantly to increased understanding between the people of Great Britain and China.'

When his secretary had finished, Needham signed the letter and handed it to me.

'Show it to the Visa Section as soon as you can. These things take weeks. You haven't much time.'

Back in the car, I slipped the letter in the glove compartment and checked my watch. If I put my foot on it, I could get to London before the Chinese Embassy closed for the day.

Everything was going swimmingly until, soon after Royston, I noticed a red light on the dashboard.

'Damn and blast!' I exclaimed. I knew what the red light meant. The generator wasn't functioning. I pulled into the next garage. Maybe the fan belt was loose.

Unfortunately, the problem was not as simple as that. 'Generator's packed in, I'm afraid,' the mechanic told me. 'You're running on the battery. You can probably go a few more miles if you don't use the horn or turn the lights on.'

'Will it get me to London?'

'You can give it a go.'

I almost made it. I had reached Marble Arch when the engine finally died. I coasted to a stop next to an enormous hole in the ground. In those days, the area around Marble Arch was undergoing major reconstruction. The huge underground car park was being built and a new traffic system designed. The Conservative Minister in charge was Ernest Marples. Looking at the havoc he had created, wags had already christened the area 'Marple Arch'.

I took an instant decision. Getting a new generator for a 1932 Sunbeam Talbot might take weeks. It could be very expensive. I remembered Miss Nicholson's warning about the difficulty of obtaining spare parts.

I saw a bulldozer approaching, pushing a load of rubble into the enormous hole in front of me. I jumped out of the car and ran over to talk to the driver.

'Would you push my car into the hole?' I shouted.

'Come again?'

The man had to throttle down before he could hear me properly.

When he finally understood what I was saying, he nodded: 'Cost you a fiver.'

For a fiver, it was cheap at the price. To be sure my money was spent as intended, I waited as the bulldozer pushed the Sunbeam Talbot over the edge of the pit. When it hit the bottom, it quivered for a moment and lay still. Moments later, the bulldozer started filling up the hole with the rubble.

'Thanks.' I consoled myself with the thought of the joy archaeologists might feel, generations hence, when they came upon this unexpected treasure.

'Any time, mate.'

I just made it to the Chinese Embassy in Portland Place in time.

At the reception, I asked to see Mr Chi in person.

'Ah, Mr Chi,' I began, when he came out to see me.

He interrupted at once. 'Just Chi, please.'

'Sorry, Chi.' I wouldn't allow him to put me off my stroke. I felt supremely confident. 'I have personal letter from Professor Needham for Chinese Ambassador Huang.'

I put my hand to my inside breast pocket and it came up empty. I tried all my pockets with a similar result.

'You have personal letter for Ambassador from Professor Needham?' At long last Chi sounded interested.

As he spoke, I realized what had happened. To keep it from being crumpled or creased en route I had put Needham's letter in the glove compartment of my car and it was now buried with the car about one hundred feet below the ground at Marble Arch. Buried, too, were our hopes of receiving formal permission from the Chinese authorities to enter their country from Afghanistan via the High Pamir mountains.

FOURTEEN

Three Men on a Motorcycle

Before we left England, we had our two motorcycles modified for desert and high-altitude work. We loaded the box sidecar with polythene jerry cans for fuel and water. We also stowed tents, mattresses, sleeping bags, tools, spare parts, spare tyres and quantities of vitamin tablets, dehydrated stews and curries.

As far as the 'normal' sidecar was concerned, this served as a depository for 10,000 feet of cine film, two 16mm cameras, exposure meters and range finders. There was just enough space left for our cameraman, Michael de Larrabeiti.

Michael had seen an article about our proposed expedition in the London *Evening Standard* and had written offering his services. From my point of view at least, he had an unusual background. He had been born and brought up in Battersea, had travelled around the world earning his living as a photographer and, at the age of twenty-seven, was now waiting to go up to Trinity College, Dublin. His sense of humour was inexhaustible. Already slightly bald, he tended to knot a bright yellow duster over his head.

During the course of his travels, Michael had spent several seasons with the shepherds of Provence, walking with them and their flocks on the annual transhumance between mountain and plain. He would later write some moving tales about his time in France. He would also write several novels, including that classic children's book *The Borribles*.

I once calculated that the number of books which the three members of the Marco Polo expedition have written now approaches the half-century mark, if you add fiction and non-fiction together.

Of course, being prolific is not by itself necessarily a matter for congratulation. Bob Powell, for example, my headmaster at Sherborne, gave me a stern warning on this subject when I called on him in his study to say goodbye on the last day of my last term.

'A word of advice, Stanley, as you make your way into the wide world,' he began. 'Actually, three words.'

'I'm all ears, sir.'

'The first is this. When you go up to Oxford, don't wear a college scarf!'

I already knew that at Oxford at least wearing a college scarf was strictly non-U, so I nodded agreement. I wondered what was coming next.

'My second point is about women. You may meet some at Oxford. My advice is always put your women on a pedestal.'

This gave me pause. Up to this point in my life, women had not been high on the agenda. In fact, there had been a distinct shortage of them. I was looking forward to seeing more of them in Oxford.

'Isn't that a bit uncomfortable, sir,' I quipped. 'Putting them on a pedestal, I mean?'

Powell ignored this flippancy. 'Treat women with the respect they deserve. Do you want to hear my third piece of advice? It's about writing. You may be tempted in later life to have a book published. Resist that temptation. There are far too many books as it is.'

I still think about Bob Powell whenever I send a typescript off to a publisher.

There wasn't, of course, much time for writing on our Marco Polo journey. Our job was to get to Peking and back within four months, which meant that we would be on the road most of the time.

In June we were ready to go. The Oxford term had ended. We dressed up in our expedition uniforms of black jackboots, belted black jackets, dark green trousers and powder-blue helmets with the letters MPRP – for Marco Polo Route Project – inscribed on them (in little local difficulties MPRP could be made to stand for 'military police road patrol'). We gave a party in the Exeter College quadrangle and, once the champagne ran out, headed for the coast.

Silver City Airways, who were interested in building bridges to Europe more than a decade before Britain signed the Treaty of Rome, 'comped' us a passage on their shuttle from Lydd to Le Touquet. We drove our spanking new machines with their spanking new sidecars up the ramp into the belly of the plane.

As I look back, that four-month motorcycle journey across Europe and Asia in the summer of 1961 was an A-grade experience. Ours was in every respect a supremely uncluttered existence. The task was simply to get from A to B each day. Sometimes, if we were lucky, we covered two or three hundred miles by nightfall. While our headlights still worked, we often drove after dark as well. Once, with our lights out of action owing to a collision with a herd of cows, we even drove by moonlight.

The wider world hardly impinged. We heard vaguely about the building of the Berlin Wall during the course of that summer of 1961, as well as Iraq's first attempted invasion of Kuwait, but on the whole we concentrated on finding the next petrol station or caravanserai.

In some respects we were unbelievably incompetent. For example, at Temple's Garage in Oxford we arranged for our newly acquired side-cars to be attached to the left-hand side of the motorcycles. This was fine when we were driving in England. But the moment we crossed the Channel, it was hopeless. If I wanted to overtake some slow-moving vehicle I would pull out towards the crown of the road and wait till Michael signalled that the coast was clear. If it wasn't, he would use a rolled-up newspaper to beat me back.

By the end of the first day, this proved too hair-raising even for Michael's normally steady nerves. Thereafter he rode pillion.

Nor, actually, were we good motorcyclists. I had ridden my James scrambler for several years on Exmoor so I wasn't a complete novice. But none of us had proper motorcycle-driving licences though the Automobile Association sportingly gave us the international 'permis de conduire', which looked authoritative enough.

Our first two or three days were uneventful. After leaving Le Touquet, we spent hours in Paris riding round the Arc de Triomphe until Michael had the shot he wanted. Then we took the road south to Berne in Switzerland where my uncle Zeki, whom I had last seen in Ankara two years earlier, was now installed as Ambassador.

Having been brought up in Switzerland, Zeki had the advantage of actually speaking Swiss-German, the language of choice in the Bernese Oberland.

'Sometimes the good Swiss burghers don't realize I can understand everything they are saying,' Zeki told me with a twinkle in his eye.

Zeki and Neçla welcomed us into their palatial residence. My Turkish cousins, Sinan and Selim, were especially intrigued by our shiny new motorcycles.

Alas, they didn't stay shiny for long. After crossing a mountain pass in a rainstorm, I managed to crash the sidecar into a wall at the head of the Ticino valley. It took a day and a half to repair the damage.

We picked up Marco Polo's trail for the first time in Venice.

Nothing much is left of Marco Polo's house save one ornamental Byzantine arch, but there is a plaque on the wall which says: '*Qui furono le case di Marco Polo che viaggio le più lontane regioni dell'Asia e le descrisse.*'

Having spent time in Italy during the course of my gap year, I regarded myself as an expert at the language.

'Here was the house of Marco Polo who travelled through the farthest countries of Asia and described them,' I confidently translated.

'Can you ask for ice cream in Italian, too?' Michael asked. 'I could do with an ice cream.'

We paid our homage to the great explorer, and then went on to visit the Mayor of Venice in his marble palace. Our boots clomped across the floor, one steward produced a tray of drinks and another brought out a leather-bound copy of *The Travels of Marco Polo* for the Mayor to present to us.

The Mayor also gave us a voucher for 100 litres of petrol, which lasted us all the way to Istanbul via Yugoslavia and Bulgaria.

A long afternoon's driving finally took us into Turkey. A high watchtower, and the Turkish national emblem of a crescent moon and star carved on the hillside, denoted the border.

The Turkish customs officer, clearly intrigued by all our equipment, called us into his office. He dropped a lump of sugar into his milkless tea and waited for it to dissolve. Then he dropped another lump in and waited for that to dissolve too. And a third. He spread out his hands and shrugged his shoulders.

'Ours is a poor country,' he said. 'Since we have no money for teaspoons, we must use more sugar.'

The customs officer in his way was a philosopher. He had the leisure to be one. There wasn't much traffic then between Bulgaria and Turkey.

'You are in a hurry, I can see,' he said. 'You people are always in a hurry. We Turks, in our centuries of empire, found that there is a place for negligence. We have not forgotten it today. The old Turkey of the Sultans seems to have disappeared. The fez has gone, purdah has gone, even the Arabic script has gone. But as a people, in our hearts, we have not changed. The way we drink our tea is the way we are – slow and sweet. You last longer in the end.'

After a brief stay in Istanbul, we headed east through Anatolia. By now we were well into our rhythm. We would wake at dawn, pack up our tents if we had used them (if it was a fine night we would sleep out in the open), kick-start the motorcycles, open the throttle and roar away.

Marco Polo himself did not pass through this part of Turkey. When he left Venice, he took ship for Acre, that extraordinary Crusader town which today sits almost on the border between Israel and Lebanon. If you visit the castle there, walk along the ramparts, or wander through the medieval bazaar, you are probably seeing the same sights Marco Polo himself saw.

The Marco Polo Route Project didn't have time to follow Marco Polo's detour through the Holy Land. Instead, we picked up his track again in Kayseri, in southern Turkey, and then followed his route into Greater Armenia.

After Sivas, the city where Tamburlaine crushed a thousand children beneath his horses' feet, we left behind the distinctive features of the Anatolian plateau: peasants standing on the flat roofs of their houses winnowing grain in the wind; little girls scrambling in the dust, their black hair plaited with strings, then cross-threaded to form a mat against the sun; huge dogs that jumped at us as we passed; the conical stacks of dung for use as fuel; the donkeys trotting round the corn stacks, pulling thresher sledges.

We took the old road up into the mountains and twisted uphill into the afternoon.

By now we had jettisoned one sidecar and ruthlessly pruned our equipment. Each morning, before setting off, we tossed a coin to decide which motorcycle would take the lead. This was a matter of some moment. Because of the dust clouds the first motorcycle put up, the second had to follow several hundred yards behind. That left plenty of time for the villagers to arm themselves with sticks and stones. If it was your turn to bring up the rear, you had to keep your head down, gun the engine and hope for the best.

We spent a night with some nomads within sight of Mount Ararat. I am not sure what tribe they belonged to but for centuries they had moved with their tents and livestock across national frontiers without bothering about passports or other formalities. This way of life was now under threat as governments with blind arrogance tried to 'settle' their pastoral peoples.

We took tea and yoghurt with them in their yurts, smoked their pungent cigarettes and admired the horses and camels tethered outside and sometimes inside the tents.

Seeing Mount Ararat was exciting enough in itself. How many times had I sat in church or chapel listening to the story of the Flood and Noah's Ark? But we had a professional interest as well. Marco Polo, who passed this way, claimed to have seen 'some portions of the Ark' on the summit of the mountain.

We were ready to make our own reconnaissance of the area and even try to reach the top of the mountain, but were warned off by the local military on the grounds that this borderland between Turkey, Persia and the (then) Soviet Union was a forbidden zone.

So, contenting ourselves with a distant view of the mountain, we entered Persia along the road by which Xerxes, on his way to Marathon, had left it. For a classicist, that was a reasonable compensation.

Today we call Persia Iran. We have managed to demonize it as a land of fanatic ayatollahs. That is not how we saw it then. After the harshness of eastern Turkey, we felt we had entered a country of fountains and gardens and walled enclosures, of delicacy and colour. We looked for wine and bread and found them in abundance. We drank bowls of syrup with iced noodles. As we rested cross-legged beneath the trees, boys brought us clothfuls of tender cucumbers and yoghurt to dip them into and flat bread for us to tear and eat. Goats nibbled, water flowed, apricots and peaches climbed and clung in the sun.

It was too good to last. Outside Tabriz, the front fork on one of the motorcycles snapped. It was a major mishap.

While I went on to Teheran, having succeeded in loading our damaged vehicle onto a passing lorry, Tim and Michael headed north on the remaining machine to explore the Valley of the Assassins.

Marco Polo's account of the Old Man of the Mountains, a great tyrant who held sway in a remote region south of the Caspian Sea, is one of his most vivid tales. In a secret valley, the Old Man founded a cult. His emissaries went forth, captured and drugged young men, who were then brought back to the valley where they found themselves surrounded by all manner of good things, by fountains and flowing water, by pavilions and wine, by green pastures and delightful women. Paradise on earth, in other words. After suitable indoctrination, these young men were then sent out to murder rival potentates. The unlucky victims included a Shah of Persia, a Grand Vizier of Egypt, two Caliphs of Baghdad, Raymond, Count of Tripoli, and Conrad, King of Jerusalem. Edward I of England, when heir to the throne, was almost killed by the Old Man's envoys in Acre in 1272, soon after Marco Polo left that city.

The fanatics were called 'Assassins' after the drug 'hashish', which the Old Man used when he first had them kidnapped.

Tim and Michael had failed to penetrate the secret Valley of the Assassins though, by their account, they came tantalizingly close. On the way back, Tim broke a bone in his foot as the motorcycle skidded on rough ground.

It was clear that we couldn't wait for Tim's foot to heal. Michael and I headed off on the remaining machine, which by now had been repaired, to track Marco Polo through southern Persia and on into Afghanistan. Tim planned to join us in Kabul.

From a professional point of view, we had some serious historical research to do on our way through Persia. Among other things, we were looking, however improbably, for traces of the Three Wise Men, the Magi. Marco Polo had described how 'in the city of Saba ... the three Magi are buried, in three large and very beautiful monuments side by side and above them is a square building, carefully kept. The bodies are still entire with their hair and beards remaining.'

Marco Polo goes on to say that though all three Magi were buried at Saba, only one was native to that town, the other two coming from Kala' Atishparastan and from Ava.

Scholars had visited Saba itself and no traces of the Magi had been found. Kala' Atishparastan, though known to be in Persia, had never been precisely located. But Ava apparently had. Nowadays, it was known as Aveh. We were even able to find it on the map, about eighty miles south-west of Teheran.

We turned off the main road from Teheran to Qum at Baqilabad. Leaving one motorcycle and most of our equipment behind, we plunged onto the caked and salt-encrusted mud of the desert. We drove for hours that day from oasis to little oasis, stopping from time to time to rest from the heat and the dust by the wall of some village.

In the end we found Ava/Aveh. We followed a flock of sheep into the central square of the village. Here, exhausted and oblivious of the steady stream of women who came with pitchers on their heads to draw water from a deep brick well, we flung ourselves down. Night fell. Camels padded softly by and donkeys trotted with tinkling bells.

It wasn't hard to imagine the Magi surveying the sky on a night such as this, seeing a strange bright star in the east and deciding to set out on the long journey to Bethlehem.

Did we find any convincing evidence that Marco Polo was right and that the Magi, or at least one of them, had come from Ava or Aveh? No, of course we didn't. Given our total inability to communicate in Persian, I doubt whether the villagers of Aveh even understood what we were looking for. They certainly didn't leap up to show us the embalmed body of Gaspar, Melchior or Balthazaar.

Two months later, after we had returned to England, the *Sunday Telegraph* printed my account of our journey into the Persian desert under the headline VILLAGE OF THE MAGI. I spun out the story as best I could, but frankly there was no telling for sure whether we had hit upon the right village.

Our trip to Aveh had convinced us that we could manage with just one motorcycle. When I crashed one of our machines comprehensively outside Qum, we realized the time had come for a major reorganization. We had huge camel-hide panniers fitted to the remaining machine and strengthened the pillion to carry the additional weight.

'Lean and mean!' Michael, as always, looked on the bright side.

His enthusiasm was infectious. We had had our setbacks, but we would keep going.

Two days later I woke up in the desert outside the magical city of Isfahan, on the morning of my twenty-first birthday. A mile away, I could see the Green Mosque silhouetted against the sky. The first rays of the sun caught the top of the minaret, then caressed the giant curve of the dome.

Michael lay on the ground beside me, wrapped in his sleeping bag. The first flies of the day were beginning to bother him and from time to time he moved his head in his sleep, trying to avoid them.

As I sat cross-legged taking in the scene (when would I have a twenty-first birthday again?), an old man emerged from nowhere to offer me a small green apple.

'*Hoob?*' the old man enquired as I took a bite.

'*Hoob*' was one of the few Persian words I knew. It meant 'good'.

'*Hoob*,' I replied.

Michael woke up at this point. 'Time for nosh, then, is it?'

Then he remembered: 'Happy twenty-first birthday, Stan!'

FIFTEEN

'Mango juice, sahib?'

From Isfahan we went to Kerman. Here we had two choices. We could either try to head north across Persia's great central desert – the Dasht-i-Lut – and enter Afghanistan via Meshed (which was the route Marco Polo is thought to have taken), or we could take the road through Pakistan.

Whenever we stopped at a *chai-khaneh* (teahouse) or caravanserai, we tried to get a reading on the problem. Was there a track across the desert to Meshed? we asked. Could we make it on a motorcycle?

Our spirits rose one day when, in one of the local teahouses, we discovered a brightly coloured map pinned to the grimy wall. The map was crowned with a smiling picture of the Shah of Persia and his bride, the whole being garlanded with a laurel wreath. What interested us was the broad slash of red running through the centre of the map, across the heart of the Dasht-i-Lut and denoting a broad new highway between Kerman and Meshed.

As we sipped our sweet tea in the little clear glasses we had come to know so well, we interrogated our fellow travellers.

'Road Kerman–Meshed? *Hoob*? Vroom-vroom!' we asked.

Alas, we soon discovered that the Kerman–Meshed highway was a totally fictional project and that the map was more an endearing expression of future road-building hopes than a statement of current realities.

So in the end we had no choice but to swing south and east through Pakistan before heading north again.

It might not have been the Dasht-i-Lut but the road from Kerman to Zahadan still runs through a most pernicious desert most of the way. Red dust swirled persistently. The sun beat down through the haze. You pass the bleached carcass of a camel or the wreck of a truck that has caught fire by the roadside and you thank your lucky stars that you still have fuel and water. The corrugations were the worst, jarring the spine in the most fearsome way. Occasionally we would meet seasoned travellers who would blithely advise us to 'just keep going at around forty miles an hour and you'll find you'll ride the bumps without feeling them'. Try as we might, we never found the knack. If we did reach the magic speed, there was always a dried-up wadi to negotiate just round the corner.

Michael and I fell off more times than I can count. Once, as we sprawled in the road, there was a loud honking behind us. The driver of an oil tanker had witnessed our latest accident and took pity on us.

He offered us a lift in his cab, which we gladly accepted. Somehow we managed to lift the motorcycle onto the back of the truck and lash it in place.

Michael expressed what we had both been thinking.

'Cheating, ain't it? I mean, we're not exactly *driving* the motorcycle along Marco Polo's route, are we?'

'We're not exactly on Marco Polo's route at this point, are we?' I replied icily.

That unscheduled lift through the southern Persian desert to Zahadan was a lifesaver. Refreshed and reinvigorated, we said goodbye to our kindly driver and belted on to Nok Kundi, Iran's border post with Pakistan, seventy-five miles away.

After that it was – for a while at least – plain sailing. As we drove on through Baluchistan towards Quetta, we stopped from time to time at the 'dak' bungalows and guest houses which still survived in that part of the world. There we savoured briefly and uncritically the traces that remained of the old life.

'Mango juice, sahib?'

'Yes, please, bearer, with ice.' And an easy chair on the veranda, looking at the stars through the palm trees and waiting for the water in the swimming pool to cool from the heat of the day.

'Curry and rice, sahib?' Yes, and the first clean white linen tablecloth we had seen for weeks.

The soft voice of the proprietor enquires in perfect English (he has been educated in an English school in Quetta) what time we will take breakfast in the morning and whether we will have one fried egg or two. Then we swim in the pool, while the dhobi man washes our clothes.

'We'd better make the most of this,' I said to Michael. 'It won't be like this in Afghanistan.'

It wasn't.

Actually, at this point we weren't really sure we would be allowed into Afghanistan at all. We had Afghan visas all right, but we had never received permission to take our camera equipment into the country.

Happily, we reached the frontier post between Pakistan and Afghanistan, high up on the Bolan Pass, just as the sun was setting. No one appeared to be guarding the border. Then we noticed. Around the base of the flagpole, fifty yards away, we could see a group of soldiers at prayer. Their backsides rose into the air together whenever they put their heads to the ground.

'Why don't I just unhook the chain?' Michael suggested. 'They may not notice, and even if they do, they won't be able to stop us, since they're occupied with higher things!'

He nipped off the bike. Half-expecting to hear a volley of shots behind us, we rode on towards Kandahar.

Nowadays, we read about Kandahar as a 'Taliban heartland'. This is where British troops in Afghanistan, at time of writing, have suffered the largest number of casualties. My memories of Kandahar are of a city given over to dancing and merriment.

As we rode into town on our motorcycle, we found the three-day festival of Jeshyn in full swing. The streets swayed with colour; the national flags hung in their thousands, fluttering over the flowing robes and tough brown faces of the tribesmen, who might have walked through the hills for a month to reach the big city. Horse taxis, gaily decorated with yellow or purple plumes, dashed past, shafts shifting and groaning under the weight of whole families. Everywhere there were huge portraits of the King and the Prime Minister.

Jeshyn, we discovered, meant 'independence'.

'Who are they celebrating being independent from?' Michael asked.

I'd done my homework. 'The British, actually. They nearly wiped us out in two Afghan wars in the last century.'

'Bloody good show!' Michael snorted. He looked around. 'They do seem a tough lot, don't they?'

Jeshyn was still being celebrated when we arrived in Kabul. Kandahar's local feast had been transmuted into a World Fair, with Russians and Americans competing for effect.

The Russians had already put a man in space. From an enormous globe on top of the Russian pavilion, a huge rocket appeared to erupt into the sky, blasting past the smiling faces of Nikita Khrushchev and Yuri Gagarin.

The American offering was less spectacular. The keynotes, as I remember, were education, roads and dams. They were obviously making an impact. The road from Kandahar to Kabul, which we had just travelled, had been newly built through American aid. The first traffic lights in Kabul had been installed in the city thanks to a US-financed highway project.

Of course, we weren't in Afghanistan to make a political report. We were still tracking Marco Polo.

The day after we reached Kabul Tim joined us, having flown in from Herat. Still hobbling, he undertook to make a last round of the ministries and embassies to see whether (a) the Afghans would give us permission to enter the Wakkan Corridor which debouched into Sinkiang, China's westernmost province, and (b) the Chinese would allow us to enter Sinkiang.

In the meantime, Michael and I headed north on our motorcycle into the Hindu Kush mountains. If we couldn't enter China, then at least we could see the great Buddhist statues at Bamiyan, surely one of the wonders of the ancient world.

When, a few years ago, I heard of how the Taliban had ordered the Bamiyan monuments to be blown up, I felt a real pang of grief. We saw many extraordinary sights in the course of our journeys during that summer of 1961 but the Buddhist statues in the Hindu Kush certainly came at or near the top of the list.

We left Kabul one morning and followed the Chardeh River as it flowed north through gorges and rapids. Sheep and goat paths climbed obliquely up the hillsides. Tribesmen moved among the rocks, most of them carrying rifles. Peasants crouched in pocket-sized fields, plucking the mountain hay by hand. We ate stews of grey, fatty mutton and smelt hashish in the tea parlours.

The road seemed to get narrower all the time. As the driver of the motorcycle I constantly had to make fine judgements. If you found yourself stuck behind a slow-moving lorry, you ran the risk of being blinded or suffocated by the dust. On the other hand, if you tried to overtake, the lorry driver would almost certainly pull over to try to push you off road. Good, clean fun from his point of view, but a life or death matter from ours.

The secret was to wait for a moment when the lorry driver was otherwise occupied – on a hairpin bend, for example. If I spotted a gap, I'd ram the motorcycle into a lower gear, shout to Michael to 'hold on tight' and try to cut through on the inside.

I won't say we were quivering wrecks by the time we reached Bamiyan, but we were not far off.

We parked the now horribly scarred and battered BSA Shooting Star at the foot of the cliff to gaze up at the gigantic (165-foot-high) sandstone god.

'Ozymandias, eat your heart out!' Michael said.

We spent an afternoon at Bamiyan. Before we left we climbed up inside the great Buddha, winding our way past his thighs and waist and chest, until we could actually perch on top of the statue's head in a kind of cave hollowed out of the rock.

'Alexander the Great passed this way,' I told Michael.

'I wonder if he scratched his name on the rock up here!'

Michael made to pull out his penknife but I slapped his hand down.

'Only joking!' He gave me a wry smile.

Michael was certainly an older and a wiser man now than he had been when he joined us. There were moments, for example on one of those hairpin bends when the lorry ahead wouldn't give way, when he probably wished he hadn't thrown his lot in with two callow Oxford undergraduates.

But you couldn't keep him down for long. He was like one of those rubber toys. If you knocked him over, he bounced back up.

We thought of turning back after Bamiyan but decided against it. To the north lay the multi-coloured lakes of Bandi Amir, among the highest in the world. The road grew steeper all the time; the motor-cycle laboured with the altitude. At a 12,500-foot pass, we paused and looked north, towards the Oxus and Russia, and north-east, towards the Pamirs and China. We saw that we were too late. The snows had already fallen on the land ahead. On a motorcycle at least, even if we received all the permits we needed, we would never make it.

'This is probably as far as the Marco Polo Route Project is going to go, Michael,' I admitted. Sometimes you just had to face reality.

Michael still had his cameras. Whatever else we threw away, he hung on to those. He took a photograph of me, with the Bandi Amir Lake in the background, lighting a cigarette with a match from a Bryant and May matchbox. Bryant and May were one of our expedition's sponsors.

Not long ago my second son, Leo, was going through some photographs of our Marco Polo trip. He found the 'Bryant and May' snapshot and had it enlarged. Because it shows me looking young and keen and fit, I have placed it on 'Grandpa's bookcase' at Nethercote.

This intriguing piece of furniture is actually made from the Lincoln College boat, the one which – as I have already described – so famously won the Torpids Races in Oxford in 1898. (The victorious boat was apparently sawn up into pieces after the event and each oarsman received a section. Did 'bow' receive the 'bow' section? Did 'stroke' receive the 'stroke' section? What about the cox? History does not relate the details and there is no one left for me to ask.)

Leo's interest in my Afghan experiences arises, among other things, from the fact that he has married an Afghan: Taies. Though Taies' family escaped to the United States when the Russians took over Afghanistan in the 1970s, their links with the country remain strong and several members of the family have visited the country following the 'defeat' of the Taliban in 2003.

I little expected during the memorable weeks I spent in Afghanistan in the late summer of 1961 that I would in due course have part-Afghan grandchildren (two so far, both girls). It would be good one day to go back to Afghanistan to join in a great family reunion in Kabul, with Afghan exiles (like Taies' parents and siblings) flying in from all over the world.

Given today's headlines, it looks as though that happy day may still be some way off. Still, we must live in hope.

We left Kabul at the beginning of September. I wouldn't say we departed with our tails between our legs, as it were, but we certainly hadn't achieved what we set out to achieve.

On our last night in the city, I was sitting alone in a teahouse, writing up my notes, when a man came over and joined me at my table. We talked for a while in the all-purpose language at which we were now quite proficient. I gathered he was suggesting I should come to his house and drink some whisky. I accepted with pleasure.

His chauffeur was outside. Feeling a bit uneasy, I got in. My feeling of uneasiness increased when we drove at speed into the mountains outside the city.

As I have already indicated I was younger and thinner then, and possibly blonder too. It didn't take me long to realize what the man had in mind so I did the only thing I could think of. I pretended to be violently sick. The car stopped. The man got out. I hit him hard on the jaw. It wasn't a good blow, more of a haymaker than anything else. I bruised my right thumb badly and to this day it still has a swollen appearance.

Seconds later, I had to throw myself off the road into a ditch as the car roared past.

A few weeks later, after we had returned to England, Peter Fleming interviewed Tim and me for the BBC's Home Service. Peter Fleming was already a world-renowned explorer. He had searched for Col. Fawcett in the Amazon, and had travelled in Tartary with only a camel for company.

It was scheduled to be quite a long piece, more than thirty minutes, with a replay foreseen for *Pick of the Week*.

Fleming turned to me towards the end of our time on air: 'Tell me, Stanley, what was the worst thing that happened to you during your journey in the steps of Marco Polo?'

I wanted to say that I had almost been buggered by an Afghan, but then I thought of all the little old ladies glued to their wirelesses.

'I was kidnapped one evening in Kabul,' I replied. 'They wanted to steal my British passport.'

'Would that have been worth a lot?'

'About one hundred pounds on the black market. Maybe more.'

When we were having a drink afterwards in the BBC's hospitality room in their Langham Place headquarters, I told the great explorer that, as far as the passport story was concerned, I had been – as Robert, now Lord, Armstrong would later put it – 'economical with the truth'.

'Quite right,' Fleming said briskly. 'You should never shock your audience. Bad manners.'

Fleming didn't stay long that evening. Given his own war record (he was head of 'D' division in charge of military deception in South-East Asia), I think he thought we were a fairly raffish couple of adventurers. He checked his watch and quickly downed his drink.

'Does anyone want a lift to the War Office?' he asked.

SIXTEEN

The Grand Trunk Road; Calcutta; Bombay; Home

The journey back to Oxford from Afghanistan was considerably longer than the way out.

Just in case we never made it to China, we had arranged a fallback return route from Bombay in India. P & O, the shipping company, was one of the sponsors of the Trevelyan scholarships and their representative had recently been present at a dinner held in Oxford for the lucky few.

Over the port, I had explained our predicament.

'Problem is,' I said, 'if we can't get into China, we shall have to go on into India and come back from there. There would be three of us and our motorcycles. Do you think P & O might be able to help?'

'I'll have a word with Sir Donald,' the man obligingly replied.

In the event, Sir Donald Anderson, P & O's chairman, couldn't have been more helpful. P & O would find us berths on a ship leaving Bombay for the UK. They might not be able to offer us first-class accommodation but they would certainly do better than steerage.

Before we left Kabul, we spread out a map of the subcontinent on the floor of one of the city's many *chai-khanehs*, where men (and only men) gather to sit cross-legged on well-worn carpets, smoke tobacco and drink those endless glasses of hot, sweet tea.

'We've still got a bit of time,' I said. 'Why don't we take the Grand Trunk Road down to Calcutta and then put the bike on the train to Bombay in time to catch the boat?'

And this was precisely what we did. We loaded our motorcycle onto a truck bound for the Khyber Pass and wound our way through the Jalalabad defile down onto the plains.

It was an eerie experience. If you looked up at the towering cliffs, you saw riflemen all around. Watchtowers bristled with guns. This was the place, I remembered, where, halfway through the nineteenth century, a British army had been totally wiped out. More than nine thousand soldiers had been massacred. The sole survivor, Dr Brydon, had stumbled into Peshawar to tell the tale.

Like Dr Brydon, we almost didn't make it to Peshawar. Our papers were checked at the frontier post. Tim's were in order, but Michael's and mine definitely were not.

'Where is your entry stamp?' the official asked me brusquely when I showed him my passport. 'Why is there no entry stamp? We cannot give you a stamp to leave Afghanistan if have not entered the country.'

Of course, I remembered why we had no entry stamp. We had simply gunned our motorcycle past the border post north of Chaman while the guards were at prayer.

'But we have entered the country,' I explained patiently, 'you can see we are here.'

The official seemed unconvinced. I had a strong sensation that our luck might have run out.

Happily, Michael, quick-witted as ever, came up with the answer. He slipped a ten-dollar note inside his passport. 'Surely the solution, ossifer' – he always called 'officers' 'ossifers' as a matter of principle – 'is not to stamp our passports at all. We were never here. Simple as that.'

When we finally unloaded the bike in Peshawar, feeling we had earned a break before beginning the long journey across India to Calcutta, we decided to spend the night at the Peshawar Club.

It was another of those blissful interludes. We had a bath, then dinner in the dining room. On the ceiling, high above the chandeliers, we could see that names and regimental details had been scribbled on the ceiling.

'Even the ladies are writing their names on ladies' night,' the turbaned Sikh bearer told us. His moustache bristled with disapproval. 'It is not at all a graceful thing for ladies to be climbing up chandeliers, even with petticoat.'

Next morning, one of the Club's stewards, Roshan Khan, a member of the famous squash-playing family and himself a former world champion, gave me a game in one on the Club's courts but I failed to win a single point.

As I write these words, decades later, the last few weeks of the Marco Polo Route Project seem to be one continuous blur of movement.

When we left Peshawar, Tim and Michael both climbed onto the motorcycle behind me. For the next several hundred miles – in fact all the way to Calcutta – I had not one but two pillion passengers. Driving was more fun than being driven, I'm sure. There are some advantages in being one of nature's prop forwards.

We still carried the camel-hide bags we had fitted in Persia, as well as jerry cans for fuel. As we careered down the Grand Trunk, or 'GT', Road, we must have looked like some multi-limbed Hindu god.

Michael took to crooning a home-made lyric in my ear as we ate up the miles.

> 'Magni intrepidi,' *he sang, imitating a Gregorian plain chant,*
> 'Three on one motorcycle
> Viri fortissimi,
> Stanley, Tim and Michael!'

We entered India at Amritsar, the town where in 1919 General Dyer had famously ordered his men to fire on the crowd. We paid a lightning visit to the Golden Temple then pressed on to Delhi, with a side trip to Agra and the Taj Mahal. I was already quite familiar with the Taj Mahal in the Turl in Oxford where you could have a lamb curry for two shillings and sixpence. But it was good to see the real thing.

Then we rattled on down through the great Indo-Gangetic plain. Lucknow, Cawnpore, Benares … of course most of the names have changed now.

I remember we stopped in Benares (now Varanasi) overnight. We went down to the ghats and watched pilgrims who had come from all over India bathe in the sacred waters of 'Mother Ganga'. We saw the funeral pyres at the water's edge and the flower petals floating on the scummy surface of the river.

Over the years I would go back to India many times but those first impressions will always stay with me. We might not have made it to China but in our brief stay in India that summer we found a worthy consolation prize.

We rested for a couple of days in the Tollygunge Club in Calcutta. The Club Secretary was the father of a boy who had been at school with me. Bill Pool took it on the chin when we rolled into his grand establishment one night with our tenuous claim to his hospitality.

'I expect you chaps could do with a bath,' he told us.

We would have loved to have lingered in those sumptuous surroundings but time was running out. At Calcutta's Howrah railway station, finding no room in the guard's van we lifted our motorcycle bodily into one of the carriages. Thirty hours later, having crossed the country from east to west via the great Deccan Plateau, we rode out of the station in Bombay.

A telegram awaited us in Bombay's Central Post Office: 'SS *Stratheden* sailing 9 a.m. Tuesday 20 September. Three cabin class berths reserved.'

It was the news we wanted to hear.

With two nights to spend in Bombay before sailing, we needed some cheap, preferably clean, accommodation.

I must have told Tim at some point about my Exmoor-born ancestor George Williams, the founder of the YMCA, because he suggested we should seek a room there.

'Tell them about your great-great grandpa. Maybe they'll give us a room for free.'

We weren't, I promise, scroungers at heart. But by then we were truly at the limit of our resources.

We drove round to the Y on the bike. Tim and Michael stayed outside while I went in to negotiate.

'No point in scaring them off,' Michael said.

My spirits rose when I saw a huge framed portrait hanging in the hall. I recognized the picture immediately. The high forehead, the earnest stare and the long white beard were unmistakable.

'I say,' I pointed at the painting, 'that's my great-great-grandfather hanging on the wall, looking as though he were alive. So I'm his great-great-grandson. What about a free room and some fried eggs for myself and my two friends?'

The man looked wearily at me. 'I am hearing that story about the ancestor only last week.'

We stayed at the Y anyway, even without a concession. It was a convenient base. For a couple of days we rode around Bombay, still three-up, on the motorcycle. I have a photograph of the three of us in front of the Gate of India.

Tim and Michael, sitting behind me, are both wearing the Marco Polo Route Project (MPRP) crash helmets. I am bareheaded. I had given up my crash helmet some time earlier. Michael and I had cadged some mutton stew from some nomads on our way up to Bamiyan in Afghanistan. Lacking a convenient receptacle, we had used my helmet instead.

When we left them the next day, we had given the nomads the still gooey item as a keepsake since I didn't feel like putting it back on my head. It's probably still there, up in the mountains somewhere.

Those short trips around Bombay were the last time the three of us rode together as a team. One day we stopped at a shoe shop somewhere along the waterfront. Our motorcycling boots had seen better days and anyway we would need something to wear on the boat.

'Something smart but casual, please, dear,' Michael requested.

We all bought shoes. Since this was a proper cobbler's, where they made shoes on the spot, I decided to order a last as well. They could keep it on the shelf for me. I had visions of sending telegrams to Bombay, over the coming years, asking for a new pair of brogues or whatever to be dispatched – dirt-cheap, of course.

A well-dressed Indian gentleman, clearly another customer, intervened to congratulate me on my decision.

'I am always buying my lasts here,' he told me.

This puzzled me. I thought you bought a last and that was it for the rest of your life.

'Why do you need more than one last?'

'The shape of your foot is changing all the time,' the man explained.

'Oh, is it? So how long did your last last last?' I asked.

We were all wearing our new, smart, hand-made footwear when, fifteen days later, the SS *Stratheden* docked at Marseilles. Leaving the motorcycle on board so that it could be taken on to Southampton where we would collect it in due course, we dashed for the overnight train to Paris.

Twelve hours later we were back in Oxford.

Jack, the College Porter, winked at me when I came into the Lodge.

'Bit late for term, aren't we, sir?'

'Only three days late, Jack. Might have been three months.'

My eye fell on the notice board. The notice about the Long Vacation was still there.

'*Gentlemen are reminded …*'

'Isn't it about time you took that notice down?' I said.

SEVENTEEN

'The King of France is bald'

Looking back, it's quite clear to me that I wasted a good deal of my time at Oxford. As I have indicated in an earlier chapter, when I first went up I had sketched out in a half-joking way three ambitions, viz. win a rugger blue, become President of the Union and gain a first in Classics.

Originally, I had told myself that I wanted to achieve all three objectives. As time passed, and after a tough internal discussion, I quietly agreed with myself that achieving just one of them would still be a satisfactory result.

As I have explained, I didn't even get to first base as far as the rugger blue was concerned. My performance in the Oxford Union wasn't much better. Though I had been a member of the Library Committee, I had never spoken from the Dispatch Box. (The Oxford Union seeks in all matters to emulate the House of Commons.) Now, as I began my third year at Oxford in the autumn of 1961, I had to recognize that the third of my mental goals, getting a first in Greats, had also been kicked into touch. I had switched horses in midstream: from Classics to English.

In later life I have sometimes asked myself why I chickened out in this way. Had I forgotten Hughie Holmes, housemaster of Lyon House, Sherborne, and his stern warning to me not to let my Classics drop? 'Hard wood grows slowly', Hughie had written. Instead of heeding his advice, I had gone for the soft option, conifer rather than oak or mahogany.

Of course, not everyone in my time at Oxford saw the study of English Language and Literature as a soft option, the equivalent, say, of Media Studies today. I am only speaking for myself. I had probably been influenced by men like Bob Powell, who had an almost mystical view of the value of Greats.

Yet I couldn't screw my courage to the sticking point. Having gone through the grind of Mods for my first five terms, I flinched from going on in the same way with Greats for a further seven terms. Deep down I knew I had taken the easy way out. Surely English, like lunch for Gordon Gekko (played by Michael Douglas) in *Wall Street*, was for wimps?

Dacre Balsdon, who would have taken me for Greats had I continued with Classics, wrote me a charming letter after I had announced my intention to switch schools, but I could tell I had gone down in his estimation.

If I had gained a first in Mods, the story might have been different. I might have stuck it out, lured by the glittering prospect of a 'double first'. (Strictly speaking, getting a 'double first' means getting a first in the finals of one undergraduate subject, e.g. Classics, as well as a first in another undergraduate level degree, e.g. Mathematics. But even in my day people were using the term more loosely to indicate a first in Mods, followed by a first in finals.)

In the event, I didn't get a first in Mods. On the marks awarded, I gained a perfectly respectable second, but no better than that.

Oddly enough, one of my best results was in the Logic paper, which I had taken as an option.

Exeter did not have its own tutor in Logic so I had been farmed out to Magdalen, where an urbane don called John Simopoulos held weekly seminars.

Simopoulos liked to raise the tricky question of the King of France's hair. '"The King of France is bald". Is that statement true, false or meaningless?'

As undergraduates we had different views on the matter.

Simopoulos also introduced us to the syllogism.

'"*All women are mad*," he would say. "*My wife is a woman. Therefore my wife is mad.*"'

This sort of syllogism was known as a Barbara, since it contained three As. Barbaras were totally kosher. If all women were mad, it was perfectly valid, at least in syllogistic terms, to claim that one's wife was mad as well.

I wish I still had my notes on Simopoulos's lectures. Unfortunately, I didn't take any at the time. Luckily, John Weston, who had been Head of School at Sherborne a couple of years before me and was then at Worcester, lent me his. When the Mods results were announced, I found out that I had been awarded an alpha double minus in the Logic paper (or was it an alpha double minus query minus?).

As I shall later reveal, this was not the last time I had cause to be grateful to John Weston, who in due course left Oxford for a glittering career in the Foreign Office and, after that had come to an end, has become a noted poet.

The only other paper in which I got an alpha mark was Greek Verse Composition. I might have had an alpha-beta or two in other subjects but this was not enough to tip the balance.

My tutor, after I switched schools, was Jonathan Wordsworth. In July 2006, after I had started writing this memoir, Jonathan Wordsworth sadly died at the young age of seventy-three. Obituaries appeared in several newspapers, recalling his contribution to scholarship, particularly his books about his namesake and relative William Wordsworth, but also the strong and positive influence he had had on his pupils at Exeter, like the poet James Fenton and the novelist Martin Amis.

Jonathan was a tall, good-looking Fellow with long, dark hair, only a few years older than I was. Though he lived with his wife and family in a rural vicarage some miles outside Oxford, he had a room at the top of Palmer's Tower, a medieval edifice on the east side of the main quad. To get to him, you had to climb up a narrow, winding staircase. Getting down was worse. As I was a scholar, I had to wear a long gown during tutorials. This tended to become caught up in your legs and it was easy enough to fall flat on your face as you negotiated the stone steps.

It was easy enough anyway to fall flat on your face with Jonathan. In Oxford in those days, and probably still today, you read your essay out at the beginning of the tutorial.

Normally Jonathan would not interrupt. He would stretch out his long legs in front of him, roll his eyes and occasionally sigh but usually he allowed you to finish saying what you had to say.

Usually, but not always. Once I began an essay with the words: 'Keats is nothing if not sylvan ...'

'In that case, he's nothing,' Jonathan slapped me down.

Unless you had written a very long essay, or had read very slowly, there was usually time for some exchange of views over a glass of sherry or whisky between tutor and pupil before the allotted forty minutes was over. These golden moments are, of course, the basis of the famous 'tutorial' system, which – in my day at least – made Oxford and Cambridge the envy of the world.

I don't think Jonathan was specially impressed by his new pupil, refugee that I was from the Classics.

Sometimes, he would get up while I was still reading out loud and leave the room. His footsteps would echo on the stairs. He might pause for a while in the quad, engaging passers-by in conversation, like the Ancient Mariner ('He stoppeth one in three'). Still seated in my chair high up in Jonathan's rooms in Palmer's Tower, I would hear his deep baritone voice and an occasional barking laugh. Then he would climb noisily back up.

'Have you finished yet?' he would ask, addressing me as a nanny might a child on the potty.

Once, when a particularly poor essay irritated him, he asked me: 'Why on earth did you change to English? Why didn't you stick to the Classics?'

'I changed to English because I've always wanted to write very badly.'

'Well, you've certainly succeeded.'

Sometimes I thought of that room, perched above the quad, as Withering Heights.

If, in the end, Jonathan started to take me seriously, it was entirely due to an extra-curricular effort on my part.

One day, early in May 1962, I wrote a long romantic poem that by some fluke won the University's top poetry prize, the Newdigate.

They didn't award the Newdigate very often. If the entries weren't good enough, the prize went unclaimed. When people asked me, as they did, who else had won the Newdigate, I would pause and scratch my head.

'Let me see. Matthew Arnold, Oscar Wilde ...' I would allow my voice to trail off, to make it clear that to win the Newdigate was to join a very select band indeed.

To explain just how and why I happened to write a prize-winning romantic poem in the early summer of 1962, I must deal with the romance first.

I had, by the beginning of my third year at Oxford, a fair number of undergraduate women friends. We tended to meet at the Cadena in the Cornmarket for tea, went to the cinema in Walton Street, or concerts in the Sheldonian.

This was all very satisfactory. I was an innocent boy from Exmoor. Apart from the Pony Club dances (one of which had ended with my disastrous crash at Morebath Manor), I hadn't met any girls during the holidays. And, during term time, Sherborne boys had been strictly separated from the Girls' School, though occasionally you might bump into a brown-bereted young woman accidentally on purpose in Cheap Street on a Saturday afternoon. So it was certainly a great joy to meet so many intelligent and attractive women in Oxford and to have long and often interesting conversations with them.

I couldn't help noticing, however, that some of my Exeter contemporaries had regular girlfriends with whom they were seen around college or in town.

Bill Gissane on Staircase 5, for example, had a devastatingly beautiful blonde lady friend called Zena, who would stretch herself languorously like a cat in the front quad after a late breakfast in Bill's rooms. How did he do it? I asked myself. The amazing thing, from my point of view, was that Bill was actually reading Science or Medicine or something.

Then there was an American called Brad Hosmer, who had rooms on Staircase 2.

Brad at the time was a serving member of the United States Air Force. He parked a Studebaker in the Turl and at weekends drove out to the USAF base at Brize Norton to keep up his flying hours.

Brad's batting average was high. In my second year I too had rooms on Staircase 2 (right at the top, next to a wild, kilt-wearing Scotsman called John Davidson-Kelly) and I would sometimes pass Brad's latest comely squeeze on the stairs.

'What's the secret, Brad?' I once asked him, as he was dashing out to Brize Norton, already dressed in his smart blue uniform.

'Dead simple, Stan.' He paused just long enough to let me know the key to all successful male–female relationships. 'Just find something you have in common.'

'What kind of thing are we talking about here, Brad?' I asked, trying not to sound too naïve.

'Well, take apples,' Brad explained. 'You meet a girl. First thing you do is ask her if she likes apples. Nine times out of ten, she'll say, "Yes, I like apples".'

'Then what?' I asked.

'Then you say: "Hell! That's amazing! I like apples too. Let's go to bed!"'

'And that works?'

'Hole-in-one fifty per cent of the time!'

I wasn't a golfer, but I knew that 'hole-in-one' was a golfing term. There was no time to ask Brad for further explanations since his Studebaker was already heading for the High, exhausts snarling.

In later life, Brad went on to become a senior general in the USAF. I read about him in the Exeter College Register. I still wonder if he uses that line about apples.

Soon after this conversation with Brad Hosmer, I had to go to London for the day. On the train, on my way back, I found myself sitting opposite a very attractive young woman called Sarah, who was at Lady Margaret Hall (LMH). I had seen Sarah around the college, being squired by Chris, a lawyer in my year.

'How's Chris, then?' I asked.

'Fine, thanks.'

After that, the ice broken, we chatted away. Soon after the train had left Reading, I remembered Brad Hosmer's advice. Find some point of common interest.

'Pretty awful place, Reading?' I nodded in the direction of the passing Huntley and Palmer biscuit factory. 'Paris is much nicer, isn't it? Do you like Paris?'

'Yes, I do like Paris!'

'Hell!' I exclaimed. 'I like Paris too! Why don't we meet at Heathrow airport next Friday morning, catch a plane to Paris and spend the weekend there?'

In those days, the bus from Orly brought you to the terminus at Les Invalides. Sarah and I made our way along the Left Bank towards the Pont St Michel. I left her sitting with her bag in a café on one of the little winding side streets.

'You stay here,' I said. 'I'll go and find a place for us to stay.'

I probably sounded more confident than I actually felt. Sarah and I hadn't actually discussed the 'modalities' of our little expedition before setting off. When I found a suitable hotel, was I going to ask for two separate rooms? Or was I going to ask for one room, with two beds? Or one room with a double bed?

There was no one to ask for advice. I couldn't get hold of Brad. We didn't have mobile phones in those days. In any case, he was probably practising a bombing run thirty thousand feet over Oxfordshire.

When I found a sweet little hotel off the rue de l'Université, I decided to go for broke.

'*Une chambre double, s'il vous plâit.*' I handed over my passport.

'*Et le passport de madame?*'

'*Madame a toujours son passport.*'

'*Il faut la chercher, monsieur.*'

I went back, feeling nervous, to fetch Sarah and her passport. What would happen, I wondered, when we returned and they realized that we weren't man and wife? Would they refuse to give us a double room? Would they insist on a 'twin' or even two singles?

As it happened, my anxieties on this score proved wholly superfluous. I tried to retrace my steps from the rue de l'Université to the Pont St Michel as precisely as I could, only to find myself hopelessly lost. Sarah, I knew, had been sitting at a table on the corner of one of those little streets …

I met her at a reception in Brussels fifteen years later quite by chance. She still looked tremendously pretty.

When she saw me, she gave a start, then smiled frostily: 'Oh, hello! Whatever happened to you that day in Paris?' she asked. 'I waited for ages but you never showed up!'

'I'm so sorry, Sarah. I just got muddled by all those little streets on the Left Bank. I just couldn't find the café where I left you. All the cafés looked the same.'

EIGHTEEN

'May Morning'

The memory of that debacle in Paris stayed with me some time, but, a few months later, I was ready to try again.

This time I wrote to my parents from Oxford: 'Will be bringing Penelope for the weekend.'

Penelope was reading English at Somerville. We had both of us gone to the Examination Schools in the High to hear J. R. R. Tolkien lecture on *Beowulf*. A small, white-haired gentleman, he was barely visible behind the lectern. Suddenly there was this tremendous explosion of sound as he began to recite the opening lines of *Beowulf*, that great Anglo-Saxon saga which was compulsory reading for all students of Eng. Lang. and Lit.

'*Hwaet!*' Tolkien boomed. '*Hwaet! We Gardena in geardagum theod-kuninga eft gefrunon ...*'

After that he paused and translated for the benefit of those of us who hadn't yet got past the opening lines. '*Lo! We the people of the Spear-danes in the old days heard of the people-kings ...*'

The lecture room that day was crowded. Indeed, I suspect the great Tolkien's lectures on *Beowulf* were among the most popular in Oxford, even though *The Lord of the Rings* and its author had not then acquired the cult status they have today.

I say 'suspect' because I was not a particularly reliable authority on the popularity of various lecturers. Apart from John Simopoulos's Logic seminar, that brilliant Tolkien performance was the only lecture I remember attending during my four years at the university.

As we pushed our way out into the High when the lecture was over, I found myself next to a striking auburn-haired young woman. Once more, Brad Hosmer's pearls of wisdom came to mind.

'*Hwaet* did you think of Tolkien's lecture?' I asked.

'Great!'

'I thought it was great too. Care for a cup of coffee at George's in the Covered Market?'

Paris, I thought, was jinxed. I proposed Somerset instead. A few days later, Penelope and I made our way down to the farm for the weekend.

It was a tortuous cross-country run from Oxford to Exmoor in those pre-motorway days and my vehicle was in any case not a speedy one. Having deposited the Sunbeam Talbot in a hole one hundred feet below Marble Arch, as I have already described, I had acquired an old London taxi instead with a top speed of around fifty miles an hour.

After driving for several hours in heavy rain, I heard a whimpering behind me. I slid the glass panel open.

'Anything wrong, Penelope?' I shouted.

'I didn't know it would take this long,' she sobbed.

My mother, of course, welcomed her with open arms when at last we arrived, around 11 p.m. She plied her with a cup of Horlicks and packed her off to bed.

Penelope stayed in bed most of that weekend, but not with me, I hasten to add. As far as relationships go, ours could not have been chaster.

My analysis of the situation, then as now, was that the journey down to Somerset in the rain did for her. Maybe it *was* a bit odd, my sitting up in the cab of the taxi like that for hour after hour, occasionally shouting to her through the hatch.

The high point of that weekend at Nethercote in May 1962 was the walk Penelope and I took to the top of Dunkery on the Sunday morning, when she was at last feeling better. At over 1700 feet, Dunkery Beacon is the highest point on Exmoor. You can see for miles in all directions: Wales to the north, Dartmoor to the south, with a raft of prehistoric barrows nearer to hand, lurking amid the heather.

This was the romantic moorland setting which I ruthlessly expropriated for my Newdigate poem.

The year I entered the contest, the poet and author Robert Graves was chairman of the judges and the selected topic was 'May Morning'. You had to stick to the general theme denoted by the chosen title, but after that the form, content and length of the poem were up to you.

It remains something of a mystery to me why I entered for the prize at all, apart of course from wanting to win. When I was at Sherborne I had had a couple of poems published in *The Shirburnian* but that was largely because I was the editor at the time. I had also written that mawkish poem about Mykonos during my gap year, as well as the occasional sonnet during fallow periods in the college library. But by no stretch of the imagination did I consider myself a poet.

The only explanation I can think of is that my long-dormant Muse suddenly woke up that morning on Exmoor and said, 'let's get this ode on the road', or words to that effect.

I need to be precise about the timing.

Penelope and I finished our walk on Dunkery, where we had climbed to the very top of the cairn, at around 11 a.m. We picked up the Sunday papers (*Telegraph* and *Express*) from the box at the bottom of the drive and were home by 11.30. My father had already gone to the pub so I knew lunch wouldn't be till two o'clock at the earliest.

I settled Penelope with the papers by the fire in the Middle Kitchen.

'My mother's in the kitchen. If you need anything, you'll have to shout. She's rather deaf. She had a hearing aid, but she keeps taking it out and putting it down and the dogs eat it. Actually, that's happened more than once. The dogs seem to like the taste. The trouble is the insurance company won't pay up any longer.'

'Where are you going?' Penelope looked nervous, as though she was being left alone in a room full of rats.

As a matter of fact, there were still quite a lot of rats at Nethercote in those days. If you were sleeping upstairs, and the fleeces weren't being stored on the billiard table at the time, you could sometimes hear the rats scurrying on the green baize cloth. I was convinced they actually enjoyed pushing the balls around because, occasionally, there would be a thud as a ball fell to the wooden floor of the landing through one of the many holes in the pockets.

My mother regarded rats as supremely intelligent animals.

'If a rat wants to steal an egg,' she explained, 'it will lie on its back clasping the egg to its bosom. Then a second rat will get hold of the first rat's tail and drag it, still clasping the egg, wherever they want to go.'

Sometimes my mother would lie on her back and clutch her bosom with both hands to demonstrate a rat's egg-stealing prowess. Having gained her half-blue at Oxford for judo, she remained proud of her physical agility almost to the end of her life.

I cast a quick glance around the room.

'I'm pretty sure there's no wildlife around in here this morning,' I reassured Penelope. 'Anyway, I'll be just next door in the Back Kitchen. Give a shout if you see something. I'll be finished by lunch.'

It was actually quite cold in the Back Kitchen but I didn't stop to make a fire. I sat at the long oak table and wrote 'May Morning', my Newdigate Prize entry, in one swell foop.

For a minute or two, before putting pen to paper, I thought about trying my hand at blank verse. Some of the world's most sublime poetry had been written in blank verse. Shakespeare and Milton sprang to mind. But then I thought: no. The judges might as well have their money's worth. I decided to go for rhyme.

And I didn't just choose any old rhyme. I went for 'rhyme royal'.

The reason I knew about 'rhyme royal' was that Jonathan Wordsworth had explained it to me in my last tutorial, three days earlier.

My essay had gone better than usual. Jonathan started looking at me as though he hadn't made a mistake after all in taking me on.

'Form versus content. That's the heart of it,' he said. 'Take Chaucer's *Troilus and Criseyde*, for example. You might think that rhyme royal Chaucer uses is highly formal but actually it gives him tremendous flexibility. You can write ABBCCAB or ABCABCA or any other combination.'

'And the seventh line just has to rhyme with one of the preceding lines?'

'Good man! You got it!' One could never be sure whether Jonathan was being sarcastic.

That morning in the Back Kitchen at Nethercote I decided that if rhyme royal was good enough for Chaucer, it was good enough for me.

In quick succession, barely pausing for breath, I produced fourteen seven-line rhyming stanzas, or ninety-eight lines of verse altogether. I finished just as I heard my father's Land Rover drive into the yard.

My father glanced at his watch as he entered the kitchen. He always wore the watch on the inside of his left wrist, a habit he had picked up when flying in the war. It meant you didn't have to take your hand off the joystick or whatever in order to check the time. Not that having his hand on the controls had saved him from having that ghastly prang at Chivenor.

'Actually, I'm not late, actually, am I?' My father had noted the pained look on my mother's face.

As he washed his hands at the sink, his glance fell on Penelope and me, waiting for our lunch.

'Hello, Stan. Hello, Penelope,' my father said. 'Had a good morning?'

I don't know about Penelope but, as it turned out, I did indeed have a very good morning.

My mother had an old portable Smith Corona which her own parents had given her for her twenty-first birthday and she typed 'May Morning' out for me that afternoon before Penelope and I set off for the return journey to Oxford. She wound some carbon paper into the machine. The carbon had seen better days.

'Will the original and just one carbon do?' she asked me.

'Can you make it two carbons?' I replied. 'Apparently they need to deposit a copy of the winning poem in the Bodleian. Not that I'm going to win.'

'Of course you are, darling.'

My mother typed away quite professionally. (I think Grandpa Williams had optimistically paid for a secretarial course as well as a typewriter when my mother left Oxford.) No mean stylist herself, from time to time she showed her appreciation by taking her hands off the keys and clapping.

'"Cathedrals, *arched like lambs* …"! That's exactly right! How clever of you, Stan! When you look at the newborn lambs jumping around in the meadow, their backs are just like that … arched, like the roof of a cathedral.'

Her typewriter having seen better days, my mother noted that the capital 'Ss' were rather faint on the carbon copies and the capital 'Ws' didn't appear at all.

'The judges will have the original, won't they?' she asked anxiously.

A few weeks later, I was crossing the Exeter College quadrangle when the Rector, Dr K. C. Wheare, buttonholed me. Wheare was a kindly, humorous Australian who had already been head of the college for several years when I arrived.

'Ah, Johnson, come and have a sherry!'

Over a drink in the Rector's Lodgings he told me the good news.

'They've awarded you the Newdigate. Splendid news! An Exeter man hasn't won the Newdigate for generations!'

Word got around college quickly. John Badcock – or 'Badders' as we knew him – who was then the President of the Junior Common Room, invited me to recite my winning effort to a crowded JCR after dinner one Sunday evening. I stood up behind the same threadbare sofa that Alan Bennett had used as a stage prop when he tried out his sermon and other sketches.

> 'Soft on that hilltop we awoke', *I began,*
> 'And in each other saw the world below
> Soft had we climbed, spoke
> Not a word, made no sound, though
> The morning cried aloud for praise.
> On this, most glorious of days
> Silence was the only God we might invoke ...'

I started on the next verse as various well-tanked-up members of the Exeter College Rugby Club arrived hotfoot from the beer cellar on Staircase 2.

> 'Perversely precarious, determined to cheat
> Topographical delimitation,
> We climbed up the cairn till our feet
> Surmounted all terrestrial equation.
> We were high, we were free, we were proud
> And all our emptiness was a crowd
> Filling what was beneath.'

'Topographical delimitation!' heckled Steve Malone, the Exeter lock forward. 'Call that poetry? Give me *Julie* any day!'

Badders tried to keep order. He was a fair-minded man.

'Give him a chance, please, Steve.'

Unfortunately, the very next line proved to be my undoing.

'"*And I myself*", I continued, "a *dubious thing of youth* ..."'

'Ho ho!'laughed Steve Malone. 'Ho bloody ho! Stan Johnson, the "dubious thing of youth" – that's rich!'

Now I want to make it clear that I have nothing against Steve Malone per se. For some years after I left Oxford I used to have a pair of rugger shorts with the nametape S. D. Malone sewn inside the waistband. I must have picked up his shorts in the changing room and he must have picked up mine. I was still wearing those shorts well into the 1980s so there was certainly a bond of shorts between us.

But in all fairness I don't think Malone and his mates gave my Newdigate poem the consideration it deserved.

They kept heckling and barracking until Badders was forced to call it a day when I was about halfway through.

'Thanks so much, Stanners,' he said. 'Brilliant stuff, no doubt. But we'd better hear the rest of it some other time.'

Oddly enough, the reception 'May Morning' received in the JCR didn't deter me in the least. I was on a high. Jonathan Wordsworth, on learning that I had won the Newdigate, had in due course read the poem and pronounced it 'an appealing pastiche'. Coming from Jonathan this was praise indeed.

'Don't you mean "appalling"?' I asked.

'No, as a matter of fact I don't.'

I sometimes sensed him eyeing me speculatively during our tutorials as though there might be more in me than met the eye.

Dacre sent me a gracious note: 'You have done much honour to yourself, your parents and your college.'

Good old Dacre! They don't make dons like him nowadays. Unmarried, he devoted his life to his students. Even though I wimped out on Greats and so wasn't his pupil, he sometimes asked me to a concert, followed by dinner in his rooms. Today, you'd probably have to have a chaperone, bachelor dons being highly suspect.

Dacre's books on Oxford and on Rome remain classics. I enjoyed his novels too, particularly *The Day They Burned Miss Termag* and *The Pheasant Shoots Back*. This was a man who was always young at heart.

Dacre had very kindly included my parents in his list of people to whom I had, in his words, 'done honour'.

To tell the truth, my father was pleased, but also a little concerned, by the news of my success in the Newdigate. When we next met, he said he was worried that I 'might have got in with a poetry set'. Though I tried to reassure him by saying that the only poetry set at Exeter was the rugby club singing dirty songs at full voice, I don't think he was convinced.

My mother, on the other hand, was delighted.

'I knew it wouldn't matter about the "Ss" and the "Ws"', she said. 'How much is the Newdigate worth?'

'Twenty-one guineas. That's what it was in 1806 when the prize was first established. That's what it still is today. If the University paid out the true value, it would be worth a fortune.'

'Don't worry! Put it all on the Derby!' my mother advised. 'When I left Oxford, I fell in love with Fitz. He was Irish and my parents disapproved so I had to break it off. They sent me out to South Africa on a cruise to get over him. On the way out, I dreamed that a horse called Escort won the Derby. Every year for the last thirty years I've looked to see if there's an Escort among the runners. Well, this year there is!'

It was too good a chance to miss. Escort's odds were 66–1. I went into a betting shop and staked all twenty-one guineas.

On the afternoon of the race, I went punting on the Cherwell with Helena Wills, taking a portable wireless with me. Helena was one of the stars of my days at Oxford, a Zuleika Dobson figure. I think winning the Newdigate must have given me a temporary glamour, otherwise I can't imagine what she was doing in my punt on Derby Day.

We were passing through the stretch of water known as Parson's Pleasure (ladies had to keep their eyes down to avoid the sight of nude male bathers) when the radio commentator let out a yell.

'Great Scott!' we heard him shout. 'There's been a tremendous mix-up as they came into the fifth furlong. The favourite has fallen! Five other horses have fallen! Escort, the rank outsider, is in the lead!'

I couldn't believe my luck. I pulled up the punting pole and waved it in the air, showering Helena with muddy Cherwell water.

For a while, I thought Escort was actually going to win. But some of the other runners made a late surge and in the end Escort came a very respectable fourth.

'Still, a place is better than nothing,' Helena said. 'At 66–1 you'll still clean up.'

'I put all twenty-one guineas on Escort to win. That's what my mother dreamt.'

My Derby Day setback was soon forgotten when I received a lovely letter from Robert Graves, the chairman of the Newdigate judges.

I picked it up one morning in the College Lodge. The envelope carried a Spanish stamp and had an address printed on the back: Canellun, Deya, Majorca.

Graves had retired to live in Majorca in the 1920s with a succession of 'muses' but his fame continued to grow. Though best known for his historical novels about the Emperor Claudius, I was aware that he was also a serious poet, a major literary figure. I imagined him putting pen to paper before climbing down the steep cliff for his afternoon swim in the clear blue Mediterranean.

'Dear Johnson', the great poet and author of *Goodbye to All That* wrote, 'yours was the only entry for the Newdigate which showed any poetic understanding.'

Stuff Steve Malone, I thought!

The next time I recited my poem was at the Encaenia on 27 June 1962. The Encaenia was the annual ceremony at which Oxford awarded honorary degrees. That year at least it was a big deal. The list of honorands included some real A-list figures, such as Charlie Chaplin, Yehudi Menuhin, Graham Sutherland and Dean Rusk, then US Secretary of State.

The University rules stated that, before the degrees were awarded, the winner of the Newdigate should recite his prize poem, in the event the prize had been awarded.

A few days before the ceremony I received a letter, in Latin, from the Public Orator, Mr Bryan-Brown, suggesting that in view of the pressures of time, I might like to limit my recitation to a brief extract.

I wrote back by return, also in Latin. 'The "tempus" might be "breve", I protested, 'but the "ars" was "longa".'

'*Vel totum vel nihil*,' I concluded. As far as I was concerned, it was all or nothing.

Quick as a flash, the Public Orator sent back the message: '*Tunc nihil*.' Then, nothing!

If I wanted to play hardball, he could play hardball too.

In the end we compromised. I was allowed to choose seven out of the fourteen stanzas, or forty-nine lines altogether.

I remember that morning so well. The Sheldonian was being refurbished so the Encaenia was being held in the Town Hall instead. Normally Harold Macmillan, the then Prime Minister who was Chancellor of the University, would have presided but he was indisposed that day so the Pro-Chancellor, Professor A. P. Norrington, stood in.

I was seated, with other University prize-winners, in the front row of the gallery, wearing my subfusc (dark suit, white shirt and white bow tie) and a peony that Helena Wills had very kindly brought round to my lodgings in St John Street that morning. Down below us, every seat in the Town Hall was taken.

As the clock in the tower of the University church, St Mary the Virgin, struck eleven, Norrington lifted his mortar board.

'*Ite! Petite!*' he said to the Senior Proctor which, being translated literally, means 'Go and seek them!'

'*Ite! Petite!*' The Senior Proctor in turn urged the bulldogs and a small procession set off into the High Street to bring in all the honorands, those great and good men who lingered on the pavement outside, waiting to be inducted into one of Oxford's most arcane rites.

To the delight of those present, Charlie Chaplin gave us an ironic version of his famous waddling walk as he proceeded up the aisle to take his seat in front of the Pro-Chancellor. Dean Rusk, the US Secretary of State, looked solemn, as well he might given the problems the US was then experiencing in Vietnam. Yehudi Menuhin, who was about to receive an honorary doctorate in music, looked particularly splendid in the LL D gown.

When they were all in place, Norrington once again took off his mortar board.

This time he waved it not at the Senior Proctor but in the direction of the balcony.

He gabbled away in Latin. After studying the language for so many years, I ought to have picked it up straightaway.

'*Newdigatus poema ... scholaris Exoniensis ... Stanleius Patricius Johnsonius ...*' Norrington intoned. It sounded like one of those pseudo-Latin sketches in *Private Eye*.

In the body of the Town Hall, some of the faces looked up in my direction.

'*Newdigato premio laureatus Stanleius Johnsonius!*' Norrington waved his mortar board more vigorously.

A hand twitched my scholar's gown and the winner of the Gaisford Greek Verse Prize sitting behind me whispered urgently, 'It's your turn now! Off you go!'

I have never suffered from stage fright. I have always appreciated these full-dress performances. You have a strange sense of power. No wonder Hitler enjoyed Nuremberg. There they all were, about a thousand people in the body of the hall, all in their finery, waiting for me to spout away.

So spout away I did. In a funny way, truncating the poem seemed to improve it. Of course, I kept in the classical allusions, the references to Troy, Agamemnon and 'Hellenic signatories' – with an audience like this, it was best to play safe. But I also retained some of the – dare I say it? – more lyrical passages as well.

I was particularly keen on the last stanza and I gave it some welly.

My first poem about Mykonos, written three years earlier during my gap year, had not been one of my best. Still, it seemed a pity to lose that Cycladic magic altogether, and I had worked in a reference to the island in 'May Morning':

> 'So once in Mykonos at dusk,' *I recited,*
> 'I thought May Morning came
> And once upon a Persian mosque
> I felt I knew some name
> Of God when in the tiles of Holy Writ
> It circled one whole minaret
> And streamed to heaven again.'

I heard later that, at this point in my determinedly moving perform-ance, Dame Lucy Sutherland, Principal of Lady Margaret Hall, had taken out her handkerchief to dab the tears from her eyes.

K. C. Wheare very kindly arranged for me to attend the Encaenia lunch afterwards, held in All Souls, one of the most beautiful of the Oxford colleges. There were drinks in the garden before lunch, the Warden, John Sparrow, presiding.

Professor James Fawcett, All Souls' Domestic Bursar, sought me out. He was tremendously polite.

'Ah, Johnson,' he said, 'I'm responsible for the seating arrangements at lunch. I've put you next to my daughter. I hope that's all right.'

'Of course it is.'

Opportunistically, during the pre-lunch drinks, I went round the honorands and other dignitaries inviting them to sign my Encaenia Programme. As I look at this document today, I see that it contains an astonishing array of autographs. Charlie Chaplin wrote 'Bravo!' and signed himself 'Charles Chaplin', pocketing my fountain pen in the process (I didn't pluck up the courage to ask for it back). Yehudi Menuhin wrote, 'To a companion of the day'. Robert Graves (whom I met that day for the first time) repeated his congratulations and added his signature. Dean Rusk, Graham Sutherland and Leonide Massine, the choreographer, all followed suit, as well as University high-ups like Norrington and Maurice Bowra.

I told Bowra that reciting his Turkish lyric about two red-legged partridges had once helped me out of a hole in Ankara.

'Splendid, dear boy! Splendid!' He seemed genuinely pleased.

A few minutes later, we went into lunch. As I listened to the long Latin grace, I caught sight of my neighbour's place card out of the corner of my eye: Charlotte Fawcett, Lady Margaret Hall.

I couldn't see much of her face because it was hidden by a mass of tawny hair.

As we sat down, she turned to me and smiled: 'I'm Charlotte.'

'I know. Your father already told me.'

Halfway though lunch, one of the college servants brought me a note which Stephen Spender had scribbled on his menu card. He had missed the ceremony, but had arrived in time for the lunch.

'Dear Mr Johnson', he wrote, 'I did not hear your poem but friends whose judgement I trust tell me it is very good. Please will you let me have it so I can print it in *Encounter*?'

The college servant was still hovering. I pulled from my pocket the text I had proclaimed that morning.

'Could you take this back to Mr Spender, please, with my compliments?' I felt very grown up.

Spender was as good as his word and 'May Morning' appeared, in its abbreviated version, in the August 1962 edition of *Encounter*.

NINETEEN

A Waistcoat Made of Rabbit Fur

Jonathan Wordsworth brought a reading party of Exeter College undergraduates down to Nethercote during my last Long Vacation in the summer of 1962. There were eight people in the group, myself included, all of us expecting to take our final examinations in English the following year. The party included Eric Davis, an American, and Stephen Gill, both of whom went on to distinguished academic careers, as well as Quentin Guirdham, who was enjoying a promising career at the *Financial Times* when he died of a heart attack at a tragically young age.

My parents had bought East Nethercote from the Stevens a few years earlier, so we now had two houses in the valley as well as some extra land, notably the inverted V-shaped wedge which previously had separated the two sides of West Nethercote.

It was in the East Nethercote farmhouse, a building of much the same age and character as West Nethercote, that the reading party conducted its business.

One evening Quentin led a discussion of 'May Morning', subjecting my poem to a lengthy, if light-hearted, textual analysis. Apart from that, we all buckled down, conscious that time was marching on.

Jonathan presided over our 'study sessions' at East Nethercote with his usual intelligence and sardonic humour. He was also, underneath that often caustic exterior, an extremely kind man. For example, having met my younger sister, Birdie, at Nethercote that summer, he went out of his way to try to ensure that she herself had a crack at getting into Oxford.

This was always a long shot. Birdie had followed our mother to Cheltenham Ladies' College, but on the whole hadn't much enjoyed it.

She had left school without taking any A levels and was marking time at Nethercote when the famous reading party arrived.

Jonathan immediately recognized her potential, encouraged her to apply to Oxford and for some months gave her individual coaching. During this time Birdie stayed with the Wordsworths in the house outside Oxford where she was treated as a member of the family.

In due course, she applied to St Hugh's – my mother's old college – and sat the entrance exam. In the end, St Hugh's turned her down, but with some very kind words. I am sure that the fact that she came as close as she did, starting virtually from scratch, owed much to the attention Jonathan devoted to her.

With the last Long Vacation over, I returned to Oxford for my fourth and final year.

My first two years had been spent in college, the third in lodgings in St John Street. For my last year, five friends and I had taken over 82A St Aldates, a medieval rabbit warren of a house, which faced the St Aldates entrance to Christ Church Meadow.

My room was on the first floor, with magnificent moulded ceilings and an unsurpassed view over the Meadow. I could sit for hours at my desk, gazing out onto the vast open spaces and the magical skyline of domes and spires beyond.

I was lucky too in my housemates who, by any standard, were an intelligent and gifted group of people. Heathcote Williams was already a published author. Colin Lucas, my friend and contemporary from Sherborne who had gone on to Lincoln, would become Master of Balliol and Vice-Chancellor of the University. Eric Davis would return to America to be an English teacher in a well-known private college near Boston. Colin Henfrey would become a Professor of Anthropology at Liverpool University. John Amos would work for the BBC and the *Financial Times*, before taking up law.

From my point of view at least, the house share worked perfectly. We didn't get on each other's nerves, in each other's hair or tread on each other's toes.

I don't want to over-egg this. From the purely practical point of view, ours was a fairly squalid existence. We had a tiny, antiquated kitchen on the mezzanine floor where the hot water was constantly in short supply. We didn't do much cooking. This was just as well, because no one ever attempted to wash up.

At the end of the holidays, I had brought my books and clothes back from Nethercote in a huge cabin trunk. This was the same trunk that my mother had taken with her on the Union Castle liner in 1932, when she had been dispatched to South Africa to recover from her undesirable romance with Fitz, the Irishman. Once I had unpacked it, I stored it on the landing outside the kitchen. The NOT WANTED ON VOYAGE stickers could still be seen on the lid of the trunk, as well as labels saying Miss Y. E. I. Williams. On the rare occasions when any of us did try to make a meal, the used plates, cups or dishes tended to be thrown into this strange receptacle. By the time we left at the end of the year, the trunk was completely full and several stout hands were needed to cart the contents away to the rubbish tip.

My London taxi had served to bring both the cabin trunk and me from Nethercote to Oxford. It was also good to have the vehicle during the term time for trips to London or even farther afield.

One day Eric Davis asked me whether I would be able to drive him in my taxi to the Shakespeare Memorial Theatre at Stratford-on-Avon, where he was planning to see *As You Like It*. As an inducement, he said he had a spare ticket and I could have it.

'Who else is going with you?' I asked.

Eric was a bit vague on this point. 'I'm working on it,' he said. 'I may bring a girl from LMH along.'

The 'girl from LMH' turned out to be Charlotte Fawcett, whom I had sat next to at the Encaenia lunch.

About a week after the trip to Stratford, Charlotte invited me to tea in her room in college. She was now in her second year, reading English.

Charlotte was a painter. *Isis*, the weekly University magazine, frequently carried her cartoons and sketches. She wore a waistcoat made of rabbit fur and, in general, had a bohemian air about her. She spent most of the time during my visit that afternoon resting one foot on an upturned waste-paper basket.

'College rules,' she explained. 'You have to keep one foot on the ground at all times if you have a man in your room.'

We were married about eight months later in the Register Office in Marylebone Road, London.

My mother and father drove up to London for the day.

Charlotte had already been down to Nethercote. My mother had picked her up at Dulverton station.

'I almost crashed on the way back,' she told me. 'I kept peering sideways at her, trying to see her face through her hair.'

My father thought I was too young to get married (I was still only twenty-two). A few weeks earlier, while I was carrying out some farming chore at Nethercote, he had muttered something about 'lambs to the slaughter'. But his heart wasn't in it. Charlotte's ebullience and eccentricity soon won him over.

When we had finished with the Register Office, Charlotte's parents, James and Bice Fawcett, gave a party for us in the garden of their London home in Cavendish Avenue, St John's Wood.

After that, we went potato picking in Kent for our honeymoon. B., that versatile young woman who had come with us to Nethercote over a decade earlier, was now married to John Paine, as I have already mentioned. John had a farm on Romney Marsh in Kent. He had expressed mild disbelief when I rang to say that Charlotte and I were getting married and wanted to pick potatoes for our honeymoon. But when he realized I was serious he and B. had welcomed us to their farm and reserved a place for us on one of the potato-picking teams.

'It's a long day,' he warned. 'You'll start at eight and knock off at four and it's pretty back-breaking work.'

It was. There you are, bent almost double, scrabbling away at the potatoes with your bare hands, all the while trying not to put clods of earth or rotten or green potatoes in the bags. The great potato-digging machine is churning along the rows, turning up more and more of these tubular monstrosities until you feel you can't last another minute.

Looking back, I realize that picking potatoes on one's honeymoon was possibly eccentric. It was not as though we needed the money. I was still flush from my Oxford days. All I can say was that it seemed like a good idea at the time. In any case, we had a second honeymoon a few weeks later on the *Queen Mary*, bound for New York.

Towards the end of my last summer term, in between preparing for the wedding and swotting for finals, I heard that I had been awarded a Harkness Fellowship.

This meant two years travel and study in the United States. My chosen field of study was creative writing and the destination was the State University of Iowa where possibly the most famous of America's 'creative writing workshops' was to be found.

I have often wondered why I was awarded a Harkness Fellowship, which at the time was certainly the best remunerated and probably the most prestigious of postgraduate awards tenable in the United States. After all, I hadn't got a first in Mods, hadn't edited *Isis*, hadn't been President of the Union etc.

In retrospect, I think four factors were important.

First, whereas most applicants put in for the better known universities and the more traditional fields of study, e.g. business administration at Harvard, I was going for creative writing at Iowa – both unusual, if not actually eccentric choices. Second, good old Kenneth Wheare, the Rector of Exeter, had, without actually perjuring himself, written me a reference in which he predicted that I would 'do very well indeed' in my finals. Third, I had won the Newdigate, which was clearly relevant to my chosen field of creative writing. Fourth, I attached to my application form a photograph of myself taken by the Marco Polo Route Project cameraman, Michael de Larrabeiti.

The photo showed me sitting, pen in hand, under a bush in the Persian desert. My head is raised to the camera; my face is grimy with travel. Half a dozen nomads are peering over my shoulder, squinting at the paper, which is already full of my jottings.

If anything tipped the balance in my favour, I am convinced it was this photo.

Winning a Harkness meant that all real decisions about life and work could be postponed for another two years. That was fine by me. I had come to the end of my time at Oxford without having any clear idea about what I wanted to do for a career.

It was more complicated for Charlotte. She had just completed her second year at Oxford. She had one more to go. If she accompanied me to America for the next two years, she would lose the chance of finishing her degree.

I never heard a word of complaint from Charlotte and her family. I don't think I even realized myself at the time what a tremendous sacrifice I was asking of my new wife.

We left Southampton on 23 August 1963, arriving in New York five days later. Charlotte had already been to America quite often. Before going to All Souls, James Fawcett had worked for the Foreign Office, being posted to New York where the United Nations was newly established. He had also served in Washington, DC, as General Counsel of the International Monetary Fund. The family – Charlotte had three sisters and a brother – had accompanied him on these travels.

But America was, literally, the 'New World' for me. I would still urge any young man or woman with no immediate compulsion to take paid employment to head west across the Atlantic. You can learn more in a year or two in America than you could possibly imagine.

The Harkness people had sent a spanking new Chevrolet Bel Air Automatic down to the quayside to meet us. The man handed me the keys.

'We've booked you in at the Carlisle Hotel for tonight. I gather you're going on to Iowa in the morning. Don't forget to drive on the right!'

I knew about driving on the right. What he didn't tell me is that you can't start an automatic while it's in gear.

I stalled the car crossing Fifth Avenue and couldn't for the life of me work out how to start it again. As the honking behind me grew louder, a friendly policeman strolled over.

'Where are you headed?'

'The Carlisle. Can't seem to get the car started.'

'Put it in park or neutral before you turn the key.'

That evening at the Carlisle, where we had eventually arrived, Charlotte and I celebrated our arrival in New York by ordering room-service dinner: jumbo prawns and giant T-bone steaks. When we had finished, I rang down to reception to tell them to pick up the trolley outside our room.

The trolley was so large and there was so much debris on it that it took the two of us to push it outside. Charlotte by that stage was getting ready for bed.

As we manoeuvred the trolley into the corridor, the door to our hotel room shut behind us.

'I'll get another key from reception,' I said.

'Be quick! I've got no clothes on,' Charlotte urged.

I was quick but I was not quick enough. The man had come for the trolley while Charlotte was still crouching behind it. I'm not sure which of them was the more embarrassed.

That was the end of our first day in America.

TWENTY

A Poet in Iowa; Mexico; New York City

The State University of Iowa is in Iowa City, Iowa, over a thousand miles from New York. Charlotte's mother, Bice Fawcett, was the daughter of a distinguished American palaeographer, Professor Elias Lowe. One of her sisters, Patsy, lived in New York. One of Patsy's sons, Jon, who happened to need a lift to Davenport, Iowa, volunteered to drive with us. For the next thirty hours, we crossed the flat, open heartland of America, marvelling at the sheer immensity of the country.

Halfway across Pennsylvania, while Jon was at the wheel, a highway patrol car pulled us over and a policeman wearing a wide-brimmed Smokey the Bear hat strode languidly over to tell Jon he had been speeding.

'You'd better come with me,' he told us.

The policeman got back in his car and we followed him to a little white clapboard hut about ten minutes off the turnpike where a large, smiling woman who was the local justice of the peace was waiting.

'How are you all today?' she greeted us, as a spider might greet a fly.

At the back of the hut, a man – possibly her husband – munched on a corn on the cob. He wore wide red braces over a plaid shirt.

If Jon was nervous, he disguised the fact. 'We're fine, thank you.'

The policeman who had arrested us typed out the details of Jon's offence. Then the smiling lady JP read it out, giving the details of the law which had been infringed and ending with the impressive statement that Jon's was an 'offence committed against the peace and dignity of the Commonwealth of Pennsylvania'.

'You all have a nice day,' she said as she waved us back onto the road. The policeman who had arrested us tipped his hat.

'Fifteen dollars. Could have been worse.' Jon was philosophical. 'If we'd been black it might have been a different story.'

Jon's comment took me by surprise. I feel rather ashamed that I arrived in America in September 1963 virtually unaware of the social and political revolution that was about to shake the country. The civil rights movement was gathering speed. Soon it would become an unstoppable force. And I knew almost nothing about it.

It was my turn to drive. I kept well below the speed limit, watching the rearview mirror, while Jon fiddled with the radio.

'Listen to this,' he said.

From the car radio came a low, haunting melody. I didn't know the song; I didn't know the singer, but I was gripped. Totally gripped.

'*How many times can a man turn his head?*' the singer asked, '*and pretend he just doesn't see?*'

It was the first time I had ever heard Bob Dylan. The first time I had ever heard 'Blowin' in the Wind'. Charlotte was ahead of me here. She'd been on CND and anti-apartheid rallies. She'd had a left-wing boyfriend who'd been President of the Oxford Union. But I was a tyro, a complete novice.

When the song came to an end – with its final haunting refrain – I realized that something was indeed 'blowing in the wind'.

Next day, as we were driving through Illinois, I heard 'If I Had a Hammer' for the first time and experienced much the same sensation. There was a new sound out there. According to Bob Dylan and Co. it was the sound of freedom! *All over this land!* It seemed a good time to be in America.

We found a flat at 908 East Washington Street, Iowa City. Charlotte unpacked her easel and paints and enrolled in the university's art department. I headed off to the Poetry Workshop.

I now regret that I didn't make more of my time in Iowa. As a writer, I could have learned a great deal. Iowa City was billed at the time as the 'Athens of the Mid-West' and a large measure of the credit for this was due to Professor Paul Engle, himself a poet and the founder and director of the Writers' Workshop. He had managed to bring writers and poets to Iowa from all over the US and from many countries outside it.

There was no doubt that Engle and Donald Justice, his close colleague on the Workshop staff, regarded the practice of poetry as a high calling.

I agreed with them at the time. I agree with them now. I had a chance to make a go of it. Winning the Newdigate had been an auspicious beginning and I could have built on that. I could have put in the hours, learned the trade, sent off my poems for publication in small specialist magazines and journals and pocketed the few dollars they might have commanded by way of a fee. I could have been a contender.

In practice, things didn't work out that way.

The Workshop used to meet, unpretentiously, from 2.30 to 4.30 every Monday afternoon in a smoke-filled Nissen hut on the banks of the Iowa River. Attendance was not compulsory but thirty or forty students were likely to appear. In the course of the preceding week, a number of poems would have been submitted. Of these, five or six would have been chosen and duplicated for consideration by the class.

One of the poems discussed that first day was my own. Professor Engle was careful to point out that the poems on the worksheet were not necessarily chosen for their poetic merit.

'They may be chosen because they're very *bad* poems,' he explained, laughing.

Turning to me, he said: 'I'm going to ask Mr Johnson to read his own poem to us.'

My offering that day was a scant six lines, entitled 'New York Harbour'. I had been inspired to write it by the memory of the buoys bobbing in the water as the *Queen Mary* came in to dock in New York a few days earlier with Charlotte and me on board. Though Charlotte knew America well, this was the first time I had seen the extraordinary Manhattan skyline.

> 'Harbour buoys,' *I recited*, 'rung by sea-swells
> Sound to me across half a continent.
> With a few muted dongs among themselves
> This conical fraternity
> Passes gentle off-shore judgement
> On the difficult city.'

Engle opened the discussion. 'This is a nicely subdued and understated poem. There is what I take to be a deliberate flatness about it. Flatness.'

He looked towards me for confirmation. I nodded, not sure what was coming next.

'It is, of course, a very English poem,' Engle continued, 'quite apart from the spelling of the word "harbour". It shows a strange disregard for geography. The author is presumably locating himself in Iowa as he writes. Iowa may be Mid-West, but it is not Mid-America.'

Donald Justice, seated next to Engle in front of the class, noticed a hand raised at the back.

'Go ahead,' he said.

I turned my head to see a bearded man with his hand raised. He looked like Allen Ginsberg. Maybe it was Allen Ginsberg.

'I would like to know in what way the poem benefits from the reference to the poet in the second line,' the man asked.

I fumbled an answer. 'I was there, that is what I was thinking. I don't see why …'

Justice came to my aid. He spoke with a soft Southern accent. 'I think a form of signature is permissible in a poem. Alfred Hitchcock, as we know, frequently appears in his own films. And Teniers, I believe, often included in his paintings a small picture of himself urinating.'

There was laughter in the room. I felt somehow that it was at my expense.

For a time discussion centred on the words 'conical fraternity'. 'This is heavy and old-fashioned,' said Justice. 'A Victorian circumlocution, like "finny tribe".'

'But surely,' Engle interjected, '"conical" is a misprint for "comical".'

'Not exactly,' I remonstrated, 'I was describing the shape of the buoys. They were cone-shaped, hence "conical".'

I could have survived the Poetry Workshop. As the weeks of that first semester wore on, I came to understand that there was method in the madness. When you had to stand up in front of the class and defend, or at least explain, every line, every word, in the poem you had submitted, you tended to take the trouble to get it right. Or as right as you could. As the term went on, I felt I was making progress.

But on 22 November 1963, an enormous spanner was thrown into the works.

The State University of Iowa in my day had 11,000 students. As was the case with most universities, students scored points for taking different classes. When term began we had joined an endless line of undergraduates waiting to register. The queue wound in and out of the trees on the campus before reaching the doors of the Field House.

Above the entrance to that building was a portrait of a stern, bespectacled man and the message VIRGIL R. HANCHER, PRESIDENT OF THE STATE UNIVERSITY OF IOWA, WELCOMES YOU! Twelve years later, when I was visiting China for the first time, I saw the giant portrait of Chairman Mao on the Gate of Heavenly Peace in Beijing and I couldn't help thinking of President Virgil R. Hancher.

We shuffled under the arch, casting a respectful glance upward at the University President's stern visage, to find ourselves in a huge hall where every conceivable course or combination of courses was offered.

I was meant to be 'majoring' in creative writing, so I signed up as planned for the Poetry Workshop. For my 'minor' subjects, I decided to concentrate on golf and the piano. Basically, you needed a certain number of points to graduate and it didn't matter how or where you scored them.

As far as golf was concerned, I don't think I ever actually picked up a club. Soon after we arrived the weather turned cold, with the temperature dropping well below freezing, and we began to realize what people meant when they talked of Iowa having a 'continental climate'.

I had better luck with piano. I hadn't tried to play the piano since my last term at Sherborne and I was keen to take it up again. Once a week, I went to the Music School for an hour's lesson with Wendell Temple.

There weren't, I have to say, very many African Americans at the State University of Iowa at that time, either as students or staff. The Rock Island Line – a 'mighty fine line' in the words of the popular song – ran through the town and I suspected that Wendell lived, as most of the black population then did, on the other side of the tracks. He was a slim, graceful man, about fifty years old.

One day, when I was struggling to master a Chopin Prelude, there was a loud bang on the door of the room and a distraught young man burst in.

'The President's been shot!' he shouted.

My immediate reaction was that he meant the President of Iowa University. 'Oh, my God! Not President Virgil R. Hancher!' I exclaimed.

'No, President Kennedy! In Dallas!'

179

At this point my piano teacher, Wendell Temple, literally fainted. As his forehead hit the keyboard, the noise reverberated through the room. Moments later, he recovered and sat, sobbing, on the stool.

'President Kennedy was the only man who cared a damn about my people and now he's gone.' The tears rolled down his cheeks.

So, for the record, that's where I was when President Kennedy was shot.

For the next three days, like most of America, we stayed glued to the television screen. As a spectacle, it was unbeatable. We followed the swearing-in of Lyndon Johnson as the new President, a distraught Jackie Kennedy standing beside him in the cabin of Air Force One still wearing her pink bloodstained suit. We followed the journey back to Washington, the sombre homecoming, the solemn pomp of the funeral and the unbearable pathos of little John Kennedy saluting his father's coffin. If there was any one person who held a troubled nation together at that time it was the CBS anchor man, Walter Cronkite, whose familiar rocky features and gravelly voice provided a stable point of reference in a disintegrating world.

Just when you thought things couldn't get worse, they did.

For once, Charlotte and I had turned the television in our apartment off. There was only so much we could take and we needed a break. The student couple who lived downstairs obviously still had their television on because we could hear the distant rumble of Cronkite's voice as he kept up his amazing broadcasting marathon!

Suddenly, we heard a tremendous shout from downstairs. 'Shit, man, no! Jesus, FUCK! Oh, my God!'

Charlotte and I leapt to our feet. We had already made the acquaintance of the couple who lived below us, so we dashed out of our door, down the outside staircase and banged on theirs.

A distraught Jerry beckoned us into the apartment. Jerry's partner, Kate, barely registered our arrival. She was transfixed by what was happening on screen.

'They've just shot Oswald!' Jerry screamed. 'They've fucking shot Oswald!'

He pointed to the bloody figure on the floor. The police were still scuffling with the assassin, Jack Ruby. As we watched, they managed to subdue him and bundled him off.

Moments later, the station replayed the actual moment when Oswald was shot. You could see Ruby jam his gun into Oswald's ribs and the grimace of pain on Oswald's face.

Nowadays, of course, we've got used to death in the living room, live on screen and brought to you in the comfort of your own home! But for Charlotte and me the cold-blooded execution of Lee Harvey Oswald was a first.

We stayed downstairs with Jerry and Kate for the rest of the morning. Jerry ordered in some pizzas and French fries.

By the time of Kennedy's assassination, Charlotte knew that she was pregnant. I wrote to the Harkness people in New York, asking them to agree to a change of plan. They had very kindly awarded me a fellowship to study creative writing at the State University of Iowa. Would they mind if I changed to economics at Columbia University in New York?

Looking back, I suspect it was the (welcome) news of Charlotte's pregnancy that led me to this change of tack. I decided that if I was going to have the responsibility for bringing up a family, I ought to have a decent job. I didn't think that writing poetry for the rest of my life was going to butter enough parsnips.

Lance V. Hammond, who ran the Harkness Programme, soon wrote back, broad-mindedly agreeing to my proposed change. Charlotte and I flew to New York for Christmas. We stayed with Charlotte's aunt, Patsy, and her husband, Merlin, who had an apartment on Central Park West. While we were there, we found a loft to rent on West 23rd Street and I signed up to study economics at Columbia when the new term began in a few weeks' time.

A day or two later, we were on the road again.

One of the requirements of the Harkness Fellowship was that a Fellow should travel around the United States for at least three or four months. Since Charlotte's baby was to be born in June, it seemed sensible to get some of the travelling done first. Columbia's second semester didn't begin till 1 February, so we had time to get the first few thousand miles under our belt before then.

'Let's head for Mexico!' I said.

'*Olé!*' Charlotte replied.

Actually, the Harkness rules said we weren't allowed to take the car across the border, so we left it in Laredo, Texas, and caught the Greyhound bus south.

It took us fourteen hours to reach San Luis Potosi and another six to Mexico City, where we visited the national archaeological museum and the cathedral, as well as the great pyramid at Teotihuacan. We took a bus to Taxco and Puebla, before returning – a few days later – to the capital.

Charlotte was suffering from morning sickness and the altitude in Mexico City didn't help either. She didn't welcome the prospect of the long ride back on the bus to the United States.

One night, a man called Boris Litwin and his wife invited us to lunch in their beautiful home in San Angel.

I must explain about Boris. He was a Russian who, like Trotsky, had come to live in Mexico. Trotsky had met an unfortunate end, being murdered with an ice pick, but Boris was still going strong. Boris Litwin's daughter, Barbara, was the girlfriend of Peter Herbert, one of my Exeter College friends. (Peter shared a room on Staircase 2 with Brad Hosmer and presumably had heard Brad's theory about apples more often than I had.) When she heard that Charlotte and I were planning to visit Mexico, Barbara had written to insist that she should say 'hello' to her parents. Mexican hospitality being what it is, the Litwins seemed to be delighted to entertain us.

At that first lunch, I mentioned to the Litwins that Charlotte and I were planning to return to the United States the way we had come. By Greyhound bus. All twenty hours of it, barring floods, earthquake, ambush or mechanical breakdowns.

Boris Litwin didn't say anything, but he looked accusingly at me. I knew what he was thinking. How could I subject my pregnant wife to another twenty hours or more on the bus? Where was my sense of chivalry?

Two days later the Litwins invited us again, this time for dinner. They showered us with presents. I remember a shawl, a wicker basket, a poncho for Charlotte and some silver ornaments.

Just as we were saying goodbye, overwhelmed by their generosity, Boris Litwin thrust two Mexico City–Laredo air tickets into our hands.

'You can forget about the Greyhound bus now!' he told us.

It was Charlotte who, on the spur of the moment, came up with an idea for repaying Boris Litwin for his kindness.

'If our baby is a boy,' she told him, as we gratefully accepted the tickets, 'we'll call him Boris!'

So we flew in comfort to Laredo, recovered our car, drove on to Iowa City to pack up our things, and then headed back across country to New York, arriving the day before the new semester started at Columbia University.

The loft on West 23rd Street met our expectations in every way. It was a spacious place, sixty foot long and twenty-five foot wide. It contained: a bath on stilts and a yellow out-of-tune piano with the motto '*Vive La Fun!*' painted glaringly on its lid. The lavatory, with a marble hand basin, was concealed from the rest of the room by some large abstract canvases. Bird cages hung from the ceiling and soot crept in through the windows.

There was a terrace at the back populated by metallic sculptures. It was easy enough to climb up from street level. Once I woke to find a large black man standing over the bed.

'I say,' I protested, 'we're trying to sleep. You wouldn't mind leaving us alone, would you?'

Happily the man took the point and climbed back through the window onto the terrace. It was often too hot to sleep with the windows shut. Having the occasional unwanted visitor was a small price to pay.

The loft was situated immediately above a café known as the Star Bar. A neon sign, advertising that lively establishment, flashed outside the street side window till 4 a.m. every night. Downstairs, we could hear the music of the Beatles blaring out on the jukebox (the Beatles visited New York that spring and took the city by storm). 'I Wanna Hold Your Hand' was a particular favourite. They turned up the volume full blast. Sometimes we wanted to curse the Liverpool Fab Four.

The noise from the (almost identical) loft upstairs was different, but in its way no less distracting. The apartment there was occupied by Karen, an artist. Night after night, we heard her walking to and fro in clackety shoes across her floor (which was also our ceiling).

One day I met her on the stairs and jokingly challenged her.

'You seem to be walking around a lot at night, Karen. What are you doing?'

'I'm watering the plants in the window boxes. The kitchen tap's a long way from the window. I don't have a watering can.'

'What do you use?

'I use an egg cup.'

Assailed from above as well as below, in the end we were forced to wear earplugs in bed.

I remember waking up one morning, several months after we had returned to England at the end of our time in New York, to find a small pink object on my pillow. Somehow, like a journalist in present-day Iraq, an earplug had become embedded while we were living in our loft on West 23rd Street and I had forgotten to remove it!

Columbia University was on Morningside Heights, around 116th Street. Walk east a couple of blocks and you were in the heart of Harlem. The contrast with Iowa City couldn't have been greater.

Apart from economics, I attended seminars in international affairs. I remember one well-attended seminar given by Professor Neustadt. Dick Neustadt already had a powerful reputation among the academic community. He later founded the Kennedy School of Government at Harvard, where the staff tended to practise what they preached by commuting from Boston to Washington. They were called 'in-and-outers'.

The main theme of Neustadt's lecture that day was a surprising defence of the new President, Lyndon Johnson. Johnson, Neustadt argued, had started well. He had taken up measures that Kennedy himself would have had no chance of getting past Congress and by sheer bullying willpower had forced them through.

'Those poor people over there,' he gestured in the direction of Harlem, 'may do better under Lyndon Johnson's "Great Society" than they would have done under Kennedy.'

I was sitting at the back, near the door. There was a Viennese restaurant on Amsterdam Avenue that served a superb apple strudel, but you had to move fast in the break between lectures to find a seat.

I put up my hand. 'You've talked about domestic issues, Professor Neustadt, and I'm sure many people agree with you. But why is President Johnson so awful on foreign policy?'

Twenty minutes later I was sprinkling cinnamon on my apple strudel in the Viennese café when a tall, well-groomed man came over to my table. He was wearing a smart blazer and a cravat and sported a monocle. Clearly English.

He held out his hand. 'I really loved it when you asked why President Johnson was "so awful on foreign policy". Those bloody academics! Serves them right!'

'Why don't you join me?' I asked.

Brian Johnson was studying for a Master's in International Relations at Columbia. He was engaged to an American woman, Pamela Pomerance. A few months later, Charlotte and I drove up to Cos Cob, Connecticut, where the Pomerance family had a large estate, for the wedding. Even though Brian and Pam are no longer together, Brian and I have remained firm friends. Some years ago, he decided to become a full-time artist and lives with his new wife, Disie, in Italy. He still dresses tremendously smartly, though the monocle appears to have been consigned to the dustbin.

My attendance at the Richard Neustadt seminar was, I have to admit, more the exception than the rule. Though Columbia was one of America's great universities and I was proud to be enrolled in it, I didn't spend as much time there as I should have done.

One of the problems was the difficulty I had parking our Harkness-provided car in downtown New York.

You could park your vehicle for free on most streets around where we lived (at the junction of 23rd Street and Seventh Avenue), if you could find a space, but you couldn't leave it there for long. You had to move it every few hours. In the mornings, for example, you could park on one side of the street. In the afternoons, you had to park on the other.

So I found myself constantly nipping out of lectures to take the Seventh Avenue Express downtown in order to move the car across the road.

Of course, we could have turned the car in and relied on public transport, but we welcomed the freedom it gave us to leave New York at weekends. In any case, if we were to meet the terms of our contract, we still had a lot of travelling to do around the US and we would need the car for that.

Coming back to Boris Litwin: five months after we moved to New York, on 19 June 1964, Charlotte gave birth to the long-anticipated baby in the New York hospital, situated by the river around East 70th Street.

In those days there wasn't so much pressure on expectant fathers to be present at the birth of their offspring. But I had no objection in principle and had attended the last lecture of a course of lectures Charlotte had been taking on natural childbirth.

As it turned out, this was strong meat. A woman called Ms Mensker propped two huge charts on the table which she called Birth Atlases and regaled us with horrific details; 'Well, by now, those little light contractions are way over. She'll really be working now. There'll be a dime's worth of caput – that means head – showing, perhaps even a quarter. Boy, you're making progress!'

When it was time for questions, I had one of my own. I'd been doing my homework.

'You say Dr Spock advises that the new baby should sleep in a separate room. But we live in a loft on 23rd Street. We only have one room.'

Ms Mensker took it in her stride. 'I guess we don't want to knock Spock, but this is one time we're gonna have to.'

After that enthusiastic tutorial, I was all set to do my share of back rubbing and so on when the time came. Unfortunately, as it happened, I missed the birth itself because I had stepped outside for a moment to get a pizza on Second Avenue. When I got back, I was told that the new baby was already safely wrapped in swaddling clothes and lying in the nursery in a cot, along with half a dozen other new arrivals.

As I peered through the glass, I found it difficult to determine which our child was. The babies were lined up so that all I could see was the soles of their feet, which were uniformly black.

Just for a moment I thought there had been a mix-up and somehow Charlotte had given birth to an African–American or Puerto Rican child. I asked a passing nurse for guidance.

'We dip the feet in ink to take their footprints as soon as they are born,' she explained. 'We want to avoid mix-ups. You can't use the babies' fingerprints. Not when they're newborn. They're too soft.'

A few minutes later, another nurse entered the crèche, picked up one of the bundles and carried it along to a tearful but joyful Charlotte. I realized with relief, as she cradled the child, that all was in order. Even then the blond hair was unmistakable.

We registered the baby with the US authorities, as well as with the British Consulate, thus ensuring future dual citizenship. Next day, I wrote to Boris Litwin to tell him that the new arrival had weighed in at over nine pounds and was doing well.

'We have named him Boris as we promised,' I wrote, 'as a small gesture of recognition for your kindness to us in Mexico. The full name is Alexander Boris de Pfeffel Johnson.'

Litwin wrote me a charming letter in response, saying how pleased he was.

Though Mr and Mrs Litwin have died, as indeed has my old friend Peter Herbert, I am still in touch with their daughter. Barbara, who lives not far from us in London, for many years continued to work for the Mexican Embassy even though handicapped by multiple sclerosis. The last time we met, she told me that every time she sees Boris Johnson on television or reads one of his articles in the *Daily Telegraph* (or presumably now hears a London Mayoral pronouncement), she is reminded of her father, Boris Litwin.

TWENTY-ONE

The Secret Ink Crystals

We didn't in the end spend two full years in America on the Harkness Fellowship as we had originally planned. In fact, I resigned my fellowship a year early. The reason I did so was that Charlotte had discovered that under Oxford University's rules you had to graduate not more than twelve terms after matriculation. In practice she could therefore finish her degree even though she had taken a year off.

With the decision taken to return to the United Kingdom in time for the new academic year, we realized that our Harkness travel quota might be somewhat truncated. While Charlotte and the new baby stayed with friends near New Palz, in the salubrious country atmosphere of upper New York State, I drove south to New Orleans with an American friend called Herschel Stroyman.

My Chevrolet Bel Air was a large car. At night, I tended to stretch out in the front while Herschel took the back.

Once when we were bedded down in the car by the side of the road a few miles from Memphis, Tennessee, we were woken by a powerful spotlight trained on the windows.

'Come on out!' a voice shouted.

'Shit!' Herschel exclaimed. 'I hope it's not the police.'

A few weeks earlier three white civil rights workers from New York had been murdered on their way south, not far from where we were. Their car, like ours, had New York licence plates. Though no one knew for sure who was responsible, the finger of suspicion pointed at the local constabulary.

We stumbled out, blinking in the light.

It was indeed the police, but for once they were in a forgiving mood. They didn't murder us; they didn't even beat us up. They examined our papers and, finding them in order, suggested we might care to move on smartly to wherever it was we were going.

'It ain't such a good idea to sleep by the highway down here! Least-wise, not if you're from up north!'

We drove quickly on to Mississippi. Most of the road signs in the 'Magnolia State' were riddled with bullet holes.

'They're only practising,' Herschel said.

New Orleans, when at last we got there, seemed like heaven. The British might have torched the town in 1815 but the inhabitants didn't seem to hold it against us. There is even a street named after General Pakenham, who did the torching, except – when we were there – the name was spelled 'Packinghome'. Perhaps it still is.

On that particular trip to the American South, we covered four thousand miles in six days. After leaving Herschel in Manhattan, I rejoined Charlotte in the country in upper New York. It was more of a pit stop than anything else because next day we put Alexander Boris on the back seat of the car in his carrycot and headed for New Hampshire, Vermont and Canada.

We didn't see the whole of New England. We didn't see the whole of Canada. But we gave it a college try.

On 29 July 1964, I wrote to my parents: 'I must say Alexander Boris is fantastically well behaved and I catch myself completely forgetting he exists. He sleeps in the back of the car as we travel hundreds of miles, and sometimes we don't even stop while C. feeds him.'

Towards the end of August, we handed the car back to the Harkness people in New York and flew back to England. We found a flat in Oxford, in a new development in Summertown, just off the Banbury Road.

Mrs Waites, who lived in the house next door, offered to look after Alexander Boris, while Charlotte went off to college each morning.

'The Principal of Lady Margaret Hall still insists on calling me Miss Fawcett,' Charlotte complained to me one day, 'even though she knows I'm married and have a baby.'

With a wife and child to keep, I realized that the time had come for me to get a job.

I did a term's teaching at Northfield School, a few miles outside Oxford. It was my first experience of state education and it was certainly a salutary one. I don't think I was ever, properly, in control of my class. You were always on a knife edge, anticipating the worst. If you tried to shout the kids down, it only made matters worse. I soon realized how astonishingly lucky the masters at Sherborne had been. If they couldn't keep control of their classes by the force of their own personality, they at any rate had a whole system of sanctions to help them, up to and including a headmaster's caning.

There was one memorable moment, in early November 1964, when I was standing in front of the class, trying fruitlessly to get my charges to pay attention to something I was writing on the blackboard. It was no use. The noise level continued to escalate and I felt a deep blush working up from my collar to my ears. What on earth, I thought, was the point of having been Head of School at Sherborne, vice-captain of rugby, editor of *The Shirburnian*, Senior Classical Scholar at Oxford and so on and so forth, if I couldn't get a bunch of sixteen-year-olds to stop talking and arsing around for even two minutes?

I understood then the despair teachers can feel when they have to get up in the morning and face another day in the classroom.

That particular morning, just when I was on the point of throwing in the towel and exiting stage left, pursued by howls of derision, there was a sudden blissful hush in the room. I couldn't believe my luck. Maybe this was the breakthrough I had been waiting for.

'Good morning, boys,' a deep voice boomed behind me. 'Good morning, Mr Johnson. How's everything going?'

I turned round to see that the headmaster had entered the room.

That was the only time during my brief career as a schoolmaster that the class I was taking stopped fooling around long enough to listen to me.

The other money-spinning activity I undertook after our return to Oxford was some academic piecework.

I had been walking one day along South Parks Road towards the town centre when I saw a pretty white brick building just the other side of Keble College with a notice outside which said: Oxford University Research Institute for Agricultural Economics.

'This looks promising,' I said to myself.

I was particularly interested in the 'agricultural' part of the Institute's title. Part of me always felt guilty that I hadn't turned to farming as a career. My parents were still soldiering on at Nethercote, trying to keep the wolf from the door, and I was gallivanting around the world. Maybe doing 'agricultural economics' would be a way of showing that my heart, anyway, was in the right place.

Dr Margaret (Peggy) Haswell, senior tutor at the Institute, was surprisingly encouraging. She was a bronzed, practical woman who had spent much of her life in Ghana, studying cocoa prices.

'How much economics do you know?' she asked me.

I explained that in theory I had studied economics at Columbia University, New York, for a semester, though in practice I had spent much of my time parking the car.

'What about agriculture?'

Here I scored better. I talked knowledgeably about lambing and silage.

At the end of the interview, Dr Haswell said: 'It seems fine to me but I'll have to ask Professor Clark who's really in charge here.'

Colin Clark, then the director of the institute, was an extraordinary man. A Roman Catholic, he had – as far as I remember – six children and, perhaps not coincidentally, believed that population growth was the key element in forcing economic and social change. His massive volume on that theme was required reading.

In due course I received a letter saying I had been admitted as an Oxford University graduate student with a view to sitting the examination for the Diploma in Agricultural Economics (Dip. Ag. Econ.) in June the following year. More to the point, Dr Haswell promised me a small allowance if I assisted both her and Professor Clark in bringing out the Institute's *Quarterly Bulletin of Agricultural Economics*.

Though well regarded by those who followed such matters, this was an abstruse publication to say the least. The so-called 'cobweb theorem' of agricultural production (output following prices in an endless spider's web) had first been enunciated in its pages and other even more arcane ideas had also received an airing there. Mine, Dr Haswell admitted, would be a dogsbody job of checking proofs, researching data and so forth, but at least it would bring in a few pennies.

Since beggars can't be choosers, when I wasn't teaching at North-field I was sitting in a little cubicle on South Parks Road correcting galleys with a blue pencil.

I hadn't thought I would be back in Oxford only a year after leaving it but I said to myself, remembering Walter Cronkite's famous nightly sign-off from *CBS News*, 'that's the way it is!' (Strange how the large, solid figure of Walter Cronkite still stuck in one's mind even though there was now an ocean between us. No wonder Americans regularly voted him top of their 'most admired persons' list.)

Working part-time as a supply teacher in an Oxfordshire secondary school, while supplementing my income with a kind of 'internship' at the research institute, wasn't on the face of it a very brilliant start to my career.

Casting around for a way to improve the situation, I remembered a conversation I had had at the last Trevelyan dinner before we left for America. These dinners for Trevelyan scholars were black-tie affairs, as I've already mentioned. We dined in splendour in one candle-lit college hall after another. Our sponsors, the captains of industry, made a point of joining us. Maybe they hoped that when we graduated we would join Shell, BP, ICI or whatever.

That particular evening, I found myself sitting next to one of the directors of Guest, Keen and Nettlefolds, now known as GKN.

'What are you going to do when your Harkness Fellowship is over?' Mr Pearson asked. He paused and tapped the side of his nose meaningfully. 'Just give me a call when you get back. With your background, I'm sure they would be interested.'

I wasn't sure at the time exactly who 'they' were and it didn't seem to be the moment to enquire. However, almost a year and a half later, I telephoned Mr Pearson in his office at GKN. He wasn't there, but I left a message. A few days later he rang me back suggesting it might be a good idea if I 'popped round' to a certain house in Carlton House Terrace, St James's, for a chat with a gentleman called Sir Ian Murray.

There are some moments in your life that you remember with total clarity. Falling over during the Gay Gordons at the Morebath Manor Pony Club dance, for example. Or tackling C. M. Payne on the Iffley Road rugby ground in my Oxford Seniors Trial. Another such moment was being shown into an elegant panelled room in Carlton House Terrace to be interviewed by a tall, distinguished man in a pinstriped suit. I could see his bowler hat and umbrella in a stand by the door.

'You realize,' Sir Ian said, as I sat down, 'that we will offer you the most intensive training in clandestine techniques known to man.'

I am not on the whole a man who says 'no'. On the contrary, when people end their sentences with a proposition, I tend to agree. In this particular case, I found the formula irresistible. The most intensive training in clandestine techniques known to man! As a recruiting line it was up there with Lord Kitchener's 'Your country needs you!'

Of course, it wasn't just the idea of working with all the gadgets and gizmos that appealed to me. I knew there was a totally serious side as well to the pitch being made. We were in the middle of the Cold War. Nobody was talking then about the collapse of the Soviet empire.

'You may have to do things in the course of duty,' Sir Ian told me that morning, 'that you wouldn't normally do. You may, for example, have to break the law, for the greater good, of course. How would you feel about that?'

I said I felt fine about that, as long as a greater good was indeed involved, and they could count me in.

I had to go to Gieves in Savile Row to have a suit made with room for a shoulder holster. There was a bad moment when the old boy hovering with the measuring tape asked me which side I would be carrying my gun. When I hesitated, he asked patiently (he had seen it all before): 'Are you right-handed or left-handed, sir? If you're right-handed, you'll want to wear the gun on the left.'

'Of course,' I said.

When I got back to Oxford, Charlotte asked me where I had been.

'I'm afraid I can't tell you that,' I replied.

'Who did you see?'

'I can't tell you that either.'

Nor could I tell her where I was going. At the crack of dawn, every Monday morning for the next nine months, I got into our battered old Ford Prefect (PYB 313), said goodbye to my little family and tootled off into the unknown.

'Hope your tutorial goes well,' I would shout as I pulled out into the Banbury Road. (By now Charlotte had only a few months to go before her finals.)

'Yours too,' Charlotte would call back, 'wherever and whatever it is.'

New recruits to an officially non-existent organization, we not only couldn't tell our spouses were we had been or where we were going. We couldn't even ring them up or receive calls.

Most of the people who trained us had fought in the war. Secrecy and sabotage were second nature to them. I'm not an expert, but I would say they were very good at what they did.

They might have been patriots, but they weren't stuffy or pompous.

There were ten new boys (no girls) in my group. They sat us down in a classroom (I can't say where) on our first day for our very first training session. I hadn't, up till then, given a great deal of thought to the subject of blackmail. That was to change.

The lecturer on that occasion was a gentleman of soldierly bearing who, we learned, was generally known as 'the Colonel'. He fixed us with a steely eye. The very first words he uttered that morning – indeed, the very first words I heard on this, the first morning of my new life – were: 'Never try to blackmail an Egyptian! It's totally pointless. If you've got some photographs of him in a compromising situation, he'll be delighted. He'll probably ask you for some copies so that he can send them to his friends!'

We were all issued with notebooks to record any pearls of wisdom which might come our way, so that morning I wrote on the first blank page: 'Never try to blackmail an Egyptian.'

Later that morning another lecturer taught us how to avoid being blackmailed. 'Don't be photographed in a hotel room in Moscow with someone who isn't your wife. If you can't keep your trousers on and you think you've been compromised, for heaven's sake call your head of station pronto!'

'Head of station may be called "Pronto",' I wrote in my notebook.

When I returned to Oxford at the end of the first week, Charlotte said: 'I know I can't ask where you've been or where you're going. But can I ask you what you've been doing?'

We'd already been taught how to answer that one: 'Oh, you know, bits and pieces, odds and ends, one thing or another,' I replied.

'Sounds fascinating!' Charlotte went next door to pick Alexander Boris up from the wonderful Mrs Waites.

Actually, Charlotte was right. It *was* fascinating. 'The most intensive training in clandestine techniques known to man' lived up to its billing. Most of these techniques remain, even today, so secret that I would risk running foul of the Official Secrets Act were I to reveal them.

However, there was one tried and trusted method of gathering information that we learned about in Week Three which I do feel able to talk about without being sent to the Tower for treason.

The official topic that morning was 'Information Gathering'. The lecturer was a sandy-haired gentleman, around fifty years old, with a distinctly Slavic accent.

'You don't always need to be ultra-sophisticated ven you're gathering intelligence,' he told us. 'Of course, the keyhole or directional microphone may be useful. Or the telephone tap. Or digging a tunnel under enemy headquarters … But sometimes, much simpler methods may be effective. Imagine you have a reason to be in someone's office. So you go in. You take a copy of *The Times* with you. You sit opposite your target and you have conversation. Meantime, you've put *The Times* down casually on the chap's desk. When it's time to leave, you stand up, pick up your newspaper, making sure you've gathered up any top-secret memos which may be on the desktop at the same time! Get it? Any questions.'

Nowadays, of course, *The Times* has been downsized, so it might not be so useful. Even the *Guardian* has a new, compact version. But the *Daily Telegraph* would still serve the purpose.

Towards the end of our training, we moved to a military establishment on the south coast to practise blowing things up. We learned how to attach high explosives to railway lines in order to derail trains. A nearby disused viaduct was a useful prop.

'Ideally,' our instructor told us, as we gathered in the gloomy arches of the viaduct one rainy morning, 'you'll blow the line just as the train is coming over the viaduct.'

'Like in *The Bridge on the River Kwai*?' I ventured.

The instructor ignored me. 'Remember, you lay the explosives on one side of the track, not both. You want the train to topple over, and all the carriages come crashing down. If you blow both sides of the track, the train may just settle down on its haunches, as it were, without toppling over.'

Nowadays, we call that kind of behaviour 'terrorism', at least when the other side is doing it. That's not how it seemed to us then. Blowing up trains seemed to be not only morally right, but good clean fun as well.

It was at this very same military establishment on the south coast that I met Patrick Fairweather for the first time. Patrick had joined the Foreign Office at more or less the same time I joined the officially non-existent organization, which I believe I may still not be allowed to name. Probably because he had a military background – he had served in the Marines as well as the Paratroop Regiment – Patrick had been designated by the Foreign Office as a kind of liaison officer to our training group.

In that capacity, Patrick participated in one of the more complicated training exercises that took place towards the end of our training period.

The exercise was to be held in the north of England. The Colonel had given us a final briefing. 'Remember you'll be under cover. Deep cover. If you meet someone you know, for Christ's sake don't give any sign that you recognize him!'

I bought a long plastic mackintosh before boarding the train since I knew it would probably be raining wherever we were going. I walked through the train, wearing the mac and trying to look inconspicuous. As I did so, I spotted two or three fellow trainees. We studiously ignored each other.

Patrick Fairweather, our liaison officer, had entered into the spirit of the exercise by disguising himself as a merchant banker. He was sitting in a first-class compartment, puffing on a cigar. There were a couple of other people in the compartment with him.

I slid the door open. 'I'm terribly sorry to interrupt, but can anyone tell me if this train is going to Darlington?'

Patrick told me later that it was all he could do to keep a straight face.

We all had different assignments that day. Mine was to blow up the power station in Blyth, a town on the Northumberland coast, about thirteen miles north of Newcastle.

The 'blowing up' part of the mission went fine. I found my way into the power station at dead of night, climbed up the metal service ladder and rammed the plastic explosive (pretend, not real of course) into the spot where the rotating shaft exits from the turbine.

'Shove it up the elephant's backside as far as you can!' the instructor had told us.

Back in town, I bought a Souvenir-from-Blyth teaspoon to crush the secret ink crystals, found envelope and paper and wrote my report. I then wrote a cover letter at right angles to the secret ink letter.

'Dear mummy and daddy, I don't think my marks are very good this week, but at least I am having a good time. You will be pleased to hear we beat Marlborough 18–6.'

After I had posted the letter, I was allowed to read the second part of my mission orders.

'After blowing up Blyth power station, head for Hexham across moor.'

I destroyed the mission order by swallowing it. To avoid carrying any incriminating evidence, I filled a salt cellar in a late-night café with the remaining secret ink crystals. I was, however, reluctant to jettison the Souvenir-from-Blyth teaspoon, so I stuffed it in the pocket of my plastic mackintosh.

It's strange, isn't it, how the smallest things can trip you up? I had kept the souvenir spoon because I thought I would give it to Charlotte when I got home after the exercise was over. A modest gift, admittedly, and not really much compensation for my protracted absences. Still, I said to myself, it's the thought that counts.

I was about five miles from Hexham, marching along the highway in a cheerful frame of mind, when I came across a red Austin Healey sports car parked on the shoulder of the road. A young woman with blonde hair and a short skirt had the bonnet open and was peering inside in a disconsolate manner.

'Anything wrong?' I asked.

'Can't seem to get it started,' she replied.

I turned the key in the ignition and the engine gave a healthy roar.

'Oh! It seems to have started now!' she exclaimed. 'Thank you so much! Can I give you a lift somewhere?'

There was nothing in my mission orders which said I had to actually walk to Hexham. As far as I knew I just had to get there by whatever means. So I said: 'That's great. My name's Stanley. No, it isn't actually, it's Bunwell. Jeremy Bunwell, er ... I mean Buncroft ...'

I almost forgot my cover name in the heat of the moment but it didn't seem to matter. We bowled merrily along in the direction of Hexham and were only a mile or so from the town when we ran into a roadblock. Blue lights flashed everywhere.

I won't pretend that the next ten hours were pleasant. My guess is the police had simply been told to pick me up and give me a hard time. Looking back, I have no doubt that the young lady in the Austin Healey had also had her instructions, though how much she knew wasn't clear. At least, I said to myself when it was all over, the police sprang their trap on the open road. They didn't wait for the Austin Healey woman to inveigle me into her hotel room somewhere!

What really let me down that night was the Blyth souvenir teaspoon. During the first two or three hours of interrogation in the Hexham police station, I thought I stuck to my cover story quite well. I made it clear that I had a good reason for being in Blyth and a good reason for heading for Hexham. But the man who was interviewing me kept on harping on about the teaspoon. Why on earth would I be carrying such an item unless for a nefarious purpose?

'Might you have needed it,' he slyly suggested, 'for crushing crystals to make secret ink?'

In the end, I cracked. If they hadn't taken my trousers away, I might have toughed it out. But, frankly, when you've been hours in a police cell in the north of England in just underpants, shirt and socks, and it's perfectly clear that the interrogators are quite soon going to move up to the next level, you look for a way out. It might not be Abu Ghraib but it was certainly alarming!

In his briefing, the Colonel had told us: 'One last thing, chaps. I'm going to give you all an emergency number. But let me make one thing absolutely plain. It *is* an emergency number. I don't expect you to use it except in an emergency!'

I would probably have used the number even if I'd still had my trousers. As it was, after one of the breaks, my interrogator came back into the cell with a scrap of paper in his hand.

'Found this in the pocket of your trousers,' he said. 'Does it mean anything to you?'

'What don't you just ring it?' I said wearily. I'd had enough by then.

A couple of days later, when we had all returned to London, we had the debriefing. I was relieved to find out that I was not the only trainee to have called the emergency number, though some had lasted longer than I had before throwing in the towel.

I gave Charlotte the teaspoon.

'Oh, Blyth. How interesting,' she said. 'Have you been there? Or am I not allowed to ask?'

'Yes, I mean, no. Well, sort of.' Even at home it wasn't easy to keep the story straight.

The Blyth business worried me. I felt I hadn't done well, particularly the way I'd got into the car with the girl. I wondered if I was cut out for the career I had chosen.

One Sunday Charlotte and I went to tea at Patrick and Maria Fairweather's house in Richmond, Surrey. By then, Charlotte had graduated from Oxford, with a very respectable second in English Language and Literature. A few weeks later (on 3 September 1965) she had given birth to our daughter, Rachel, in St John and St Elizabeth's hospital, St John's Wood, London, only a stone's throw from the Fawcett family home in Cavendish Avenue. We chose Sabiha as a middle name, in honour of my step-grandmother, Ali Kemal's second wife. So it was as a family of four that we set out that day from Oxford to Richmond.

While Charlotte and Maria and the children were upstairs (the Fairweathers had two girls, Catherine and Natasha, the same age as Alexander Boris and Rachel) Patrick and I walked in the garden.

'One of the things I find so difficult,' I told Patrick, 'is this question of cover. People ask me what I'm doing. Officially, we're meant to mumble, turn the question, be evasive or whatever. But I don't think it's very convincing, do you?'

Patrick gave this some thought. 'Why don't you say you work in the Foreign Office?'

'Fine, but what if they ask what my job is there?'

'I'll get back to you on that.'

A few days later, I received a three-word message from Patrick. Happily, it wasn't encoded. I didn't need a one-time pad to decipher it. It said simply: 'Sudan desk officer'.

Before we officially graduated from the course, we were taken on a familiarization visit to King Charles Street where the Foreign Office's magnificent building is located. I didn't see Patrick Fairweather on that occasion. Being about to be sent to Rome for an initial diplomatic posting, the first step in a distinguished diplomatic career, he was otherwise occupied.

But I did see Hugh Stephenson. Hugh Stephenson, known as 'Tiggy' to more intimate friends, had been at Oxford a couple of years before me and had joined the diplomatic service on coming down from university. In later life, besides being a long-distance yachtsman, he would become the first ever Professor of Journalism at a British university.

I bumped into Hugh as I was walking down one of the Foreign Office's long marble corridors.

'Good heavens, Stanley! What are you doing here?' Hugh asked.

I remembered Patrick's advice. 'I've joined the Foreign Office, actually, Hugh.'

'That's good news! What are you doing?'

'I'm the Sudan desk officer.'

Hugh looked puzzled and a little irritated.

'No, you're not. I am!'

TWENTY-TWO

'I'm a horribly serious person'

I still have a letter my mother sent to Charlotte and me on 18 June 1965. I can see her hurriedly writing it at the kitchen table at Nethercote, then jumping into the car to clatter down the bumpy track to the letterbox at Larcombe Foot (where the Nethercote drive meets the Winsford–Exford road).

She must have caught the post that day because the letter containing her warm congratulations arrived in time for Alexander Boris's first birthday. She also posted a hammer and pegs, writing: 'I purposely chose a toy requiring intelligence, but if he [Alexander Boris] once discovers the joy of hammering crockery I fear he will lose interest in the pegs! So keep your egg-shell china out of reach.'

My mother had some words for us too. Charlotte having just taken her finals, my mother wrote: 'How wonderful it must feel to have schools over. I can remember how I felt at the end of the last afternoon of the last day. And I want to tell you how much we admire and respect you both for tackling the examinations on top of your other commitments.'

Both? I think my mother was over-egging it there. Charlotte's achievements had indeed been commendable. There were not many other undergraduates in those days who sat their finals with a baby less than a year old in tow, while being seven months pregnant with another.

But my mother had included me too in her paean of praise and, for the sake of accuracy, I must make it clear that my achievement in taking and passing the Oxford University Diploma in Agricultural Economics was in no sense commensurate with Charlotte's. For the last six months at least, I had done absolutely no studying at all. I hadn't even been in Oxford. I had been gadding around the country learning how to be totally inconspicuous and acquiring the rudiments of 'tradecraft', as John Le Carré would have called it.

In the circumstances, I hadn't expected to take the diploma at all. However, one Saturday morning in early June, a letter from the examiners arrived informing me that since I had 'pernoctated satisfactorily' I was entitled to sit the exam.

Which is what I did. I had to miss three days of week twelve of the most intensive training in clandestine techniques known to man but it turned out to be worth it. Apart from the Statistics paper, which was horribly hard for someone who had barely achieved a pass in O level Mathematics (echoes of 'this unfortunate boy'), I did reasonably well – well enough, anyway, to qualify for the diploma.

'If it hadn't been for the Statistics, you might have got a Distinction,' Peggy Haswell told me when the marks arrived. 'You did particularly well in the Development Economics paper. I'm not sure what you're doing at the moment, but why don't you apply to the World Bank? Here, wait a moment, they sent me a brochure the other day about a scheme they have. The Young Professional Programme, they call it, if I remember right.'

I watched her rustle around her crowded desktop looking for the brochure. If I'd had a copy of *The Times* with me, I could have scooped up all the documents in the approved fashion and studied them at my leisure. But I didn't. I had to wait till she found what she was looking for.

I took the brochure away with me. Charlotte and I pored over it. The World Bank, it seemed, was recruiting so-called Young Professionals from all over the world, bringing them to Washington, and training them on the job ('the most intensive training in development economics known to man'? I wondered) before integrating them into the Bank's operating departments.

'So what does the World Bank actually do?' Charlotte asked.

I flipped back to the beginning of the brochure and read out what it said: '"Based in Washington, DC, the Bank is the largest and oldest organization providing development finance. It began operations in 1946 and so far has made almost 500 loans, amounting to $10,000 million, in about 80 countries."'

'What are the loans for?'

'Basically, I suppose, to make life better for people. That's the theory, anyway,' I replied.

Charlotte studied the brochure. 'It says a postgraduate degree achieved with distinction in a substantial discipline is highly desirable. Do you think your Diploma in Agricultural Economics will qualify?'

'Let's see.' It was a long shot but I sent off for the application forms anyway.

In due course I was invited to an interview at the World Bank's European Office in Paris. It must have gone well because, on 21 October 1965, I received a telegram: 'Committee decision favourable; letter follows offering appointment effective March seven. World Bank.'

Can I begin to explain how momentously important receiving that telegram was to me? I'll try.

Deep down I'm a horribly serious person. I may not be a left-winger. I've certainly never voted Labour in my life and can't imagine doing so now. I doubt if I was any more radical forty years ago than I am today. But the idea of working for an organization like the World Bank really gripped me. With billions of dollars at its disposal, this was an institution that could change the face of the planet. I had been lucky enough to see by then a good deal of the Third World. I had followed Marco Polo through Asia and hitch-hiked my way across South America. I reckoned I knew something about the poverty in which so many people lived. Here was a heaven-sent opportunity to set out on a new course.

I take my hat off to the people who ran the officially non-existent organization that I may still not be allowed to name. They must have been deeply irritated by my decision to accept the World Bank's offer. They had just put a lot of time, money and effort into training me and I had walked right out of their life.

There were probably some security considerations too. I had handed back all my notebooks, but how much had I retained in my memory, which could never be expunged, at least until the onset of Alzheimer's?

Sometimes I wonder what happened to Sir Ian Murray. Once, a year or two later, I saw a small advertisement in *The Times*: 'Would the gentleman who inadvertently removed my umbrella from the Reform Club last Saturday kindly return it? Sir Ian Murray, Bt.'

I wondered whether Sir Ian Murray Bt was his real name. As for the advertisement about the umbrella, it could have been a coded message. Or again, it could have been genuine. These were murky waters.

Long after I had handed in my papers, I found myself recalling the lessons I had learned during my brief career as a spy. How, for example, could I ever forget the very first words of the very first lecture I attended: '*Never try to blackmail an Egyptian*'? Even now, over forty years later, if I am ever tempted to entertain dark and secret thoughts about blackmailing Egyptians, I put them firmly out of my mind.

That autumn, Charlotte and I were living in London. After leaving Oxford (for the second time) we had rented a flat in Crouch End, an area of London which has become fashionable now but which was quite affordable then, even for a family of four.

The Sunday afternoon after the World Bank telegram arrived I drove from London to Ascot, where 'Sandy' lived, in some trepidation. I knew what I wanted to say to Sandy. I wanted to tell him that I was about to resign from an organization to which he had given much of his working life before I had given it a proper try. I wasn't sure how he was going to take it.

In the event, Sandy was superb. He was more than superb. He made me feel right about it when I wasn't really feeling right about it at all.

'Stanley,' he said in his unmistakable Eastern European accent, 'if I vas in your shoes, I vould do the same thing.'

There are certain times in your life when you feel you have been granted a last-minute reprieve. This was one of them. I don't know if I would have been any good as a spy – probably not, I thought, and my incompetence might have cost people their lives – but now I didn't even have to find out.

Since we didn't have to go to Washington till the end of February, Charlotte and I decided to leave London to spend the winter on Exmoor in a rented cottage, high up on the edge of Winsford Hill, that magnificent stretch of moorland a few miles from Dulverton.

It was good to be in the depths of the country for those last few months in England. Charlotte painted. Alexander Boris pottered around in the snow (it was a rough winter and we spent our time keeping a wood-burning stove going) and Rachel, from pram or high chair, kept a keen eye on things. I profited from the break by writing my first book.

Bearing in mind the months spent at the Writers' Workshop in Iowa, I opted for fiction rather than non-fiction. Specifically, I was aiming to produce an international thriller, as it would now be called, but with a light-hearted, almost satirical touch.

Each morning I scribbled away in longhand, then, after I had finished a first draft, typed it out on the old Smith Corona typewriter that my mother had been given for her twenty-first birthday.

Bearing in mind my duties of lifelong confidentiality and wishing anyway to be on the safe side, I decided I should check with my erstwhile employers that they had no objection to my having a book published. Of course, I remembered my former headmaster Bob Powell's strong views on this question ('Never publish a book, it's unforgivable!') but decided to ignore them.

Around the middle of January, I took the train to London for an interview with a security officer.

We met in an office near Lambeth Bridge. The man's face seemed familiar to me and suddenly I realized why. He was the spitting image of Field Marshal Montgomery of Alamein. Was he Monty's double? I wondered. (Actually he was Monty's younger brother, Brian.)

'So you're writing a book, are you?' he harrumphed. 'Do you have to? We're not very keen on books.'

'It's a novel,' I explained.

'Ah!' The man's mood brightened visibly. 'You mean it's fiction, a bit of fantasy?'

'You could call it that.'

We left it at that.

Before we left for Washington, Jo Hone advised me to send the book to Heinemann. Jo was a producer at the BBC who had handled the talks I had given on the Home Service over the last couple of years. Some of them had been quite long. I had, for example, recorded a twenty-minute piece about my gap year travels in South America that the BBC broadcast during a Promenade Concert interval. The most recent, called 'Don't Knock Spock', had included a description of Alexander Boris' birth in the New York Hospital.

Over a long and bibulous lunch near Portland Place, Jo told me he had a friend at Heinemann called Bill Holden, a director of the firm. Would I like to meet him?

In due course Jo very kindly took me to see Bill.

'I'll see what I can do,' Bill said.

Bill obviously handed over my MS to a colleague because, a few weeks after we arrived in Washington, I heard from Roger Smith, one of Heinemann's editors, asking me to make some changes. He quoted the outside reader's report. 'This has a really brilliantly funny plot. Unfortunately ... puns are made for their own sake, characters are dropped for long periods, and jokes carried on far too long ...'

'This makes excellent sense to me,' Roger wrote, 'and I hope it does to you.'

It did. I did some more work on the book, among other things changing the title from *Eat before Reading* to *Gold Drain*. I worked on the characters and cut out some of the jokes.

Roger wrote off to Robert Graves for a publicity puff and Graves wrote back by return. Roger sent me a copy of Graves' letter, adding, 'We're going to include the whole of it on the back flap.'

Which, in due course, is what Heinemann did. Those who don't have a copy of *Gold Drain* to hand may be interested to know that Robert Graves' ringing endorsement read as follows: '*As Professor of Poetry at Oxford not many years ago I attended a College undergraduate debate and heard a lot of nonsense talked: until someone with an American voice chipped in with very good sense. Afterwards I asked: "Who was that?"*

"Oh, that was Stan!"

"Who's Stan?"

"The fellow who went to China on a motorbike last Long Vac."

The next time I met Stan was in the Sheldonian Theatre, having unwittingly helped to award him the Newdigate Prize for Poetry. He had come to read out his entry, the only one that year which made poetic sense.

Now he is in Washington, married with two children, and, I gather, advising the US Government on its monetary policy. I am sure his advice will make sense.'

Graves ended his encomium by saying: '*At any rate, his* Gold Drain *is the most complicated and best-written send-up of the modern spy-novel that has yet appeared. It makes such good sense that nobody need try to challenge him in that line of country.'*

I wrote to Heinemann before *Gold Drain* was actually published to say that, though I was absolutely delighted by Graves' letter, (a) I wasn't actually an American, (b) I was working for the World Bank, rather than the US Government, and (c) I had recited my Newdigate poem in the Oxford Town Hall rather than the Sheldonian, since the Sheldonian was being refurbished in 1962.

Heinemann wisely decided not to write back to Graves in Majorca asking for a redraft and printed the letter as they had received it.

Does an author, I wonder, always have fond memories of his first published book, as of, say, his first girlfriend?

I certainly enjoyed writing *Gold Drain* and was pleased with the reception it got. The reviews were generally favourable. The *Sun* wrote: 'The author not only writes with sweet precision but ties up every loose strand in the convoluted fantasy. A near miracle of plot work.' The *Yorkshire Post* called it: 'A nice little tour de farce.' *Punch* said it was 'funny and intelligent too'.

TWENTY-THREE

How to Double the Number
of Pyramids in Egypt

Charlotte and I arrived in Washington on 22 February 1966: George Washington's Birthday.

The World Bank put us up at the Dupont Plaza Hotel, just off Dupont Circle.

Next day, Sunday, we woke up to see that it was snowing heavily. After breakfast, I looked in the Yellow Pages and found an advertisement for a supermarket selling children's goods called 'Kiddie Cut-Rate'. I rang them up and discovered that they sold two-seater child buggies. The address given in the Yellow Pages was Tysons Corner, Virginia. I had no idea where Tysons Corner was.

'Can I get there by public transport?' I asked.

The voice at the other end of the line seemed doubtful. 'You could try.'

I returned to the hotel that afternoon chilled to the bone from several hours on unheated buses, but otherwise triumphant. For the next several months, if not years, we pushed Alexander Boris and Rachel about in the two-seater buggy. They took it in turns to sit in the front seat.

The Dupont Plaza served as a temporary home for a dozen or so other Young Professionals (YPs) who joined the World Bank at the same time as I did. A multi-national group, we included in our number two Britons, two Indians, two Italians, one Pakistani, a Swede, a South African, a Dutchman, a German, a Swiss, a Greek and a Frenchman. Most of them were married and several had children.

During our stay in the hotel, which lasted about a month, the YPs inevitably saw a good deal of each other. Though we all had different assignments as we started our new careers in the Bank, we tended to keep in touch even after we had left the Dupont Plaza. We learned quite soon that other, older Bank staff members regarded the YPs with some suspicion. They had had the hard grind; we seemed about to be offered glittering rewards before we had truly earned them.

Once Richard Van Wagenen, a lanky Dutchman from the Bank's Administration Department who was formally responsible for us, had to send us a message saying it might be advisable for the new YPs not to use the select Vice-Presidents and Senior Staff Dining Room quite so often. Modesty was not one of our strong points.

The President of the World Bank when I joined was George D. Woods, who before coming to Washington had made his career with the First Boston Bank. (By convention, an American was always President of the Bank while a European, usually a Frenchman, was head of the Bank's sister organization, the International Monetary Fund.)

After a few days' orientation, I learned that my first assignment was to be with Mr Woods' principal Economic Adviser, Irving Friedman. Mr Friedman could not have been friendlier. He had known my father-in-law, James Fawcett, when, only a few years earlier, James had been General Counsel to the IMF, and he seemed to be pleased to take me on.

Friedman's main concern in those days was to ensure the successful replenishment of the World Bank's soft loan affiliate, the International Development Association (IDA). IDA 'credits', as they were called, were on concessionary terms whereas Bank loans carried the market rate of interest. I worked alongside an immensely clever Indian, Bimal Jalan, who knew the answers to questions lesser mortals hadn't even thought of asking. In later life, Bimal became the Governor of the Central Bank of India, an ineffably grand position.

The central idea of the YP course was to give us maximum exposure to the different facets of the World Bank's operation. In my case, six months in the Office of the Economic Adviser to the President was followed by six months in the South America department, working on the Colombia desk.

In those days, Colombia had not achieved the international renown as a haven for kidnappers and drug barons that it enjoys today. On the contrary, it was one of the World Bank's favourites. At that time, the

Bank lent more money to Colombia than to any other South American country. One loan followed another in rapid succession: for power generation, for highway construction, for agricultural development. Colombia borrowed money across the board. World Bank staff members were constantly on the plane to Bogotá.

On one occasion I found myself taking part in a mission to Colombia to discuss a loan to Incora, the Colombian land reform agency. Incora had been set up to deal with the whole question of 'latifundia', the traditional system of landholding which ensured that a very small percentage of the population owned a very large proportion of the land.

Incora was headed by Enrique Peñalosa, who would later be Mayor of Bogotá. Enrique was a charismatic man, determined to change the system of land tenure and willing to use the resources of the World Bank to do so. Sitting in on the negotiating sessions as more experienced Bank staff fleshed out the terms and conditions of the loan was an eye-opening experience.

In the eighties and nineties, long after I had left Washington, the World Bank and the International Monetary Fund were completely demonized by the environmental movement. They were seen as the instigators of huge projects that turned into environmental and social disasters (trans-Amazonian highways, mega-rice projects in Indonesia etc). That wasn't how I saw the Bank in the sixties. When I worked there, I had a sense of that organization's tremendous potential for good.

On the way back from Bogotá, we stopped in Cartagena, an extraordinary medieval Spanish city on Colombia's Caribbean coast. I went swimming in the sea one afternoon with Ray Frost, who, as head of the Bank's Colombia desk, had been leading our mission. Frost's mother, Dora, had *en deuxièmes noces* married Hugh Gaitskell, leader of the Labour Party. Struck down by a heart attack in January 1963, Gaitskell had been succeeded by Harold Wilson as leader of the Labour Party. Wilson, at the time I joined the World Bank, was Britain's Prime Minister, having been elected in 1964 after the Profumo scandal sank Harold Macmillan.

As I splashed around in the warm Caribbean surf, looking back at the ramparts of the old Spanish city (today Cartagena is a World Heritage Site), the British political scene seemed, happily, very far away.

I would sometimes joke in later life that I left Britain in the sixties to get away from Harold Wilson and the 'socialist nightmare'. This was an exaggeration but, like most exaggerations, it contained a grain of truth. The great grammar schools were going to be abolished; the unions were tightening their grip on British industry. It was a good time to be out of the country.

Towards the end of 1967, I moved from the Bank's South America department to the Projects Department to join the Indus Basin Team. This was a fascinating assignment, demonstrating how an organization with the power and resources of the World Bank could literally change the face of a country, if not a continent.

The origins of the Bank's Indus Basin Project lay in the fight that had broken out between India and Pakistan in 1961 over the waters of the Punjab rivers. At Partition, India had found herself cut off from the headwaters of the rivers which flowed through her territory and, in due course, had gone to war to get them back. A key part of the peace settlement was that the World Bank should help Pakistan build two dams, one on the Jhelum and one on the Indus itself. The Bank would also fund some massive link canals that would transfer the water across country from Pakistan in the west to India in the east. That way Indian water supplies would be safeguarded.

In November 1967 I flew to Pakistan with other members of the Indus Basin Project team. We had two objectives. The first was to review progress on the Jhelum River Dam, known as Mangla.

The day after we arrived in Islamabad, we were driven into the mountains to the dam site. We climbed, on foot, to the top of the half-constructed spillway and looked down into the steep valley below. The dam's turbines would generate massive amounts of power; the reservoir would fill with millions, if not billions, of cubic feet of water. Pakistani peasants would be able to irrigate their fields. Electricity, generated by the dam's turbines, would enable them to put in thousands of tube wells where surface irrigation was lacking.

All seemed to be going to plan and we returned to our hotel that night in an optimistic frame of mind.

The second part of the mission was much more complicated: to discuss the question of World Bank finance for the second dam, this time on the Indus itself.

The stakes were high. Never before had the mighty Indus been dammed. The geologists and engineers had already identified a site high up in the mountains, at a place called Tarbela. Here they hoped to build one of the largest dams in the history of the world. Instead of the floodwaters of the Indus running waste into the Indian Ocean, they could be trapped behind the dam in a giant mountain reservoir.

Once the massive link canals were completed, transporting huge volumes of water from west to east, the poor peasants of India as well as of Pakistan would find their whole lives transformed.

But there was still a major question mark over the whole scheme: even if the project was viable in engineering terms, was it viable economically as well? The World Bank was bound by its statute only to fund projects which could generate an acceptable economic rate of return. The cost of building the dam, high up in the mountains, would be enormous. Billions of dollars would be needed. Would the Tarbela Dam generate sufficient economic benefits to set against the huge financial outlays?

This was, of course, the kind of question World Bank staff were trying to answer all the time. The system of project appraisal was highly developed and the procedures were tried and trusted. Preliminary missions were followed by in-depth investigations. 'Yellow-cover' reports became 'green-cover' reports as the process of internal and external consultation continued. Finally a 'grey-cover' report would be put before the Bank's powerful Loan Committee for approval.

Tarbela was a project of exceptional magnitude. Apart from the massive amount of money involved, successful conclusion of the Indus Basin Project (hopefully helping to avoid future water wars between India and Pakistan) would do wonders for the World Bank's international prestige.

'There's a lot riding on this, folks!' Bob Sadove, the Indus Basin Project team leader, told us as we gathered for an early morning strategy session in our Islamabad hotel.

Sadove, an American, was determined to go down in history as the man who brought the Indus Basin Project to a successful completion. His deputy was an Englishman, Chris Willoughby, who was similarly single-minded. I was awed by Chris's dedication. The lights in his office would be burning night after night long after all of the rest of us had gone home.

Besides agriculturalists and engineers, the team that day also included a brilliant young German economist and statistician, called Heinz Vergin. Heinz's job was absolutely vital. He had to struggle through the most complicated calculations to establish whether or not the Tarbela Dam was likely to generate an acceptable economic rate of return. If it wasn't, then – in his view – no matter what the political considerations might be, we shouldn't be putting it forward to the World Bank's Board of Directors for approval.

Heinz had arrived in Pakistan in a pessimistic frame of mind. In those pre-computer days, he had been cranking his machines for weeks.

That morning he told us that he feared the worst. 'Let's look at the siltation rates first. How much capacity are we going to lose in the reservoir from siltation, and over what period of time? What about power? If the reservoir silts up, that affects how you run the dam, the flow of water through the turbines. And that in turn affects how much power you can generate and how much water you have available for irrigation.'

Heinz kept his gloomiest news to the end. Even assuming the dam didn't silt up and you could maintain power and irrigation, the problem of salinization had to be taken into account. Irrigation famously produced salt-encrusted deposits in arid soils, and that in turn would slash agricultural yields dramatically, wreaking havoc with the calculations of economic benefit.

'You could even get a negative rate of return,' Heinz concluded sombrely.

'You might not want to mention that today when we meet WAPDA,' Bob Sadove warned.

WAPDA was the Pakistan Water and Power Development Authority that would be responsible for Tarbela if the project went ahead. Later that day, we met in their Islamabad headquarters, the World Bank team sitting on one side of the table, the Pakistanis on the other. Down the far end on our side, Heinz Vergin tactfully kept his reservations to himself.

The first discussions of the project went well. Though many more meetings would take place before the construction of the Tarbela Dam was finally approved, the message that day was clear. This was something that was going to happen.

I was the low man on the totem pole and I don't recall saying anything useful during our meetings. I learned a lot, however. For example, I realized that, when you're dealing with economics, you can usually juggle the numbers (or adjust the basic assumptions) to achieve the outcome you are looking for. By the time the Tarbela Dam finally went to the Board for approval, the projected economic rate of return, after some judicious tinkering, had been jacked up to a respectable four and a half per cent.

Just how closely, I wondered, did the members of the World Bank's Board read the documents that were put before them before approving a loan? Did they just nod them through, knowing that anyway, given the Bank's constitution, a handful of the main donors (such as the United States and the United Kingdom) had a majority of the votes and that those countries could do more or less what they liked?

In the spring of 1968, when I had been in the Bank for over two years, my friend Mark Cherniavsky and I decided to test the hypothesis that on the whole the Bank Board members didn't read the documents as closely as they should have done.

Mark, an Englishman who had joined the Bank as a Young Professional a few months before I had, served as Secretary of the all-powerful Loan Committee. In that capacity, he was responsible for the flow of documents reaching the Committee as well as the agenda of the meetings.

The first meeting of the Loan Committee to be presided over by the World Bank's new President, Robert S. McNamara, formerly the United States Secretary of Defense, was due to be held on 4 April 1968, Mr McNamara having succeeded Mr Woods at the beginning of the month.

Mark very decently agreed to have printed up on official Loan Committee stationery as a 'grey-cover' report a document that I had prepared entitled 'United Arab Republic – First Tourism Project'. The covering memorandum, which I had also drafted, indicated that the

Executive Directors were asked to approve a loan of $100 million to the UAR (the new official name for Egypt).

I was not personally present at the meeting of the Loan Committee that day but I heard later from others who were. Most members of the Board, it seems, were ready to nod the project through. Financing the 'tourist sector' was a new departure for the Bank. Perhaps more important, they were especially keen to be seen to be authorizing a big loan to Egypt. The Bank's reluctance a few years earlier to help Egypt build the Aswan High Dam had led directly to the nationalization of the Suez Canal and the disastrous Anglo-French invasion in November 1956.

However, some Board Members who took the time to study more carefully the document I had prepared were, I understood, intrigued to learn that the $100 million was to be spent on financing three new pyramids.

Paragraph 9 of my Executive Summary stated: '*While it is obviously not realistic to make a simple linear extrapolation of the foreign exchange earnings that will result from doubling the number of available pyramids in Egypt, the Appraisal Report points out that, as long as the necessary complementary facilities are provided in an integrated package, i.e. hotel accommodation, night-clubs, tour-guides, camels etc., the revenues accruing to the Egyptian economy from increased tourist expenditures will be substantial. It is calculated that the internal marginal rate of return from the construction of an incremental pyramid will be approximately 9.762%.*'

I had been equally enthusiastic where the non-quantifiable benefits were concerned. '*It is anticipated that the construction of such a large and prestigious project would have a great impact on political and tribal unity … from an international point of view, the project might result in a substantial lessening of tension in the Middle East as a whole.*'

I was told that Robert McNamara had actually opened the discussion of the proposed loan when Pieter Lieftinck, the Bank's Dutch Executive Director who had a reputation for picking up details in the Board papers, including typos and spelling mistakes, called for the floor.

'Mr President,' he began, 'I would like to point out that the date of the document we are considering is 1 April 1968!'

Mr McNamara had not apparently been amused by the jolly jape I had played that day. My immediate boss, Bernard Chadenet, a Frenchman, who was in charge of the Projects Department, had himself been present at the Loan Committee meeting. Though he had appreciated the spirit of fun in which I had submitted the paper and had done his best to protect me from the repercussions, I sensed he did not regard my future in the World Bank as being exceptionally secure.

'*Ce n'est pas évident. Il faut voir.* Let's see' was his cryptic comment when he called me in to see him in his office after the meeting.

As it happened I had arranged to play squash at lunch time that day with an American friend, Alan Novak.

'Come and see my new office in the State Department,' Alan said, after he had soundly thrashed me in the somewhat foetid YMCA squash court on G Street.

As the Chief Assistant to the Assistant Chief, Alan had a grand room on the seventh floor of the State Department building in Foggy Bottom. He propped his feet on the desk. A US flag stood in a brass stand in the corner.

'Gene's out of town today,' Alan said. 'Tell me what's up. Something's bothering you. I could tell by the way you kept fluffing your serve.'

I told Alan about the events of the morning. When I had finished, he looked thoughtful.

'What do you know about the world's population problem?' he asked.

'Actually,' I replied, 'I've just written a paper on the subject.'

'Not another spoof, I hope?'

'No, I suggest the World Bank should make population control one of its priorities. With population growth rates at three or even four per cent per annum, the countries who were the Bank's clients are most often running to stand still. I'm arguing that the World Bank should start taking the population explosion seriously and actually try to do something about it by funding birth control and family planning programmes around the world.'

'Sounds just the thing,' Alan said. 'Why don't you send it to me? We might have something for you.'

I heard back from Alan by return. 'I've talked to Ray,' he said. 'Ray liked the paper. He thinks you should see Mr Rockefeller.'

ABOVE: Band-i-Amir lake, Afghanistan. Our BSA 500cc twin-cylinder Shooting Star is looking the worse for wear.

BELOW: In front of the Gateway of India, Bombay. Tim Severin is sitting behind me and Michael de Larrabeiti, the Marco Polo Expedition's photographer, brings up the rear.

Charlotte Fawcett as an undergraduate at Lady Margaret Hall, Oxford, May 1962. We were married a year later.

Charlotte reading to Alexander Boris and Rachel, c.1970.

Alexander Boris, Joseph, Rachel and Leo – my four children by my marriage to Charlotte. This photo was taken on a skiing holiday in Meribel, France, around 1985.

Alexander Boris has borrowed my crash helmet! This photograph was taken around 1970.

With the Duke of Edinburgh at the opening of the European Conservation Year, Strasbourg, February 1970.

Representing the EU (as it now is) at a meeting of the United Nations Environment Programme Governing Council, Nairobi, May 1976. I escaped the next day for a prolonged safari in the Masai Mara and Serengeti.

With President Junius Jayawardene of Sri Lanka in Colombo, 1979, at a meeting to discuss the world's population explosion.

Sir James Scott-Hopkins, MEP, introduces me to the Pope John-Paul II, Rome, 1980.

With Joanna Lumley, campaigning to save 'baby seals', Trafalgar Square, c.1982.

With President George Bush Senior at the White House, Washington DC, May 1990, at an environmental conference.

Mrs Thatcher endorses my campaign to be elected as an MP in Teinbridge in the May 2005 General Election.

David Cameron comes down to Newton Abbot to support my efforts to become MP for Teinbridge in the May 2005 General Election. I received 21,593 votes, unfortunately not quite enough to dislodge the Liberal Democrat incumbent!

ABOVE: Jenny and I were married on 27 February, 1981, and lived happily ever after.

LEFT: Campaigning to save marine turtles at the WTO meeting held in Seattle, USA, December 1999. We were drenched by police water-cannon, but we succeeded in derailing the meeting.

BELOW: On the ice-flows in the Gulf of St Lawrence, Canada, February 1982. A few weeks later the European parliament called for a ban on the import of seal products.

ABOVE: At Nethercote, 18 August, 2000, my sixtieth birthday. This was a great family gathering including my six children and their spouses and all (then) available grandchildren. (The current total of grandchildren is eleven). Jenny's mother, Lois Sieff, is on the left.

BELOW: With Jenny and our children, Julia and Max, in London, June 2007.

In 2008 my son Boris – the mayor of London – was the subject of the BBC's genealogy programme *Who Do You Think You Are?* As well as outlining our strong Turkish connections, the BBC's researchers found that Boris and I are directly descended from King George II of England. My mother's mother, Marie Louise Caroline Helène de Pfeffel, was the daughter of one Karoline von Rothenbourg. Karoline's father turned out to be none other that Prince Paul of Württemberg, himself a direct descendant of King George.

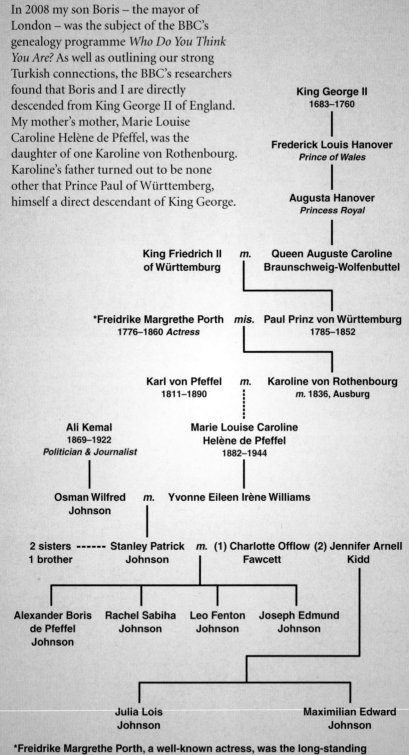

King George II
1683–1760

Frederick Louis Hanover
Prince of Wales

Augusta Hanover
Princess Royal

King Friedrich II   *m.*   **Queen Auguste Caroline**
of Württemburg   **Braunschweig-Wolfenbuttel**

*Freidrike Margrethe Porth   *mis.*   **Paul Prinz von Württemburg**
1776–1860 *Actress*   1785–1852

Karl von Pfeffel   *m.*   **Karoline von Rothenbourg**
1811–1890   *m.* 1836, Ausburg

Ali Kemal   **Marie Louise Caroline**
1869–1922   **Helène de Pfeffel**
Politician & Journalist   1882–1944

Osman Wilfred   *m.*   **Yvonne Eileen Irène Williams**
Johnson

2 sisters ------ **Stanley Patrick**   *m.*   **(1) Charlotte Offlow (2) Jennifer Arnell**
1 brother   **Johnson**   **Fawcett**   **Kidd**

Alexander Boris   **Rachel Sabiha**   **Leo Fenton**   **Joseph Edmund**
de Pfeffel   **Johnson**   **Johnson**   **Johnson**
Johnson

Julia Lois   **Maximilian Edward**
Johnson   **Johnson**

***Freidrike Margrethe Porth, a well-known actress, was the long-standing
mistress of Paul Prinz von Württemberg**

Ray Lamontagne, who had been at Yale Law School with Alan, was now working in New York as an associate of John D. Rockefeller III, the noted philanthropist. Mr Rockefeller, it emerged, had just been appointed chairman of a national policy panel set up by the United Nations Association of the United States (UNA-USA) to report on how the United Nations and its system of agencies (which included the World Bank as a so-called 'Specialized Agency') could tackle the world's population problem.

The membership of the UNA-USA panel was blue chip. The Rocke-fellers were probably the richest and most famous family in America and persuading John D. Rockefeller III to serve as chairman was a great coup. George D. Woods, whom Robert McNamara had succeeded as President of the World Bank, agreed to be vice-chairman. The panel included many of the 'great and the good' in the United States foreign policy establishment.

My job would be to serve as 'project director'.

'Basically, you'll have to do all the work,' Ray explained. 'You'll have to make sure the research gets done, draft the report, steer it through the panel and make sure Mr Rockefeller knows everything he needs to know.'

I flew to New York for a first meeting with Mr Rockefeller. Room 5600, 30 Rockefeller Plaza, was discreetly opulent. I thought I recognized a Titian, a Rembrandt, two Picassos and a Braque but they were hung without ostentation. Mr Rockefeller himself was modest, almost to the point of being self-effacing.

He poured me tea from a priceless Ming teapot. 'Now you're the expert, Mr Johnson. We shall be relying on you to steer us through the thickets.'

'I'll do my best,' I said. Truth to tell, I was a little overawed.

The move to New York, where I would be based in the UNA-USA office at the junction of 45th Street and First Avenue, naturally meant leaving Washington. In some respects, this was a wrench. Charlotte and I had enjoyed our time in the nation's capital immensely. Soon after arriving we had bought (for $25,000 which I borrowed from the Bank's Credit Union) a white clapboard house on Morrison Street, just off Connecticut Avenue in NW Washington. We had a garden (or 'yard') front and back and a fairly plentiful supply of au pairs who were able

217

to arrive in the United States on G-IV visas, thanks to my employment with the World Bank.

By then, having proper household help had become essential. Charlotte was pursuing her own painting career vigorously and in any case we now had three children, not two, since Leo had joined Alexander Boris and Rachel in September 1967, being born in London during our home leave.

I was conscious of the fact that Charlotte and I had already exceeded the 2.1 or 2.2 children necessary for long-run population stability but I salved my conscience by arguing that the population explosion was taking place in the Third World, not in the West where, if anything, the problem in the future was likely to be declining fertility rates.

If Washington in those days was an easy place to live, it was also a very stimulating one. We had many friends among the British press corps. Tony and Carol Howard, David and Suzan Watt, Charles and Dip Wheeler, David Spanier, John Graham and Dominick Harrod spring to mind. Working for various media outlets, such as the *Observer*, the *Financial Times*, the *Daily Telegraph* and the BBC, they all did their best to ensure that the British public was not starved of US news.

We also had many American friends. Some of then worked on Capitol Hill, some as lawyers, some – like Alan Novak – as aides to highly placed government officials. On the first Tuesday of each month, as many of us as were able would meet in an upstairs room of the Occidental restaurant on Pennsylvania Avenue. We would drink dry martinis before lunch and cognac after. Most smoked as well. I tried once or twice but couldn't master the art. But even without a cigarette in one's hand, it was hard not to feel the buzz.

I have stayed in contact with Alan and Katie Novak over the years. Quite apart from his crucial role in getting me the job as project director of the national policy panel on world population, Alan was the inspiration for the lead character in my second novel, which Heinemann published in 1968 as *Panther Jones for President*. The opening paragraph of the novel reads (in part): 'Hersch Feldman, a short round man, bounced. No other word could describe his progress. He had bounced from Orthodox Brooklyn, through Princeton, to Trinity, Oxford, on a Rhodes. He had bounced back across the Atlantic and, landing as always on his feet, had come out top of Yale Law School ...'

Alan was not particularly pleased by 'short round man', but he approved of the rest of the description and was amused by the book's plot which centred on an ingenious scheme to replace a Johnson-type President with a Black Power activist. I like to think the book would have been a bestseller if President Johnson hadn't announced on the eve of its publication (31 March 1968) that he wouldn't be standing again.

'I shall not seek, nor shall I accept, the nomination of my party for another term as your President,' Johnson intoned.

I am sure that short sentence, tacked without any advance notice onto the end of a long televised speech, delighted millions across America. It didn't delight me.

Today, with Barack Obama's successful bid for the White House preoccupying the world's media, I can't help thinking the plot of *Panther Jones for President,* involving, as it did, the replacement of an unpopular President with America's first African–American leader, was remarkably prescient, even though it took four decades for the dream to become reality.

If Washington when we arrived there at the beginning of 1966 was an interesting, sociable place, it had become by the time we left – halfway through 1968 – increasingly tense. After a good start with his 'Great Society' programmes, Lyndon Johnson and his administration were becoming bogged down in Vietnam. Riots broke out in several major US cities and Washington was not exempt. Though the leafy suburbs of Morrison Street escaped unscathed, the streets burned ten blocks from the White House.

Charlotte in particular was shaken by the violence. When the assassination of Martin Luther King was followed in quick succession by that of Robert Kennedy, President Kennedy's brother and the man who looked set to gain the Democratic nomination now that Lyndon Johnson had withdrawn from the race, she told me she had had enough.

'Why don't we go back to England?' she asked, as we sat in front of the television one morning looking at Bobby Kennedy's crumpled body lying on the floor in the kitchen of the Ambassador Hotel, Los Angeles.

'Give me a year,' I replied. 'I'll do by best to have us all back in England by then.'

Leaving Washington to go to New York wasn't exactly going home, but at least it was a step in the right direction.

TWENTY-FOUR

'Eighteen rupees and a transistor radio'

We rented a house on Harbor Island, Norwalk, Connecticut. It was a magical place, with its own jetty, looking out over Long Island Sound. The birdlife was extraordinary. As the sun rose, we would watch the geese flying over the water, long necks outstretched. Nearer to shore, wading birds splashed and gabbled. At night, in the far distance, you could catch the gleam of Manhattan's skyscrapers.

The house had its own large garden, fenced with white palings, as well as a flagpole overlooking a small private beach. Somewhere along the line I had accumulated enough breakfast cereal box-top tokens to write off for a large white towel embroidered with the words BIRDS EYE BROCCOLI SPEARS and an accompanying illustration. Occasionally, when we saw the binoculars of passing yachtsmen trained in our direction, we would gather as a family by the flagpole and ceremonially hoist the towel. As the pennant, with its distinctive emblem, was unfurled, I would encourage Alexander Boris, Rachel and even little Leo to come to attention with a smart salute. Vreni, the Swiss au pair who had come to help with the children, joined in and sometimes let out a yodel for good measure.

I am not sure what the passing yachtsmen made of our little ceremony but we enjoyed it anyway.

The first meeting of the UNA-USA national policy panel on world population was held in New York on 27 June 1968. We met in the oak-panelled East Room of the Century Club at 7 West 43rd Street. The Century Club was then, and probably still is, quintessentially part of the American East Coast establishment. It positively reeks of old money and old families, while providing a haven for some smart new arrivals, including businessmen with philanthropic tendencies and high-powered academics jumping on and off the public affairs carousel.

All the panel members who attended that first morning were, I believe, conscious of the magnitude of the task that confronted them. If they weren't, Mr Rockefeller soon set them straight.

He opened the meeting by reading out in his slow, careful way, pausing for emphasis when he felt emphasis was needed, a letter that U Thant, then Secretary-General of the United Nations, had recently written. "'*I hope*,'" Mr Rockefeller read, "'*that the distinguished Panel you have put together will be able to plan new and constructive approaches to one of the most pressing problems of our generation and age.*'"

My job as project director was to sit next to the chairman and give him whatever help he needed in steering the meeting in the right direction. I wasn't exactly daunted by the task, but I was certainly conscious of the ironies. Most of the panel members were big-hitters in their various ways, men who were honoured in the habitations. I was just a young whippersnapper, not yet twenty-eight years old. One of the main objectives of the panel was to advise the US government on how to approach the world's population problem and yet I wasn't even an American.

I have to hand it to Mr Rockefeller. He never made me feel I was out of place or not up to the job. He was always immensely courteous with an understated sense of humour. He didn't often laugh out loud, but sometimes you could hear a quiet chuckle. He was the oldest of the five Rockefeller brothers, though possibly not the best known. His brother Nelson had been governor of New York; David had run the Chase Manhattan Bank; Laurance was a noted conservationist; Winthrop had been governor of Arkansas. For my money, John's contribution to society was every bit as valuable as that of his siblings. Though he had many other philanthropic interests, trying to tackle the world's population problem was one of his priorities. Through the Rockefeller Foundation and the Population Council, and now through the UNA-USA panel, he devoted much energy to this endeavour, with considerable success.

When Mr Rockefeller had finished with U Thant's letter, he continued with his own opening statement. I had gone over the draft with him in his office the previous afternoon. We had made one or two changes and he seemed comfortable with the text he now had.

'The present rate of world population growth,' Mr Rockefeller said, 'appears to jeopardize the satisfaction of mankind's basic needs. Actual or imminent shortages of food, housing and clothing go hand in hand with conditions of congestion, unemployment, grossly inadequate educational resources, and the pollution of man's environment ...'

At this point, he paused and looked around the room. 'The question we have to consider is how the United Nations, the world's foremost international organization, is going to deal with the world's most important problem.'

I don't think there was anyone in the room that day who had any doubts about Mr Rockefeller's assessment. I certainly didn't.

As I had observed during my time in the World Bank, a developing country with a high rate of population growth and limited resources was caught in a vicious circle. It couldn't put enough money into agriculture to increase productivity because the day-to-day needs of consumption left no room for investment. It couldn't create enough jobs for the unemployed or build enough schools for exactly the same reason. Sometimes the pressures of population growth could be seen in their starkest forms of hunger, misery and disease. Sometimes the manifestation was subtler, to be found in the disappointment and disaffection of those whose expectations had not been met; in social unrest and political instability, even threatening the maintenance of peace itself.

In macro-economic terms, the case for action was, to my mind, incontrovertible. If population was rising, say, at 2.4 per cent a year (the projected average rate at that time for the less developed world), and national income was growing at 4 per cent (an optimistic assumption) it would take forty-three years to double per capita income. And since per capita income in many parts of the developing world was less that $100 per annum, even a doubling of per capita income was hardly likely to represent a satisfactory fulfilment of economic expectations.

As I look back, I can say that the year I spent as the project director of what soon came to be known as the Rockefeller Panel on World Population was, professionally speaking, probably the most important year of my life. We met five times over the course of the next ten months, always in the Century Club. The attendance of the panel members was exemplary. Their contributions to the discussions were well judged and to the point.

Best of all, from my point of view, the panel gave me a real job to do. They mandated me, at that first meeting, to visit post-haste the various UN agencies that were or might be involved in tackling world population explosion.

So, in the course of the summer of 1968, while Charlotte and the children enjoyed the delights of Harbor Island, Norwalk, I travelled in quick succession to the headquarters of the world education agency (UNESCO) in Paris, the World Health Organization (WHO) and the International Labour Organization (ILO), both in Geneva, as well as the United Nations Food and Agriculture Organization (FAO) in Rome. Then I came back to my office in New York and wrote a report for the second meeting of the panel, held in the middle of September, setting out the position as I saw it.

Many of the UN agencies, it seemed to me, had mandates that would allow them to take action on the population front but they hadn't done so. I wrote: 'Though the population cake has been sliced this way and that in an endless series of coordinating meetings, very few crumbs have as yet fallen into the lap of a hungry world. The question of mandates, of which agency should undertake which activity, has been used as a classic delaying tactic by a UN system which, taken as a whole, is reluctant to make a more impressive commitment.'

That first whistle-stop tour was to be followed by a more extensive journey through the Third World that I undertook at the end of the year. My objective was to see at first hand the impact of the population explosion in the developing world, to assess what the various countries were already doing to cope with the problem, and to make some recommendations to the panel for international action, in particular through the United Nations.

The Ford Foundation happily looked after the logistics of my trip. Dr Oscar ('Bud') Harkavy, the officer in charge of the Ford Foundation's Population Program, was also a member of the Rockefeller Panel and very happy to help in any way he could. I went to see him in his office in the Ford Foundation Building on East 43rd Street. We sat on a sofa, looking out through internal plate-glass windows onto the luxuriant vegetation of the atrium, while he ticked off the countries I should visit.

'Well, obviously you must go to India. That's where it all began. And if you go to India, you've got to do Pakistan too. That's one of the ground rules.'

'Indonesia?' I asked.

'There's not much going on there. But maybe that's one of the interesting things if you want to look at the problem from as many different angles as possible. One hundred and fifteen million people and some of the highest densities on earth.'

Thailand and Taiwan were added to Asia, and Hong Kong and Singapore were thrown in for good measure since the plane stopped there anyway.

'What about Africa?'

'As far as sub-Saharan Africa is concerned, Kenya's the only country with a formal population policy, though there have been some signs of movement in Ghana. You ought to go to Addis Ababa too, to the Economic Commission for Africa.'

We turned to South America. There I ended up with Brazil and Chile. Brazil because, with (then) almost a hundred million people, it was half of South America just by itself. Chile because, of all the South American countries, this was the one where the most liberal attitude to birth control had so far been taken.

In the event, I visited all the countries Bud Harkavy had recommended. In those pre-electronic-booking days, my air ticket opened out like a concertina as I went from airport to airport and continent to continent.

For practical reasons, since I was embarking on a round-the-world tour and was already on the west side of the Atlantic, I began with South America.

In Brazil, the leaders of the main family planning organization were still reeling from the effects of the recent encyclical. Issued by Pope Paul VI on 29 July 1968 – just a few weeks before my visit – *Humanae Vitae* maintained, indeed, reconfirmed, the opposition of the Roman Catholic Church to the use of artificial contraception. His Holiness had observed the pill's grim progress throughout the world and he didn't like what he saw. He proclaimed that every act of sexual intercourse should remain open to the transmission of life. Walter Rodrigues, the director of BEMFAM (Sociedade Civil Bem-Estar Familiar no Brasil), the main non-governmental family planning body, was practically in despair. Brazil's population was doubling every twelve years, the slums in cities like Rio and São Paulo were bursting at the seams, women were crying out for access to family planning, BEMFAM was making slow but sure progress in meeting the needs and then, wham!, out of the blue, this torpedo!

Walter Rodrigues was a large man. Six foot three, squashed into his tiny Volkswagen, he would bang his hands on the steering wheel in frustration as we drove around the city. Brazil's President, Artur da Costa e Silva, had even sent a telegram to the Pope welcoming the encyclical.

If my time in Brazil showed me one side of the family planning controversy, the ten days I spent in India showed me another.

After Brazil, I had visited Chile, then flown on through Asia following the itinerary that Bud Harkavy had suggested. I had seen a lot and learned a lot. Japan, Taiwan, Hong Kong, Singapore, Indonesia, Thailand – all these countries were in their different ways ready to support or at least tolerate family planning programmes but none of them so far had adopted a formal policy of reducing the rate of population growth.

By the time I landed in New Delhi I was looking for some more radical commitments than I had so far seen. In India, I was not disappointed.

This was a country where men like Jayaprakash Narayan – one of the most renowned of Gandhi's disciples – had likened the population crisis to a new military invasion. The late President Radhakrishnan had called the five hundred million mark a 'danger signal' that India would ignore at her peril. Prime Minister Indira Gandhi, comparing the task of raising the level of living in India to that of a man who builds his house on the sands before the advancing tide, had warned: 'Time is not on India's side.'

When I had visited India seven years earlier on my Marco Polo motorcycle ride, I had – I am ready to admit – failed to pick up on some of these encouraging signals. With a full programme of visits ahead of me, I now had a chance to make up for that omission.

India was, I learned, engaged in a massive effort to bring down the birth rate. Almost 50 per cent of the population was under fifteen years of age. The number of Indians would increase by almost 150 million in the next decade. The stork had overtaken the plough with a vengeance. As you drove around, in town or country, you couldn't miss the family planning signs with the distinctive red triangle: 'One or two – that will do!' All India Radio covered 80 per cent of the country. Twenty-two out of thirty-six stations promoted family planning over the air.

One day I visited a vasectomy camp being held in a municipal building in a Calcutta suburb. Just to see what it felt like, I joined the queue for the operating room. A welfare worker thrust a paper into my hand. I saw it was a consent form.

'*I desire to get myself sterilized*', I read. '*My wife and I understand that the operation is for our own good and for the good of our family and that we shall not be able to have any more children.*'

'Where do I sign it?' I asked.

'Here, where it says "LTI".'

'What does LTI stand for?'

'Left thumb imprint.'

I was next in line for the knife when I chickened out. Admittedly, I had three children already, which was over the limit but – who knows? – we might want to have more. Birth rates were falling in Britain. And Britain wasn't India. The situation was different there.

As I made my excuses and began to leave, one of the clinic's attendants blocked my way.

'It's a snip,' she said, trying to talk me into it.

When she saw I was not to be persuaded, she thrust a paper into my hand. It was an official document, certifying that I had been vasectomized.

'But I *haven't* been vasectomized,' I protested.

She shook her head from side to side. 'Please go next door and collect your eighteen rupees.'

Mrs Gandhi, I realized, was a harsh taskmaster. Each state, each clinic, had its sterilization targets. It didn't do to upset the apple cart.

After I had returned to my hotel, I posted my newly acquired vasectomy certificate to Charlotte, looking after our three children in Norwalk, Connecticut.

'Thought you might enjoy this!' I scribbled on the flap of the envelope.

About a week later, I was in New Delhi, packing my things for the next leg of my trip, when the phone rang.

It was the hotel operator. 'There is a Mrs Johnson on the line for you, sahib.'

Charlotte came straight to the point. 'What's all this about?'

'What's all what about?'

'The vasectomy certificate.'

I tried to laugh it off. 'Just a joke. Of course, I didn't go through with it.'

'I don't believe you.' Charlotte sounded tearful. 'It says you acknowledge receiving eighteen rupees and a transistor radio!'

Happily, the hotel operator who had kindly been listening in case there were any technical difficulties intervened: 'Please do not worry, Mrs Johnson. In India family planning programme, many people get rupees without having operation! Usually, they get the transistor radio too! The family planning targets have to be met!'

I flew on from India to Pakistan, visiting both the East Wing and the West Wing. Nowadays, the East Wing has become Bangladesh and the West Wing a popular television programme! I called on Enver Adil, the government's newly appointed family planning commissioner, and learned that the ambition of the third five-year plan (1965–70) was to achieve a 20 per cent reduction in the birth rate by the end of the plan period.

'That means,' Enver Adil told me, 'that twenty-five per cent, or five million of the overall total of twenty million, should be practising contraception by 1970. The coil continues to be our best bet, but vasectomies have caught on in East Pakistan like wildfire!'

Today, in India and Pakistan, the efforts to slow the rate of population growth and to promote family planning no longer seem to have the same urgency as they did when I was there almost forty years ago. Men and women with the single-minded drive of Indira Gandhi and Enver Adil are hard to find on the Indian subcontinent. Instead, it is China which now leads the way, not the subcontinent. This is ironic. At the time the Rockefeller Panel was sitting, China eschewed official birth control programmes. The Red Guard vilified Liu Shao-chi, who, a decade earlier, had tried to promote them.

The last lap on my round-the-world tour was Africa. I visited Kenya – which five years earlier had attained its independence from Britain. Tom Mboya, a Luo (from the tribe based in the western part of Kenya), had been made planning minister and he courageously decided to try to tackle a situation where population was growing at more than 3 per cent a year.

Under Mboya's guidance, the government had decided to establish a Family Planning Council, but there was never really any attempt to promote a vigorous policy of population control and Mboya himself, a few months after my visit, was gunned down in a Nairobi street.

If Kenya was the most advanced nation in sub-Saharan Africa in terms of promoting family planning, where did that leave the rest? In Addis Ababa, the Ethiopian capital and the seat of the United Nations Economic Commission for Africa, I was able to acquire a brief synoptic overview of the population prospects for the African continent as a whole. They were horrendous. Many of the nations of sub-Saharan Africa were, like Kenya, facing population growth rates of over 3 per cent. Things weren't much better north of the Sahara. Superstition, religious and tribal rivalries, custom and practice – all seemed to militate against a rapid and effective spread of family planning.

When finally I returned to New York, assembled all my notes, and sorted out my ideas after a hectic, fact-filled journey, I realized that my report to the Rockefeller Panel was not likely to make cheerful reading.

The members of the panel, to be fair, didn't seek to duck their responsibility. They were prepared to recognize an emergency when they saw one. In June 1969 they called for a new United Nations Population Agency to be established with an annual budget of at least $100 million a year. The *New York Times* and many other newspapers gave our recommendations front-page coverage.

I took the view then that I was unlikely ever to do anything more important in my life than the role I had played in helping to launch the United Nations' birth-control programmes. Almost forty years later, I still hold that opinion. The world's population explosion still seems to me to be the number-one issue of our time, even though the amount of effort being devoted to solving it seems to have diminished most shamefully since the time I was first involved.

Nowadays, of course, a $100 million annual budget seems chicken feed. Some houses on the smartest streets of London sell for $100 million. But forty years ago, it still seemed like a lot of money.

I think it even seemed like a lot of money to Mr Rockefeller. I remember flying down with him to Washington to present our findings to President Nixon's Secretary of State, William Rogers. (President Nixon, having defeated the Democratic candidate, Senator Hubert Humphrey, in the November election, had succeeded Lyndon Johnson in January 1969.)

We sat in an office even grander than Alan Novak's, looking out on a bright summer morning at the immense obelisk of the Washington Monument. Mr Rockefeller banged the coffee table in front of us.

'One hundred million dollars a year! That's what it's going to take, Mr Secretary.'

I realized then what an inspired choice UNA-USA had made in inviting Mr Rockefeller to chair the panel. The man had clout at the highest level. On 18 July 1969, a few days after our visit to Washington, President Nixon sent a Message on Population to Congress. The President wrote: 'It is our belief that the United Nations, its specialized agencies, and other international bodies should take the leadership in responding to world population growth. The United States will cooperate fully with their programs. I would note in this connection that I am most impressed by the scope and thrust of the recent report of the panel of the United Nations Association, chaired by John D. Rockefeller III. The report stressed the need for expanded action and greater coordination, concerns which should be high on the agenda of the United Nations.'

Scope and thrust! I liked that!

Charlotte and I threw a party at our house on Harbor Island to celebrate.

When, at some point during the festivities, the telephone rang, John Graham, the *Financial Times*' Washington correspondent who happened to be staying with us, picked it up.

'The Johnson residence,' he said. 'Who's speaking, please?'

My heart sank when I heard him exclaim: 'Rockefeller? Not John D. Rockefeller, surely? Not John D. Rocker-fucking-feller!'

He passed me the phone. 'It's for you. Man pretending to be Mr Rockefeller.'

I picked up the receiver and heard a voice I recognized.

'You seem to be having quite a time up there,' Mr Rockefeller chuckled.

It turned out he had gone to Williamsburg for the weekend. He was ringing to offer his congratulations on President Nixon's Message on Population to Congress.

I poured John Graham another drink. It seemed the best thing to do in the circumstances.

Within weeks of the publication of our report, the United Nations had established the United Nations Fund for Population Activities and in an inspired choice appointed Rafael Salas, by reputation the second most powerful man in the Philippines, to head it. The money poured in. Within months, the $100 million target had already been exceeded as other nations joined the US in offering funds to the new agency.

'Basically, we hit the jackpot,' I explained to Charlotte, as – yet again – we packed up our things and left our lovely seaside house in Connecticut to fly to London. I was sad to be leaving New York. There could hardly be a more stimulating city to work in. As far as I was concerned, it had been an amazing year. In terms of both interest and impact, it was difficult to see how it could be bettered.

But, in another way, as we headed for JFK airport, I felt that at least I was keeping my side of the bargain. As I have already mentioned, when Bobby Kennedy had been shot the previous year I had promised Charlotte that I would do my level best to get our family home within a twelvemonth. And, give or take a couple of weeks, that was precisely what I had succeeded in doing.

TWENTY-FIVE

Solid Exposure to Rainforest

We spent the rest of the summer at Nethercote. For the first time Charlotte and I had our own house in the valley, having bought Nethercote Cottage while we were still in the United States.

The cottage, as its name implies, was not a grand dwelling. The previous owner, Mr Cole, had lived there on his own until his death with an extensive collection of books about bee-keeping and animal husbandry that we inherited. Since there were only three bedrooms, we converted an internal garage into a fourth. Even then, we were short of space, so Alexander Boris acquired a small boxroom of his own in which his early doodles may still be seen pinned to the wall. His first known literary effort – a competently scrawled 'Boo to grown-ups!' – is also to be found there. (My sister Birdie lives in the cottage today.)

The main farmhouse, West Nethercote, was still occupied by my parents, while my sister Hilary, her husband, Peter Heanly, and their growing family (by now they had four sons) lived in the middle house, East Nethercote, which we had bought from the Stevens in 1957, together with 120 acres of land.

Charlotte and I, with our three children, overlapped with the Heanlys for a few months at Nethercote in the summer of 1969, after our return from America. Then, in August 1969, the Heanly family left for Australia. The four sons whom we knew as toddlers that summer, playing in the yard and swimming in the river, have all – like their parents – made their lives Down Under and have wives and families of their own. Hilary and Peter have both retained their British passports but their offspring and descendants, now scattered about the country, are Australians to the core and definitely cheer for the home side when English rugby or cricket teams come to visit.

I spent most of my time that summer writing a book about my recent travels through the Third World and was gratified when Heinemann published it under the title *Life without Birth: A Journey Through the Third World in Search of the Population Explosion*. *Life without Birth* was actually rather a silly title, for which I take full responsibility. I obviously wasn't suggesting that people should give up having babies altogether; just that we should have fewer of them. It would have been better if I had settled for something like *The Population Explosion*.

As I have already indicated, with three children of my own I was definitely conscious of the ironies implicit in writing a book about the world's population problems.

Recently, I found a copy of *Life without Birth* propping up one of the legs of the billiard table on the landing at Nethercote. After years of supporting our piled-up fleeces after shearing, the table was seriously wonky and my 364-page tome was actually performing a useful function. I see that I wrote, plaintively, in the introduction: '*I look at my guilty face in the shaving mirror as my children clatter down to breakfast … how can I face that row of small blond heads bobbing over the corn-flakes knowing that I am statistically accountable for the burdens they will add to society?*'

When the summer was over, Charlotte and I moved to London with the children. Our new address was 41 Blomfield Road, in Little Venice, conveniently close to Paddington station. Though the house belonged to friends of Charlotte's parents, Charlotte and I were able to pay the going rent for this upmarket property thanks to an extraordinary piece of good luck which had befallen us just as we were about to leave America.

On the occasion of the very last meeting of the Rockefeller Panel, I found myself talking to David 'Dave' Bell, Vice-President of the Ford Foundation. The Century Club, as usual, had laid on a very good meal and Dave was in an expansive mood.

'Would you like to go to London for a year?' he enquired over the coffee. 'The Ford Foundation could probably give you a Travel and Study Grant.'

I knew there was a London in Ontario, Canada. There might also be a London in Texas (after all, there was a Paris, Texas).

'Do you mean London, *England*?' I asked, to be on the safe side.

'Sure,' Dave Bell replied. 'We could send you to the London School of Economics.'

The Ford Foundation was as good as Dave Bell's word. As a Ford Foundation Fellow, I signed up to do postgraduate work in demography at the LSE under Professor David Glass and spent some time learning the basic skills of the trade. Birth, copulation and death, as T. S. Eliot put it, are all the facts when you come down to brass tacks. He would have made a good demographer. Nowadays, of course, migration is the other key statistic demographers have to take into account.

I didn't do as much studying as I should have done. In the first place, I often found it tricky to locate the right LSE classroom in time for a lecture, since most of the facilities are tucked away in a maze of back streets off Kingsway. More importantly, I found myself increasingly absorbed during the first few months of 1970 in the political fortunes of the British Conservative Party.

While I was still in America I had written to Edward Heath, then the leader of Her Majesty's Loyal Opposition. Was there, I wondered, anything I could do to help remove Harold Wilson from office and help the Conservatives return to power?

Mr Heath did not actually write back in person but Douglas Hurd, the former diplomat, novelist and future long-serving Foreign Secretary, who was at the time head of Mr Heath's private office, did. Douglas put me in touch with Brendon Sewill, then Director of the Conservative Research Department, and Brendon in due course invited me to join the Department as the Conservatives' first ever desk officer for the environment.

Brendon took me to lunch at the Carlton Club in St James's. 'Reggie's very keen,' he said. 'So is Peter.'

Reggie was Reggie Maudling, former Chancellor of the Exchequer and Fellow of All Souls, who had overall responsibility for the Conservative Research Department. Peter was Peter Walker, the whizz-kid who had made his fortune in the City (he was the Walker of Slater Walker) and who was now shadow Secretary of State for the Environment.

It is funny how things go in cycles. At the beginning of the 1970s all three political parties sensed, just as they do today, that the environment was becoming an increasingly important political issue. 1970 had been declared European Conservation Year. Some wags called it 'European Conversation Year' but the UN was busy preparing for the first ever world environment conference, to be held in Stockholm in June 1972. American astronauts, a few months earlier, had landed on the moon. Planet Earth, we all now knew, was a pale, fragile orb and we were busy making a frightful mess of it. Teddy Goldsmith, brother of the more famous Jimmy, had founded *The Ecologist* magazine and was working on a 'Blueprint for Survival'. The Club of Rome was studying 'The Limits to Growth'.

In due course, I found myself attending regular meetings of Peter Walker's shadow 'environment team', which included Michael Heseltine, then MP for Tavistock, as well as another MP, Chris Chataway, the man who had, with Chris Brasher, paced Roger Bannister in his famously successful attempt to run the first ever four-minute mile.

Brendon Sewill found an office for me as well as a job. The Conservative Research Department in those days kept itself at a safe distance from Conservative Central Office in Smith Square. It actually occupied two elegant buildings in Old Queen Street, just off Queen Anne's Gate. I found myself sharing a room in 34 Old Queen Street with Chris Patten and Patrick Cosgrave, both at that time full-time staff members of the Research Department.

Chris Patten succeeded Brendon Sewill as Director of the Conservative Research Department before being elected to Parliament and embarking on a career as a politician, author and, most recently, Chancellor of Oxford University.

Patrick Cosgrave was a brilliant writer and journalist, who had a penchant for wearing colourful bow ties. Each morning, around eleven, Mrs Stagg, the tea lady, would bring us our cups of coffee with two lumps of sugar apiece. Since neither Chris Patten nor I took sugar in our coffee, we would throw the redundant lumps at Patrick, hoping to dislodge his tie or at least knock it askew.

Patrick appeared to endure this daily ritual with his usual good temper though I don't think we ever actually scored a bullseye.

In February 1970, Charlotte and I, with the three children and a Dutch mother's help called Joke (pronounced Yo-Ker), drove to Strasbourg for the Opening Conference of European Conservation Year. (Nine years later, I would find myself spending a week a month in Strasbourg as a newly elected Member of the European Parliament.)

235

In due course I reported back to the Conservatives on the results of the Conference. I also drafted an article to be signed by Mr Heath and submitted to the *Spectator*, then edited by Nigel Lawson, who in due course would become Mrs Thatcher's Chancellor of the Exchequer.

'We have for some months,' Mr Heath wrote in the article which Nigel Lawson duly published in March 1970, 'been engaged in a wide-ranging study of a series of questions affecting the environment, including noise, air pollution, water pollution, land use, housing, and transport problems. This work is still continuing, but the principal guidelines for a Conservative programme in this field are already emerging.'

If you go to the *Spectator*'s offices and search through the dusty bound volumes which grace the panelled walls, you can still read Mr Heath's contribution on Conservative environmental policy. Nowadays, of course, the Conservative opposition makes a good deal more noise about the environment than it did at the end of the 1960s. And for good reason. All over the world, the environment has moved centre stage as far as public policy issues are concerned. But I still think Mr Heath's 1970 *Spectator* article deserved at least a B+.

More to the point, it set the stage for a first ever formal Conservative commitment on environmental policy in the context of a national election campaign. In the run-up to the June 1970 general election, the Conservatives published their official Election Manifesto, 'A Better Tomorrow'. In that document, the environment rated three full paragraphs. It may not sound a lot in the context of today's environmental furore. The important thing, at least as far as I was concerned, was that it was included at all.

I don't think many people (apart from Mr Heath himself) actually expected the Conservatives to win the general election that was held in June 1970.

I certainly didn't. Before polling day, I cleared my desk at the Conservative Research Department, said goodbye to colleagues and, with the family, headed for Exmoor.

I remember staying up all night in the cottage at Nethercote on Thursday 18 June 1970, watching the election results on an old black and white TV. The reception was not good since Nethercote lies in a steep-sided valley and the situation was not improved by the erratic nature of the electric current produced by our generator.

But we could see enough to know that Mr Heath had pulled off a famous victory. Next day he kissed hands with the Queen on his appointment as Prime Minister. Reggie Maudling became Home Secretary and Peter Walker became Secretary of State for the Environment, a job that involved presiding over a Super-Ministry which included housing and local government, transport and public works as well as environmental policy as such.

Among my papers I have found an invitation which reads: 'The Prime Minister requests the honour of the company of Mr and Mrs S. P. Johnson at a Reception at 10, Downing Street, on Thursday 25 June 1970, at 7.00 p.m.'

As things turned out, I was unable to go to the reception that Mr Heath, the incoming Conservative Prime Minister, gave to celebrate his victory. In fact I didn't even know that Charlotte and I had been invited. By the time the card arrived, I was in the far north of Dahomey (as present-day Benin was then called) and completely out of contact.

When I did finally return to the capital, Cotonou, I found a message from Charlotte at my hotel, asking me to telephone urgently.

I was rather worried. Had I absent-mindedly mailed her some new incriminating document? Was there to be a repeat of the 'vasectomy' fiasco?

'What's up?' I asked when at last I got through to Nethercote Cottage.

'We've got an invitation from Downing Street for next Thursday. What shall I tell them?'

'Phew!' I breathed a sigh of relief. 'I thought something dreadful had happened.'

'I thought it might be important,' Charlotte said, a bit put out.

'Please tell Downing Street I'm very sorry but I'm in Africa at the moment so unfortunately we can't come.'

Towards the end of his life, Mr Heath wrote an autobiography called *The Course of My Life*. I've often wondered if the course of *my* life might have been different if I hadn't so resolutely distanced myself – in the most literal sense – from the Conservatives' 1970 election victory. I doubt it, but I can't be sure.

I didn't actually return to England for some weeks. Dahomey was just the first stop in a journey that took me to over a dozen countries in Latin America, Asia and Africa. In Latin America, I visited Mexico, Colombia and Brazil. In Asia, I visited Turkey, India, the Philippines, Thailand and Burma (now Myanmar). In Africa (besides Dahomey), I visited Ghana and Tanzania. Apart from the occasional fleeting pit stop, I didn't finally return to England until the end of the year.

The reason for this protracted absence was not some inherent wanderlust but the need to research a book that I had undertaken to write about the 'green revolution'. Nowadays, the term 'green revolution' is usually understood as having something to do with environmental policy. But at the beginning of the 1970s it had an agricultural connotation and referred to the revolution in farming that had been brought about by the new strains of wheat and rice developed by men like Dr Norman Borlaug (who won the Nobel Peace Prize for his work in this field).

Hamish Hamilton, in London, and Harper & Row, in New York, seemed keen to publish, while the United Nations Development Programme, the Food and Agriculture Organization of the UN, and the World Bank funded the travel and ensured I was able to visit various far-flung projects around the world.

My account of this venture duly appeared under the title *The Green Revolution*, so I have no need to repeat it here. I enjoyed the research. Though I had already visited some of the countries on my itinerary during my work for the Rockefeller Panel, the change of emphasis – from population to agriculture – meant that I had to spend most of my time not in the city but in the bush.

Perhaps the most memorable part of this round-the-world trip was the Latin American sector. I had been in the Amazon before, of course, but I had never had the solid exposure to the rainforest that I acquired when researching *The Green Revolution*. I am flipping through the pages of the book as I write this and, as I do so, the image of a vast expanse of forest, stretching as far as the eye can see, comes back to me.

Over the years I have spent a good deal of time on or in tropical rainforests, but I shall never forget the day I first flew across the heart of the Amazon in a battered old DC 4.

'After an hour or two in Leticia [a small town on the Colombia–Brazil border]', I wrote, 'we take off again for Manaus. I stand in the cockpit behind the pilot and watch the jungle roll beneath the wings of the plane. This huge bowl of greenery is one of the great oxygen-producing areas of the world. My layman's understanding of ecological interdependence is that air knows no international frontiers. On a clear day when the traffic has gone to bed and a soft night wind blows, one may taste the breath of the Amazon rainforest even in places like Oxford Street …'

I went on: 'It seems so rich and so luxuriant that it is hard to believe this jungle, the ecological climax of the Amazon region, is only one step removed from a desert … Abuse this resource through random exploitation and nature may wreak a hideous vengeance.'

In the more than thirty-five years since I wrote those words, I have returned to Brazil at least a dozen times. The process of deforestation in the Amazon has steadily gathered speed. Whole states have been denuded of trees as roads have been carved through the forest with miners and cattlemen following hard on the heels of the loggers. Little did I know when I penned that first description of flying over the Amazon from Leticia to Manaus that, in a few short decades, my worst fears would be realized.

When I returned to England, the *New Scientist* carried an article I had written about the Amazon rainforest and the dangers posed by the cattle ranchers to Brazil's greatest resource. I also wrote several pieces for *The Times*.

There were other agreeable spin-offs from *The Green Revolution*. The *Observer Colour Magazine*, which had already serialized *Life without Birth*, did the same for my new book, printing long extracts on successive weeks of the account I had given of my travels in Burma. (Burma in those days was more or less off-limits to journalists and only my UN credentials secured me a visa.)

For a man who had laid down his pen in the Conservative Research Department only a few weeks earlier, I see I wrote rather breathlessly about the attractions of the Burmese Way to Socialism. 'Perhaps the best way to describe what Burma wants to be is to describe what she does *not* want to be. She does not want to turn into a country where the capital city swells up like an infected gland attracting to itself manpower which

239

cannot conceivably be employed in any productive capacity. In other words, she wants to avoid the horrors of rampant urbanization as these are to be found in Africa, Latin America and other parts of Asia ... She does *not* want to be a Western Society if this means the constant pursuit of materialistic goals and the social divisiveness produced by the differential accumulation of wealth ...'

Teddy Goldsmith's magazine, *The Ecologist*, also printed some long extracts from my Burma chapter. Jimo Omo Fadaka, one of *The Ecologist*'s regular contributors, regurgitated several pages word for word in an article entitled 'The Tanzanian Way to Socialism'. The only changes from my text as far as I could see was that Jimo put Tanzania whenever I had written Burma and Nyerere whenever I had written Ne Win.

I rang up Teddy to complain.

'Ha ha!' Teddy laughed uproariously. 'What a marvellous example of recycling. Sorry I can't talk more now. I'm watching the St Leger on television. Got a large bet on!'

As it happened, I had actually encountered President Julius Nyerere of Tanzania during the Africa leg of my world tour. I was visiting the UNDP/FAO livestock project in Dodoma, in the arid heart of the country, when Nyerere arrived to tour the region. Sensing some useful material for the book, I followed the presidential convoy in my official UN car as it went from village to village. Sometimes, Nyerere made a short speech, standing in the shade of a baobab tree. Sometimes he stayed silent. Once a little boy stepped forward from the crowd and read out some welcoming words from a scroll. I thought it was a marvel he could read at all, the child was so small. My host that morning, a Swedish water engineer called Homberg, standing next to me, said: 'It is a big work to build up a country.'

As befitted a man with such responsibilities, the President didn't travel light. Nyerere's baggage train that day included three mobile generators, four water tankers, one lorry-load of petrol and diesel, as well as the President's two caravans and a portable latrine.

Later that day, caught up in the slipstream, we found ourselves at the presidential campsite as lunch was being prepared. Nyerere himself was tucking in to the midday meal just a few feet away. A servant stood behind with a parasol, another held an ivory-handled fly whisk.

Glancing across, I saw the President looking at me with a puzzled expression on his face. He beckoned to one of the retainers. I think he wondered what I was doing there.

'We had better get going,' I said to Homberg. President Nyerere's lectures on 'ujamaa', his personal approach to economic and social development, were known to last several hours sometimes.

Gratifying though the response to *The Green Revolution* was, I soon realized that it was not easy to keep a growing family through the efforts of one's pen alone. Admittedly, living at Nethercote had been relatively cheap. While I was travelling, all three children had attended Winsford Village School (now closed). In those days on Exmoor a little money could go a long way.

But we both felt we couldn't stay on in the valley permanently. Much as we loved Exmoor, we needed a base in London as well. So at the end of the year we bought a house in Princess Road, just off Primrose Hill, London NW1, which was conveniently located right next door to the Primrose Hill Primary School. It was time for me to find a proper job.

TWENTY-SIX

A Bicycle Not Made for Two

Rafael Salas, who had been appointed the Executive Director of the newly established United Nations Population Fund (UNFPA), very kindly invited me back to New York to join him as the Fund's first public affairs officer. He offered me a high grade for my age with a commensurate salary. I was sorely tempted to accept. Having helped to lay the foundations, it would have been exhilarating to assist this particular building rise to its full height.

In fact, I was not only tempted; I succumbed. I sent Rafael a telegram of acceptance, only to countermand the message a few days later. I realized it simply wasn't on to move the family back to America, so soon after returning to England.

Rafael took my refusal in good part. For years thereafter I served as a consultant to UNFPA and, with Rafael's encouragement, eventually wrote a book called *World Population and the United Nations*, published by Cambridge University Press in 1987. Rafael's untimely death in harness that same year deprived me of a good friend and robbed the United Nations of a key player in its efforts to place population and family planning at the heart of its development efforts.

Though I didn't take up the job with UNFPA, I did in fact stay in the same field of activity. At the beginning of 1971 I joined the International Planned Parenthood Federation, the largest non-governmental organization in the world supporting birth control and family planning programmes in eighty countries. IPPF's international headquarters were conveniently located in Lower Regent Street, London, a twenty-minute ride on my Elswick Hopper bicycle from our new house. The job title was International Liaison Officer. Basically, I was meant to look after IPPF's links with the UN and its system of agencies.

IPPF in those days still had a pioneering air about it. Not so long ago, women like Marie Stopes had been publicly vilified for advocating contraception even in advanced countries like Britain. In much of the developing world, birth control advocates were regarded with a mixture of suspicion, intolerance or outright hostility.

When I joined IPPF, Julia Henderson, formerly director of social affairs at the UN, New York, had just taken over as its Secretary-General. IPPF, as an international non-governmental organization, was accredited to the UN. One of the first things Julia (with her UN background) asked me to do was to ensure that IPPF was fully involved in the preparations then being made for the first ever UN Conference on the Human Environment, scheduled to be held, as I have mentioned, in Stockholm in June 1972.

Most often the planning sessions for the conference were held in New York or Geneva, official United Nations sites. Sometimes we met in more unlikely venues. One such was a motel in Founex, Switzerland, where for two weeks in June 1971 some thirty 'experts on development and environment' elaborated a document that became known as the Founex Report.

Nowadays, those who follow the evolution of international environmental policy look back on the Founex Report as a seminal text. The report made it clear that environmental considerations should be an integral part of the development process. In other words, the rich, white Western world would get absolutely nowhere if it tried to tell the poor, coloured developing nations that they had to cut back on their development aspirations because of the damage to the environment which would be caused. The industrial world, the Founex Report argued, had to face up to the fact that if there was an environmental crisis, we had caused it.

Some of the meetings I attended for IPPF that year were not strictly within the UN framework, but were part of the general groundswell of international concern for environmental issues. I recall going to Jyväskylä in Finland for a five-day meeting that lasted five nights as well, the sun never setting at that time of year so close to the Arctic Circle. I also went to Seoul in South Korea for a conference sponsored by the *Dong-A Ilbo*, a leading newspaper and, more prosaically, to Paris and Bonn.

Since almost everyone seemed to be getting in on the 'Stockholm process', the non-governmental movement wanted to be sure that its voice too was heard loud and clear. IPPF, as a major NGO (when I joined its budget was over US $20 million), certainly felt this.

With only a few months to go before the Stockholm meeting, Julia Henderson called a senior staff meeting in the London headquarters.

'IPPF must make a statement in the Plenary in Stockholm,' Julia announced firmly. 'We need to show the links between population and environment. Stanley, you had better draft something.'

I'm probably the only person who knows how much the IPPF Statement on Population and Environment owed to the language that had already appeared in the Rockefeller Panel's recent report. Thirty-five years later, I'm ready to own up. The text was apt and it seemed a shame to waste it.

The draft I circulated to the next meeting of IPPF senior staff tackled the controversial population–environment relationship head-on.

'No nation,' the concluding paragraph ran, 'can live in isolation. The world is only just beginning to realize the dangers involved in the changing and complex relationship between man and his environment. Contamination of the streams and oceans, erosion of the soil, destruction of vegetation, the rise in the concentration of carbon dioxide in the atmosphere, indiscriminate use of poisonous pesticides and synthetic detergents, the disposal of radio-active waste – these are problems which have vast international implications. To deal with effects without dealing also with causes is inadequate and superficial. One of the root causes, perhaps the root cause, of the threat to our environment is the demands made by expanding populations in developed and developing world alike. The fact that, at the present time, we have only the haziest idea of the nature of the interrelationships involved should not provide an excuse for inaction. If the present world population of three and a half billion is allowed to grow to seven billion or more, our understanding of these things and of possible ways of mitigating their impact may come too late to be of much comfort.'

I added some useful material about family planning and women's rights, female literacy and so on, ran it past the senior staff, then sent it off around the world to IPPF's member associations in more than eighty countries.

Nowadays, of course, all it takes is one click of the mouse to engage in a worldwide consultation. At the beginning of the 1970s, life was more complicated.

The various IPPF branches, to give them due credit, took their job seriously. As I remember, a special meeting was held in the South-East Asia region to ratify the draft text which I had prepared. It was translated into several UN languages and printed up in leaflet form with IPPF's logo on one side and the specially designed homunculus, the symbol of the UN Conference on the Human Environment, on the other.

With only weeks to go before the opening of the Stockholm Conference, Julia Henderson called another meeting of senior staff.

'We have a text,' she said, holding up the now agreed IPPF Statement on Population and Environment. 'It has cost us time and effort, but I'm sure it was worth it. The question now is: who is going to deliver the statement to the Plenary?'

If you've virtually grown up in the UN system, as Julia had, words like 'plenary' have a special ring about them. For an NGO, even an important NGO like IPPF, delivering a statement in the plenary session of a major inter-governmental conference was – and probably still is – a big deal.

Some of those present that day expressed their surprise at Julia's confident assertion that IPPF would be able to address the Plenary. As I remember, Joan Swingler, a long-standing advocate of family planning in the context of female emancipation, pointed out that hundreds of NGOs would be going to Stockholm.

'Surely they won't *all* be able to speak in the Plenary?' Joan interjected.

Julia remained confident. 'I'll take some soundings. I'm sure it will be okay if we get our bid in early. I think Fred Sai should be IPPF's official spokesman.'

This time we were all on Julia's side. Nominating Fred Sai was a brilliant idea. Fred had been director of Ghana's medical services before joining IPPF as Assistant Secretary-General. He was a man of great humour and approachability. With Fred at the speaker's rostrum delivering the message, no one would accuse IPPF of preaching racist neo-colonialism (rich, white people telling poor, coloured folks to stop breeding like rabbits).

Fred was pleased and honoured to accept the assignment. 'Just make sure you give me the final version of the speech in good time, Stanley,' he told me.

'Count on me, Fred,' I said.

The United Nations Conference on the Human Environment opened on 5 June 1972 in Stockholm with an ecumenical service consisting of five hymns, five prayers and five sermons. (The longest sermon ran for thirty-five minutes; it was delivered in French on the theme 'Why Job had boils'.) Maurice Strong, the Conference's Canadian Secretary-General, then led delegates on a fifteen-minute bicycle ride around the centre of Stockholm.

Maurice Strong was an inspirational leader. Under his guidance, the Stockholm Conference adopted a world plan of action on the environment and led to the setting up of the United Nations Environment Programme in Nairobi which has done much good work since, including alerting the world to the destruction of the ozone layer and the dangers of global warming.

But I'm not sure the bicycles were such a brilliant idea. Or perhaps the idea was just too good to be practicable.

Maurice had procured over a hundred velocipedes from an industrial sponsor. They were smart white affairs with the blue Conference homunculus emblazoned on both front and rear mudguards. Maurice's concept was that delegates would pick up a bicycle whenever they wanted to get from one venue to another. When they arrived at their destination, they would park the bike in one of the specially designated bike-racks for the next person to use. A novel and imaginative form of collective transport.

In practice, things didn't work out as planned. Hours, if not minutes, after the start of the conference, most of the bicycles had disappeared. Eco-friendly delegates obviously found it more convenient to 'park' their bicycles in their own hotel rooms on a permanent basis. I remember seeing some splendidly robed representatives from Nigeria wheeling their bicycles into the lifts of the Stockholm Sheraton as soon as the first morning's session was over. Some delegates even took the bicycles as souvenirs and presumably sent them home with their luggage at the end of the conference.

It was the absence of suitable transport at the crucial moment that contributed to the fiasco over IPPF's long-planned statement to the Plenary. Basically, I had said to Fred Sai that I would meet him at 2.30 outside the conference hall at the beginning of the Friday afternoon session. As promised, I would come armed with The Speech. We would go into the hall together. I had checked that Fred's name was down on the list of speakers. IPPF was batting at number five.

I had lunch that day at the Sheraton with my old friend Brian Johnson, whom I had first met when we were both at Columbia University. While I was in the World Bank in Washington, Brian had been working for the United Nations Development Programme in New York. He had returned to England to take up a post with the Institute for Development Studies at Sussex University and had recently been serving as a consultant to Maurice Strong, hence his presence in Stockholm.

Brian and I finished a schnapps and pickled herring lunch around 2.15 p.m. and looked around for bicycles to carry us on the ten-minute ride through town to the conference. I managed to wrestle one from a reluctant delegate who had taken his machine into the coffee shop in the lobby and who seemed determined to hang on to it. But Brian had no such luck.

With time beginning to press, the obvious solution, it seemed to me, was for Brian to ride pillion on my vehicle.

We were about five minutes away from the Plenary hall and making good progress, when a policeman flagged us down. Did we know, he asked, that we were in a pedestrian zone?

'Good heavens, no! Terribly sorry, ossifer, I mean officer!' I was truly contrite.

Did we know that two people were not allowed on a bicycle unless the machine was constructed for that purpose?

'*Daisy, Daisy, give me your answer, do!*' Brian chirruped cheerfully behind me. '*You'll look sweet upon the seat of a bicycle made for two.*'

Swedish policemen are very serious. Indeed, the Swedes as a whole are a serious people.

'My name is not Daisy,' the policeman observed. 'Nor is this bicycle made for two.'

Owing to this contretemps, I was at least ten minutes late for my rendezvous with Fred Sai, waiting impatiently outside the conference centre.

'Don't worry, Fred,' I reassured him, 'there are several speakers ahead of you this afternoon. I've seen the list.'

Fred grabbed The Speech from my outstretched hand and rushed into the building to take his pre-assigned seat within striking distance of the rostrum. The vast room was less than half full. Either the delegates hadn't come back from lunch, I thought, or else, since it was Friday, they had already left town for the weekend. Sweden in June can be particularly lovely. Stockholm lies on the coast, surrounded by a thousand islands, where many fortunate Swedes have built their second homes.

A sudden doubt assailed me. What if the speakers' list had collapsed? I decided that I had better check on the anticipated timing of the IPPF intervention. I went over to the speakers' desk at the side of the room to talk to one of the officials.

'I say, you wouldn't mind telling me when you expect IPPF to be called, would you?'

A grey-haired woman of about fifty looked at me coldly. 'We called IPPF fifteen minutes ago. I'm afraid you've missed your slot.'

She reminded me of an airline captain announcing that because of the late arrival of certain passengers the plane would not now be able to take off till next week.

Of course, I tried to remonstrate with her. I'd had this problem with the bicycle, I explained at some length. We were unavoidably detained.

'Unavoidably? Why were you riding two on a bike through a pedestrian zone? If you want to get back on the list, you'll have to ask Mr Bengtsson personally.'

Mr Ingemund Bengtsson, the Swedish Minister for Agriculture, had been elected as the President of the whole conference on the opening day and, as it happened, he was in charge of the Plenary that afternoon. I tiptoed onto the platform and positioned myself behind him as he sat with the gavel in his hand.

He saw me coming. Half-turning in his chair, he said: 'The answer is no. Delegates should be present at the beginning of proceedings, if they want to speak. They should listen to the other speakers. It's a matter of good manners.'

Ouch! If I could have crawled away to lick my wounds I would have done so. As it was I had to break the bad news to Fred. We had missed our slot and, what's more, we would never get it back.

Full many a rose may be born to blush unseen but I don't think Fred saw things that way. I wouldn't say that he was disgruntled. He was too nice a man for that. But, as P. G. Wodehouse used to put it, I don't think he was particularly gruntled either.

The best I managed, after much pleading with the organizers, was to have Fred's speech, including the famous IPPF Statement on Population and the Environment, written into the record of the Conference. And there it no doubt remains.

In later life, Fred Sai became Population Adviser to the World Bank before returning to take up assignments in his home country of Ghana. As a Ghanaian delegate, he played a crucial role in the 1984 and 1994 World Population conferences, brokering many vital compromises and chairing key committees. So even though he missed his moment of glory in Stockholm, he more than made up for it later.

Still, I owe him an apology.

Peter Walker, the United Kingdom's Secretary of State for the Environment, led Britain's delegation to the Stockholm Conference and made a powerful speech. He would later be the licensed 'wet' in Mrs Thatcher's cabinet. Already at Stockholm, he nailed his colours to the mast as a modern, compassionate Conservative.

'It would be easy,' Peter Walker proclaimed, 'to obtain popularity by conserving the many good environments that exist. But the proper social objective must be to improve the environment of those who have long endured the legacy of the industrial revolution. It is for this reason that I hope we will pursue a similar policy internationally.'

Peter Walker and I had a drink afterwards. I scribbled away in my notebook since I was also moonlighting at the time as the *New States-man*'s environment correspondent. My old friend from Washington days, Tony Howard, who had succeeded Paul Johnson as the editor of the magazine, complained only half-jokingly that he had had to print my reports in three successive issues on a conference that had lasted less than two weeks.

Unlike many politicians, Peter Walker was brilliant at dealing with the press. He didn't need a battery of press officers. Instinct told him how things would play in Peoria.

Actually, I came quite close to joining the Department of the Environment as a special adviser, to help on the public relations side of the Minister's work. Peter took me to lunch one day at Buck's (marmalade pudding a speciality) and sounded me out. I was definitely interested and said I would let him know.

Within minutes of my returning to my office, more than moderately chuffed, I received a call from Ian Bancroft, then Deputy Permanent Secretary of the Department of the Environment. He sounded suspicious, if not actively hostile. 'I gather you've been having lunch with the Minister. Could you possibly come over and have a chat?'

My desk diary for some reason was balanced on the seat of my Elswick Hopper. (Remembering the Great Stockholm Bicycle Fiasco, I kept the machine in my room to stop it being stolen in the street.) As I reached out for it, it fell on the floor.

Bancroft obviously heard the commotion on the other end of the line. 'I'll have a cup of tea ready in about ten minutes, if you can make it.'

The tea was good, but Bancroft's news was not.

'I'm afraid the department takes a very dim view of the Minister's proposal to bring you in as a special adviser,' he told me.

'Is it me personally you don't like?' I asked. 'Or is that you don't like the Minister having his own political appointees?'

'More the latter,' Bancroft admitted.

That was reassuring, anyway.

Nowadays, of course, political appointees are thick on the ground in the civil service. Often they seem to run the show, like Alastair Campbell, for example. But that was not the situation then. The civil service guarded its prerogatives jealously. The civil service advises, Ministers decide. That was the theory at least.

As a consolation prize, Peter Walker appointed me as a member of the Countryside Commission, the body charged with looking after our National Parks. This was a non-paid, non-onerous position. The Countryside Commissioners met once a month in the Commission's offices in Cambridge Terrace, Regent's Park, to deal with papers prepared by the staff. Many of these related to the provision of lay-bys and toilets in the nation's beauty spots. We didn't much like either, but sometimes reluctantly we had to give the go-ahead.

The Commission's chairman was John Cripps, son of Sir Stafford Cripps, former Chancellor of the Exchequer. The staff director was a Devonian, Reg Hookway, who had played a leading role in the European Conservation Year conference I had attended a year or so earlier in Strasbourg. Reg's deputy was Adrian Phillips, who had won a Trevelyan Scholarship to Oxford at the same time as I had.

Adrian was surprised to see me. 'What on earth are you doing here?' he asked as I wheeled my bicycle into the hall to attend my first meeting as a Countryside Commissioner.

'Peter Walker appointed me.'

'Ah! That explains it.'

Today, 'Nolan' procedures in theory preclude the arbitrary exercise of ministerial prerogative. I'm so glad Nolan hadn't been thought of then. Quite apart from the interest of the work itself, my membership of the Countryside Commission enabled me to stave off a major threat to the Nethercote valley.

For years the South West Water Board had been examining the possibility of building a new large reservoir in the region to meet growing urban demand for water. It had examined many sites and had eventually come up with a shortlist of three. As it happened, each one impinged on the Exmoor National Park. Approval of the Countryside Commission was therefore necessary.

The matter came before us at the third meeting I attended after being appointed. Being a well-run organization, the Commission had sent out the papers in advance. Being a less well-organized appointee, I had failed to read them beforehand.

When we came to item five, 'Proposed new reservoir in the South West', I idly flipped through the binder to find the staff paper.

'Any comments?' Cripps asked. Like his father, he was always brisk and businesslike. 'The recommendation before us is that the Commission should agree to the siting of the reservoir on the Exe at Kemps Farm on Exmoor. Ideally, of course, we'd prefer to have no new reservoirs on Exmoor, but the demand for water in the South West is rising all the time and this seems the least bad alternative.'

Kemps! Still scrabbling through my papers, I held up my hand. Kemps was the farm at the entrance to the Nethercote valley, situated where our long and bumpy drive joins the Winsford–Exford road. A dam across the Exe at Kemps meant that the whole of our valley would be flooded. All three houses – West Nethercote, East Nethercote and Nethercote Cottage – would be under hundreds of feet of water. Much of our land would be flooded as well. Even if compensation was paid, I couldn't imagine my parents welcoming the plans. Their whole life was in the valley. I certainly wasn't in favour. Our house would go too.

I finally found the staff paper and quickly read the recommendation. 'In view of the fact that building a reservoir at the alternative sites, Haddeo and Landacre, will have major environmental and social consequences, it is recommended that the Commission agree to the Kemps site, recognizing that a reservoir in the Nethercote valley will have minimum adverse effects.'

Minimum adverse effects!

'Mr Chairman,' I spluttered, 'I feel I must declare an interest here. I actually have a house in the Nethercote valley and my parents have lived there for over twenty years.'

Cripps knew the rules. 'Do you want to leave the room while we discuss this item?'

I looked around for help. If I left the room, there was every chance that the Commission might approve the staff recommendation. I decided to stay.

Happily Reg Hookway came to my aid. 'Why doesn't the staff take another look at this?' he said in his deep Devon burr. 'We're not in a hurry. We can come back to it later.'

In due course, after further intensive consideration and consultation, the staff came up with a different recommendation, namely that the dam should be built in the Haddeo valley, not on the Exe. Admittedly more than a score of farms would be flooded, but further enquiries had revealed that, since most of the farmers were elderly and compensation would be paid, local opinion was in favour.

I was abroad on IPPF business when the Commissioners approved Haddeo as the site of the new reservoir, so the question of redeclaring my interest didn't arise. When I heard about the outcome I breathed a sigh of relief.

As far as I was concerned the moral of the story was clear. Don't go to a meeting without reading the papers first. I have tried, often unsuccessfully, to live up to this precept ever since.

The Haddeo reservoir was in due course built. Today, you can sail and fish there, though for some reason swimming is not allowed.

There was, I am ready to admit with hindsight, a certain logic in the original staff recommendation for a dam at Kemps. Flooding the Johnsons was certainly a conceivable option since, a couple of years earlier, my father, increasingly troubled by arthritis, had given up active farming. We had had a farm sale in one of the fields at the top of the farm. All the stock, live or dead – sheep and cows, tractors and carts – were auctioned off though my father insisted on keeping his brood mares, Sunshine and Serena.

I was in London at the time of the sale but I brought five-year-old Alexander Boris down to Somerset with me on the train from Paddington. We hired a car at Taunton and drove straight to the auction, coming into our top land from the Staddon side, without going up our long farm drive.

The sheep were sold off in pens, ten or twenty at a time. I can hear the auctioneer, Tom Rook of the Minehead firm James Phillips and Sons, as I write these words.

'Here's a fine pen of Clun crosses,' Tom would shout. 'What am I bid? Who'll give me twenty? Any advance on twenty?'

At one point in the sale, some of our cows escaped from their pen. There was a lot of hollering and shouting as the locals, many of whom had come over on horseback to the sale, galloped off to round them up.

I remember looking over at my father as the auctioneer worked his way through to the final lots: the buck rake, the tedder, the trailer etc. His pipe, unlit, was still clenched firmly in his teeth.

That afternoon my father, barely sixty, was witnessing the destruction of his dreams. All his life he had wanted to be a full-time farmer. When we came to Nethercote in 1951, he had at last achieved that ambition. Now, eighteen years later, he had had to give it up. Yes, he would keep an eye on the horses over the next years; yes, he would keep the place going in a practical sense, repairing what needed to be repaired – the cars, the generators etc. – but in reality we were no longer farming Nethercote.

With all the stock gone, we had let the grass to a neighbouring farmer, Fred Hayes. Fred Hayes and his wife, Rita, were good friends of my parents, Fred in particular being – like my father – a regular patron of the local pubs. The Hayes were traditional Exmoor farmers, with four sons following in the footsteps of their parents to make their careers, indeed their whole lives, on the land.

The arrangements my father put in place when we sold the stock in 1969 have endured to this day. We have a yearly grazing agreement with no guarantee of renewal on either side. But in practice it works.

Today, for example, I am in the process of negotiating an agreement with DEFRA to conserve the rare high brown fritillary butterfly on some of our south-facing rough ground above the Exe. The Hayes' cattle will be needed to trample the bracken on our 'brakes' so as to give the violets, the only food the larva of this particular butterfly will eat, a better chance of survival.

Mike Hayes, Fred and Rita's second son who keeps a special eye on Nethercote, is deeply intrigued by this new venture.

'Let's hope the butterflies come back,' he told me recently when I was explaining the DEFRA scheme. 'That'll be something, won't it?'

Exmoor farmers are nothing if not adaptable. The Hayes family certainly understands the new priorities. My father would have too. In his heart he always preferred animals to people and I'm sure he would have rated the survival of a rare butterfly at Nethercote very highly indeed.

Over the last thirty years, our valley has become a veritable treasure house of wildlife. Apart from the butterflies, actual or potential, we have loads of dormice (also on Britain's endangered species list), barn owls, heron, kingfishers, woodpeckers, buzzards and kestrels galore, not to speak of red deer, foxes, badgers and bats.

The bats, by the way, enjoy being inside the house as well as in the barns. Sometimes, our au pairs would complain about being disturbed with bats flying around in their bedrooms at night and even being tangled in their hair.

Once I sought my mother's advice. 'Tell them to put a saucepan on their head when they go to bed!'

There may even be otters on the river. They seem to be coming back on Exmoor.

If you go out into the yard at night you can hear the owls calling and, if the weather is clear, you can see the stars, Exmoor being one of the regions of the country least affected by light pollution.

My father once told Jenny (whom I married in 1981 after Charlotte and I were divorced) that the day we held the farm sale was the 'saddest day of his life'. I can understand that. I remember seeing him, looking blankly out over the penned sheep (he knew so many of them individually, some even by name), as Tom Rook auctioned them off. There was real anguish there.

My father had four children. As a matter of choice or circumstance, none of us was in a position to run the farm in the sense of undertaking the hard, tough grind of the farming year: lambing, shearing, haymaking, docking, dipping or whatever. If one of us had stepped forward into the breach, there would have been no need for the farm sale.

That afternoon, when the last lot had been sold, I looked at my watch.

'I had better head back to Taunton,' I said. 'If I get a move on, I can probably catch the 5.05.'

My father took the pipe from his mouth. He had barely spoken all day.

'Of course, old boy. Go ahead. Thanks for coming down.'

He patted five-year-old Alexander Boris on the head and turned away.

I still regret that we didn't stay on that evening for supper at the farm. We could have caught a later train. I could have been around when I was needed. But it is too late now for second thoughts.

What I recognize today about my father is not so much what he said, but what he did. He didn't want to live in a town, and certainly not in a city. He wanted to live in the depths of the country, preferably at the end of a very long drive, bumpy enough to deter visitors. And that is precisely what he achieved. Sometimes, I would be upstairs in my room, swotting away at Homer or Virgil, and I would hear the tractor rumble into the yard. Usually, this meant that there was some chore to be attended to, often involving manure of one kind or another. There were times when I pretended to myself I hadn't heard him arrive. I knew he wouldn't shout up the stairs to ask for help.

TWENTY-SEVEN

If It's Tuesday, It Must Be Belgium

One of the hazards of working in or around the United Nations for any length of time is the inordinate number of documents you accumulate. My small office at IPPF simply wasn't big enough for the piles of paper as well as my bicycle and me, so I had taken to storing all the superannuated material in the attic of our house in Princess Road, NW1.

One Saturday morning in September 1972, with the Stockholm Conference now a matter of history, if not legend, I decided to have a massive clear-out. I went up to the attic with a roll of black bin liners and filled sack after sack with documents. The attic had a roof hatch, so I pushed each sack as I filled it over the low parapet into the street below, listening out for a satisfying thump as it landed.

In theory, this was a sound time-and-energy-saving scheme, though marginally hazardous to the public. In practice, it was anything but. Though the first filled bin liner fell on the pavement, as planned, the second landed on top of a manhole cover in the street and cracked it from stem to stern. The bag and its contents continued on a downward trajectory, ending up in the cavity six feet below.

At the time I knew nothing of this. I blithely continued the evacuation of the attic, tossing at least half a dozen weighty sacks off the roof. Job done, I went down onto the pavement ready for the tidying up phase of the operation.

To my surprise, there was virtually no rubbish to be seen. By some unerring instinct, almost all the bags of UN documents, IPPF reports etc. had found their way into the underground bunker.

Most of the bags had broken apart on impact so I spent the next hour fishing out the papers by hand. I was about to emerge from the hole in the pavement with the last batch of documents clasped to my chest, when I heard a pleasant female voice calling down at me.

'Oh, hello, can I help you?'

I clambered out. 'No, actually I've finished. But thanks for asking.'

The voice belonged to Daphne Clutterbuck. An elegant, well-dressed woman, she stood there beside me, obviously wanting to continue the conversation.

'I do like your house.' She gestured towards our front door. 'I've always wanted to live in a neat, modern house like this one.'

'You can have it, if you like,' I replied. I was in that kind of mood. Also, as I have already explained, I am the sort of person who likes to say 'yes' rather than 'no'. Dionysian rather than Apollonian. Or is it the other way round?

Daphne was enthusiastic. She clapped her hands. 'May I really? How lovely!'

She thought for a moment. 'Would you like our house in exchange?'

Less than two months later, Charlotte and I moved into the Clutterbucks' house and they moved into ours. We didn't have far to go. The Clutterbucks lived in the heart of Primrose Hill village, less than five hundred yards away.

It would be wrong to say that money didn't change hands. It did. The Clutterbucks' residence was definitely a notch up from ours. By a stroke of the good luck that has dogged me all my life, soon after the house swap was agreed, I found a cheque for $10,000 in the mail from the Rockefeller Foundation. There was a covering note. It said: 'With the compliments of John D. Rockefeller III for your further work on vitally important world issues.'

By a coincidence, Daphne Clutterbuck arrived just as I was opening the letter. She wanted to discuss which items of furniture she should leave behind. I endorsed the cheque over to her on the spot. There were many ways of continuing further good work on vitally important world issues. Getting the domestic situation straight was a good start. I felt sure Mr Rockefeller would understand.

One of the advantages of moving into 174 Regent's Park Road was that we would have much more room. As far as the Johnsons were concerned, space was at a premium. Just before Christmas the previous year, Charlotte had given birth to our fourth child – Joseph. Jo was now approaching his first birthday. It was time he had a room of his own. The Clutterbucks' house had rooms for everyone – and to spare. What's more, it had a garden both front and back. What more could a growing family want?

We settled into the new house, then went down to Nethercote for Christmas. Soon after the New Year, I was back in my office.

I have to say that, thrilled as I was in all other respects, Jo's arrival presented me with a personal and even professional dilemma. I have already indicated that I had felt a certain uneasiness as the Johnson family continued its remorseless expansion. I couldn't help feeling that, for a man whose career had so far been largely spent in trying to persuade other people not to have children, having four of my own in quick succession was possibly overdoing it.

Charlotte, concentrating on getting the new house in order, was not tremendously sympathetic.

'Why don't you get a different job?' she asked.

'What kind of a job?'

'That's up to you.'

I was sitting in my office a few days later, mulling matters over in my mind – what kind of a job and where? – when, providentially, the telephone rang.

'This is the Civil Service Commission. Am I speaking to Mr Johnson?'

'You are indeed.'

'Are you aware, Mr Johnson, that a few days ago the United Kingdom joined the EEC, the European Economic Community?'

I was slightly miffed. I had worked with the Conservative Party in the run-up to the 1970 election. Though I had been concentrating on environmental matters, I was well aware of Mr Heath's firm commitment to take Britain into Europe with, *bien entendu*, the 'wholehearted consent of the British people'.

'Of course I know we've joined the EEC,' I said.

'In that case,' the voice went on, 'I must ask you whether you're ready to let your name go forward as a British candidate for a senior position in the European Commission in Brussels.'

Later that afternoon, after I had bought a smart pair of trousers at Simpson's in Piccadilly, I had a meeting with a Mr Kirkness (the man behind the voice) in the Civil Service Commission's offices in Savile Row.

'Basically,' Kirkness explained, 'we think Hannay has been able to plant a British flag on an important new post in Brussels.'

'Hannay?' I queried. I remembered the hero of John Buchan's *The Thirty-Nine Steps* had been called Richard Hannay. Had he miraculously resurfaced? Planting flags on perilous mountain summits was right up his street.

'David Hannay is Sir Christopher Soames' right-hand man, his *chef de cabinet* as they call it. Soames, of course, is one of the two new British Commissioners.'

'What's the job?' I asked.

'It's one of the posts dealing with environmental policy. The environment, as you can imagine after the Stockholm Conference, is a new priority area for the EEC. The Commission will have a special directorate to deal with environment and consumer protection. Within that directorate, there'll be a Quality of Life Division, a Pollution Division and a Consumer Protection Division. That means there'll be three Head of Division posts. At least one of those posts will be British. We think Hannay has managed to bag Quality of Life for a British candidate.'

'Quality of Life sounds right up my street,' I said. 'I'm very keen on the quality of life. How did my name come up?'

'You've just written a book called *The Politics of Environment*, haven't you?' Kirkness said. 'We keep an eye on these things, you know.'

I was sceptical. It was true that *The Politics of Environment* had been published a few weeks earlier (by Tom Stacey). It was subtitled: *The British Experience*. I had tried to cover recent developments, leading up to the creation of the Department of the Environment and including an eyewitness report of the UN Environment Conference, though I left out the unfortunate Fred Sai speech episode. Two hundred and forty pages long, the book had been handled with great efficiency by the publisher in an era when word processing was not even a distant dream.

The Politics of Environment had been well reviewed by Tony Aldous in *The Times* and by Christopher Tugendhat (later European Commissioner) for the *Financial Times*. But I didn't think that just one book could be the reason for my sudden emergence as a fancied runner in the EEC stakes.

'Lots of people nowadays write books about the environment,' I said.

'Actually,' Kirkness continued, 'UKREP put your name forward. Among others, I should add. You won't be the only candidate. Even though we believe the post will go to a Brit, the Commission wants to make up its own mind. So we'll give them a choice of two British candidates or possibly three.'

UKREP, it turned out, signified the United Kingdom's permanent mission to the EEC, then headed by Sir Michael Palliser. After further probing, I discovered that my old friend from Sherborne, John Weston, who had joined the Foreign Office after leaving Oxford and was currently assigned to UKREP, had been the prime mover in suggesting me as a possible candidate.

I made a mental note to buy John a splendid dinner in Brussels' finest restaurant if I got the job. This was the second time he had come through with the goods. (The first occasion, as I've already described, was when he lent me his Logic notes at Oxford.)

Of course, John hadn't been able to fix my appointment all on his own. My name had gone on up the line. Ewen Fergusson, the former Scottish rugby international, who was UKREP's Head of Chancery, had – crucially – endorsed the idea. When I met Ewen in Brussels a few weeks later, I was thoroughly daunted. Apart from having a razor-sharp mind, he was physically enormous. If you made the mistake of saying 'hello' to him in a genial way, he would put a giant arm round your waist and literally lift you off your feet high into the air (and even then I was no mean weight). Once, when my second son Leo was about six years old and we were all out at some 'maatjes' (raw herring) party in the Belgian countryside, Ewen picked him up, hoisted him to the sky and then dropped him into a bed of nettles. Leo didn't seem to mind.

I reported back to Charlotte that evening on the conversation I had had with Mr Kirkness of the Civil Service Commission. She was in the middle of a minor domestic crisis, our daughter Rachel having inhaled a piece of eggshell that had, as a result, lodged in her lung.

'If I get the job,' I said, 'I'm afraid it will mean moving house again. I know we've only been here a few weeks. It will mean moving *coun-*

tries, actually. We'll have to live in Belgium. On the other hand, I won't have anyone ribbing me about being a family planning expert with four children.'

As I remember, Rachel exploded into another fit of coughing at this point. I wouldn't say I got the green light from Charlotte. More like amber.

Taking silence for assent (often the best principle) I decided I had better let my name go forward anyway. By then it seemed to have a life of its own. It was jumping up and down, raring to go. It would have taken a bolder man than I am to stop it.

There was a minor blip before things were nailed down. It turned out that David Hannay (now Lord Hannay of Chiswick, a 'people's peer') had actually planted a British flag not on the coveted Quality of Life post but on the Prevention of Pollution post instead.

While I was probably fairly well suited for the Quality of Life post (what classicist isn't?), the job specifications for the anti-pollution post, as indicated by the European Commission, were for someone with a 'strong scientific background'. This was understandable given that, in the fight against pollution, knowledge of chemistry, biology, zoology, not to speak of meteorology, forestry and marine issues, is undoubtedly useful, if not essential.

Clive Gibson, who worked for David Hannay in Soames' cabinet, explained the situation to me one day in the middle of January 1973 when I was making a rapid reconnaissance mission to Brussels. It wasn't my first visit to Belgium, but it was my first visit to the Berlaymont. That huge starfish-shaped glass building next to the Rond-Point Schuman in Brussels has turned out to be the forerunner of the veritable tsunami of architectural devastation inflicted by the EU institutions on a once delightful city.

Clive, an immensely rich young man who soon retired to his ancestral estates, smoked a huge cigar and had his feet on the desk.

'As you may know, there's been a bit of a mix-up and we've ended up with the wrong job. So I hope your science is up to snuff. As I understand it, they're looking for a real boffin.'

'Well, I got Maths O level. Just.' I said. 'And I've written an article for the *New Scientist* about the destruction of the rainforest in the Amazon.'

'Splendid,' Clive enthused. 'Always knew you were the right man for the job.'

Clive Gibson continued by advising me to get my skates on. 'You have to go after these jobs in the Commission, otherwise you can find someone else has got them. Or else they're not there after all. Go and see Carpentier. He's going to be the head of the new Environment and Consumer Protection Service. As Division Chief, you'll be reporting to him.'

Michel Carpentier, a Frenchman, who had been working in the Commission's Industry Department before being picked for his new job as environmental and consumer affairs supremo, was in Paris when I caught up with him. He was attending the OECD's Environment Committee in the OECD headquarters in the Château de la Muette, not far from the Arc de Triomphe. We had a rapid exchange in the margin of the meeting.

Carpentier spoke perfect English but I chipped in with some French from time to time. My French was definitely better than my maths. After all, my mother was half-French and even though we didn't speak the language at home much, I felt comfortable with it. I would always put France top of my list of favourite countries.

I liked and admired Michel Carpentier at first sight. A man of explosive energy and dogged determination, he had thick, brown hair, worn *en brosse*, a marvellous sense of humour and the instincts of a street fighter. He was exactly the right person to lead the fledgling environment and consumer affairs directorate. Other departments in the Commission would be only too keen to reduce it to impotence. It was Carpentier's job, by fair means or foul, to make sure that didn't happen.

The interview, such as it was, must have gone well. A few weeks later, I heard formally from the Commission that I had been appointed to the new post. My full title was Head of the Division for the Prevention of Pollution and Nuisances. The grade was A3, one below the director level (A2) and two below the director-general level (A1).

Taking up my position at the beginning of April 1973, just a few weeks after Britain's accession to the EEC, I would be very much in the vanguard of the advancing troops.

'But where will the children go to school?' Charlotte asked. Alexander Boris, Rachel and Leo were still attending the primary school in

Princess Road, next door to the house we used to live in. (Thirty-five years later, when Alexander Boris ran successfully for the post of London's Mayor, he was able to recall his time at a state primary school in the Borough of Camden.)

'They can go to the European School and grow into good little Europeans,' I told Charlotte.

Bliss was it in that dawn to be alive!

TWENTY-EIGHT

A Safari and a Lost Briefcase

Charlotte and I rented a house in Uccle, one of Brussels' leafy suburbs. My Elswick Hopper had made the cross-Channel journey with us. On a fine day, it was a great joy to be able to cycle to work through the wide tree-lined avenues of the Forêt de Soignes.

The Prevention of Pollution and Nuisances Division, of which I was now in charge, was already more or less up to strength. Most of my team had, as I had not, a strong scientific background. Some had even been transferred from the Commission's own scientific research centre at Ispra in Italy.

Though 'head of division', I was easily the youngest member in the team but the others didn't seem to hold that against me. Vladimir Mandl, an Italian, dealt with water pollution. Peter Stief-Tauch, a German, looked after the air. Goffredo del Bino, another Italian, handled chemicals. Jean-Marie Junger, a Frenchman, was in charge of noise. Pierre Bonnet, also French, dealt with various highly polluting industrial sectors, such as the titanium-dioxide industry.

Pierre was infinitely patient. It was clear I knew nothing about titanium dioxide. One day, after I had been in Brussels a few weeks, we had lunch at an Italian restaurant in the nearby rue Archimède and, as we ate our *melanzana alla parmigiana*, he drew the structure of the titanium-dioxide molecule for me on the paper tablecloth.

In those days lunch was a serious affair. You left your office around a quarter to one and didn't return till after three. No afternoon meeting ever began before 3.15 (the *quart d'heure diplomatique* being very much *de rigueur*).

As we lingered over our wine, Pierre asked me how I was enjoying things. My staff, he told me, had formed a favourable impression of me.

'How very kind, Pierre,' I said. '*Très aimable!*'

French in those days was still the common language in the European Commission (and anyway Pierre Bonnet wasn't much good at English) so I told him, in French, that I in turn had formed a favourable impression of the members of my division.

'There's just one problem,' I added. 'I've not yet had the chance to meet Benno Risch. I go along to his office down the corridor but he doesn't ever seem to be there. He doesn't answer the telephone either.'

Risch, a German, was meant to be dealing with the problems of waste.

'Ah, Benno!' Pierre poured himself another glass of wine. '*Il faut lui téléphoner à la maison.*'

Later that day, I dialled Benno Risch's home telephone number. A female voice answered in German.

My German is fairly primitive. I never learned the language in any formal sense but since I had been skiing a couple of times in Austria when I was at Oxford, I was ready to give it a go. I remembered German was like Latin in that you had to put the verb at the end of the sentence.

'*Kan ich bitte mit Herr Risch sprechen?*' I began

'*Mein Mann ist in der Bad,*' the voice replied.

I realized I was talking to Mrs Risch, who was telling me that her husband ('mein Mann') was in the bath.

I thought 3.30 in the afternoon was an odd time to be in the bath when Mr Risch ought to have been in the office, but I let it pass.

'*Venn dein Mann ist auf dem Bad gekommt,*' I proceeded, '*bitte gesagt ihr nach Herr Johnson telefonieren.*'

'*Herr Johnson?*'

The German version of my new EEC business card used the word 'abteilungsleiter' as a description of my functions as 'division chief' or, in French, 'chef de division'. President Kennedy had famously said 'Ich bin ein Berliner'. So now I told Frau Risch: '*Ich bin ein Abteilungsleiter von Herr Risch.*' To make assurance doubly sure, I added: '*Ein Abteilungsleiterführer!*'

I thought adding on the word 'führer' might help, but I'm not sure it did. Several days passed. Risch still didn't appear in the office during working hours, although, according to reports, he sometimes put in an appearance in the middle of the night.

I tried once again to reach him at home. Once again, I found myself talking to Frau Risch.

She was very polite. '*Enschuldegmich. Mein Mann ist immer in der Bad.*'

I was flummoxed. Risch was apparently always ('immer') in the bath.

It was some time before I discovered the true situation. Benno Risch was indeed in the bath whenever I called. But when Frau Risch spoke of the bath, she was actually referring to the 'swimming bath' – *das Schwimmbad*! It turned out that Benno, being a versatile man, was actually building himself a swimming pool in his garden. This project had already taken several weeks and was likely to last much longer.

Silly me, I thought. I should have known. A well-trained *fonction-naire* has a clear sense of priorities.

A few months later, when his pool was finally finished, Benno Risch started coming to the office quite often in daylight hours, though he also maintained his predilection for nocturnal visits.

Early in 1975, Granada TV came to Brussels to make a programme about the European Commission at work and for some reason my division was chosen as the guinea pig. The Granada team was a high-powered affair. It included Roger Graef, Norma Percy, Brian and Anne Lapping – all of whom have gone on to fame and fortune in the world of television. They not only filmed in my office as we drafted the first 'directive on the disposal of waste'. They even managed to gain unprecedented access to the official working groups of the Council, as the directive was being discussed prior to adoption.

I had a chance to view the Granada film again recently and to realize that Benno Risch, notwithstanding his heavy commitments elsewhere, actually managed to put in fairly regular appearances when the cameras were rolling.

At one stage, about an hour into the film (it is almost two hours long), the camera shows Benno and me sitting together at the Commission's end of the long Council table, as we try to defend the directive in the Council's Environment Working Group.

Ireland held the rotating EEC Presidency at the time, so an Irish-man, Brendan Tighe, was in the chair.

'What is "waste"?' Brendan asks, sounding like Pontius Pilate asking 'What is truth?' 'Could the Commission please enlighten us?'

Confronted with this direct challenge, Benno and I confer. When we first drafted the text, we couldn't agree on a definition so we decided not to have one. (The film has already shown that crucial omission in its first twenty minutes, shot in my office in the Commission.)

'Waste is anything anyone wants to get rid of,' I say feebly.

'It doesn't sound very precise,' Brendan Tighe comments.

Then Benno Risch takes the microphone from me and speaks for a long time in German. There are no subtitles at this point but he is obviously quite convincing because the discussion soon moves onto the next point.

In retrospect, I think I misunderestimated Benno Risch, as President George W. Bush puts it. *Entschuldigen Sie!* Benno clearly won the point for the Commission that day, though it may have been a Pyrrhic victory. EU waste directives ever since have lacked a proper definition of waste and much confusion has resulted.

The Granada film was finally shown in Britain on the eve of the national referendum on 5 June, 1975 on the United Kingdom's continued membership of the EEC. The outcome of that vote was positive, by a margin of almost two to one. Did the Granada film influence the result in any way? Would there have been an even bigger swing in favour of Europe if the British electorate had not been exposed at the last minute to the raw entrails of the Brussels bureaucracy? There is no way of knowing.

What I do know is that most of Brussels was delighted that Prime Minister Harold Wilson's deft footwork had paid off and British membership of the EEC seemed now secure.

Was *I* delighted? Yes, of course I was. I had come to Brussels first and foremost as an environmentalist. After two years in my job, I had come to understand and appreciate the tremendous scope you had as an administrator to actually get things done. The Commission in those days was an astonishing place to work. In my field at least, you could wake up in the morning, go to the office, call a meeting, work on a text, run it through some desultory inter-service consultation, and within weeks discover that you had an agreed draft of a legal instrument (usually a 'directive', but sometimes the even more stringent 'regulation') which could be then sent to the Council for adoption.

Of course, in the Council, things could be tough, as the member states hacked away at the proposal. But still there was every chance that, less than a year after you had first thought of the idea, the Council would have adopted it in more or less its original form. Thereafter, the member states would be bound to translate the directive into their own national laws and if they didn't you could haul them before the European Court of Justice.

The whole thing basically was mind-blowing. It wasn't just the process that was staggering. It was the sheer volume of legislation that the process gave rise to. In 1976, Graham & Trotman published a one-hundred-page book I had written called *The Pollution Control Policy of the European Communities*. This detailed the laws we had rammed through in the previous three years. In 1978, they published a second edition of the book, now 150 pages long. Ten years later, the Dutch publishing house Kluwer took over Graham & Trotman and it published a new and expanded version of the book which I had prepared with a Commission colleague, Guy Corcelle. That book, now entitled *The Environmental Policy of the European Communities*, ran to three hundred pages. In 1995, Kluwer published a second edition, now well over four hundred pages long.

From time to time, the people at Kluwer write to Guy Corcelle and me asking whether we are going to produce yet another edition of our work. Given the volume of environmental texts that have continued to emanate from Brussels, it is hard to see how we could do so within a manageable compass, even if we had the time and energy.

In my personal prefaces to the volumes mentioned above, I paid tribute to the brilliance and tenacity of Michel Carpentier, the Director of the Commission's Environment and Consumer Protection Service. Without his vigour, determination and tough, aggressive intellect, we would never have made the progress we did in those halcyon years of the seventies.

When I returned to Brussels in 1984, after a stint in the European Parliament which I will come to in a moment, I had the good fortune to work as a senior adviser to Laurens Jan Brinkhorst, the Commission's new Director-General for the Environment. (Jenny and I have remained good friends ever since with both Laurens Jan and his wife, Jantien.) Laurens Jan had been a Minister in the Dutch Government before he came to Brussels, and when he left the Commission he was elected to the European Parliament before once again turning to national politics and joining the Dutch Cabinet for several protracted stints, including one as Agriculture Minister at a time when the Netherlands was in the throes of a foot-and-mouth epidemic, a crisis which he handled with notable calm and skill.

When I think back on the evolution of EU environmental policy, I am constantly struck by how much it owes to the dedication of brilliant men like Carpentier and Brinkhorst and, of course, to some notably able and committed EU Environment Commissioners, like the Italian Carlo Ripa di Meana and the United Kingdom's Stanley (now Lord) Clinton-Davis.

Would the member states, without the push from the Brussels Commission, have ever adopted such a mass of environmental legislation covering as it did a whole range of subjects – air, noise, water, chemicals, waste, nature protection etc? No, in my view, they certainly wouldn't have. Though individual countries might have developed their own legislation, it would never have been as coherent and as comprehensive as that adopted at the European level. And, by definition, purely national legislation would not have been continent-wide.

And yet, and yet. It is only after I left Brussels in the nineties and returned to England that I began to ask myself whether the price paid for putting all this legislation on the statute book via Brussels (admirable though most of it might be) was not after all too high.

It boils down basically to the question of democracy. The European Commission was not then, and is not now, in any sense a democratically elected body. Yet, as I have tried to show, it has tremendous power. Take the right of initiative. Under EU law, only the Commission has the right to make a legislative proposal. Unless the Commission puts forward a text, the Council is powerless.

When the Commission does put forward a text, the Council may not ignore it. The EU legislative process is like a relentless sausage machine. Drafts go in one end and fully fledged EU laws come out the other.

As an environmentalist, as I say, I applauded. That is why I went to Brussels in the first place. As a democrat, by the time my first stint in Brussels was over (May 1979), I think I was beginning to have my doubts about the whole thing.

Those doubts, I hasten to add, were not in any way cosmic. Almost all the legislation we proposed in those days under the EEC environment programme had to be adopted unanimously by the Council. I could say to myself, if a member state really doesn't like some draft law, it can veto it and the law won't be adopted. If a national parliament wants to be sure the veto is applied, it can mandate ministers as they go to Brussels.

The Danes, I noted, did precisely that. You could be sitting in a Council meeting with the Council on the point of adopting some environmental measure relating to, say, water quality when suddenly the Danish Minister would raise his hand and gloomily tell the gathering that unfortunately Denmark couldn't agree because the Danish Parliament hadn't yet given its approval.

To a *fonctionnaire*, eager to hang yet another legislative scalp from one's belt, this Danish insistence on observing democratic procedures could be totally infuriating. Looking back, I think we should all have been grateful to the Danes for insisting on the formalities.

By the 1980s, of course, the situation had changed. Environmental measures, like most other EU legislation, were increasingly being adopted by qualified majority vote (QMV) which meant that the opposition of a single member state, or even several of them, could no longer hold up the adoption of a measure.

I never thought I would look back at the days of the national veto as a golden age, but I think I do now.

I don't want to give the impression that my professional life in Brussels in those days was entirely spent in meetings. It certainly wasn't. In my day, at least, the European Commission was a very civilized place to work.

I remember arranging to play squash at lunch time at the Castle Club, Wezembeek, during my first full week at work. Since no one ever expected you back in the office before three, my partner, a Belgian called Léon, and I called it a day around 2.30. I had a shower and was changing in the locker room in a leisurely fashion before returning to my office, when I noticed that Léon was throwing on his clothes in a tremendous hurry.

I was impressed. 'Rushing back to work, then, Léon?' I ribbed. 'It's good to know that even *fonctionnaires* of long standing are still highly motivated!'

'*Surtout pas!*' Léon protested. 'My wife's got lunch waiting for me at home.'

I soon learned that going home for lunch was the norm rather than the exception. In those days in Brussels there were four rather than two rush hours. The amazing thing was that, even if you lived several miles out, as we did, you could still get home in less than fifteen minutes.

As international civil servants we were constantly on the move, not just between our homes and the office, but outside Brussels, and indeed outside Belgium. You were constantly visiting the EU member states to discuss problems they might have with a particular Commission proposal. If you didn't want your text to be blocked in the Council, the best course of action was to try to sort things out on a bilateral basis. And since the Presidency of the Council changed every six months, there were more formal visits to be paid to discuss the priorities of the incoming team. Realistically, six months is not long for radical changes of emphasis to be imposed but a country taking up the reins still has a chance to push its favourite pieces of draft legislation in the hope that they will actually be adopted during its term of office.

And, of course, we didn't just travel in Europe. With the United States (in those days at least) being such a major player in world environmental policy, we travelled to Washington for regular meetings with the United States Environmental Protection Agency (EPA).

We also went, with increasing regularity, to Nairobi, where the United Nations Environment Programme (the establishment of which had been one of the main outcomes of the Stockholm Conference) was now based. Mustafa Tolba had succeeded Maurice Strong, UNEP's first Executive Director, in 1976. Tolba stayed at the helm until 1994, building effectively on Maurice's legacy while giving UNEP its own shape and style.

It fell to me, on two or three occasions during my first stint in Brussels, to represent the Commission at meetings of UNEP's Governing Council in Nairobi. For the 1976 meeting of the Governing Council, I decided to combine work and pleasure. My old friend Adrian Phillips was now working for UNEP. He and his wife, Cassandra (Sandy), had children the same age as Alexander Boris and Rachel. We agreed that, once the UNEP meeting was over, we would embark on a major safari, driving from Nairobi through the Masai Mara into Tanzania, then continuing through the Serengeti to Ngorongoro, before returning via Lake Manyara to Kenya.

Alexander Boris and Rachel were doing well at the European School in Uccle and there didn't seem to be any problem about removing them for a couple of weeks. But Leo, still less than nine years old, was desperately disappointed to be excluded. I warned him a lion might eat him, but the prospect didn't seem to deter him.

'You and Jo must look after Mama,' I told Leo. 'She needs you.'

Charlotte and I bought Leo a transistor radio by way of compensation, but still we felt bad about it. There was, of course, no question of my taking Jo, who was still a tiny toddler.

On the morning of our departure to Nairobi, I caught sight of Leo's face as we were putting our suitcases in the car. It was too much to bear. I rang the European School. I rang Lufthansa.

There was no time to get Leo any shots or even any safari clothes. My photo album shows that he spent most of the time in his pyjamas.

I was hustling my now augmented little party into the car when Leo said: 'Hold on, Dada, I need to fetch something.'

He ran up the steps into the house and came back with the transistor radio in his hand.

'Please take it back,' he said. 'I shouldn't have it. Not now that I'm coming with you after all.'

Charlotte and I could have cried. As a matter of fact, to quote President George W. Bush once again, I think we may have 'teared up somewhat'.

We had a wonderful two weeks on safari with Adrian and Sandy Phillips and their children, Oliver and Barnaby. Adrian had his own vehicle. I hired a Land Rover in Nairobi. We had tents, cooking equipment, food, water, mosquito repellent, even a folding table to have our meals on. Over the years I have been on safari many times but that first extended trip through the Mara and Serengeti was certainly one of the most enjoyable. Elephant, lion, giraffe, buffalo, cheetah, hyena – we saw them all.

Day after day we gazed on herds of wildebeest and hartebeest that seemed to stretch across the plains as far as the eye could see. We had a competition for the best 'gnu' joke of the safari ('Gnu York! BBC Gnus …!'). I can't remember who won.

Of course, like all trips, ours had its bad moments. The worst, as far as I was concerned, came the evening when I discovered I had managed to lose my briefcase containing my cameras, passports, tickets and money.

We had crossed into Tanzania from Kenya to make the long drive from Seronera to Ngorongoro, reaching the lip of the famous crater as night fell. I was unpacking the Land Rover when I noticed the briefcase was missing. It simply wasn't there. I was sure I had piled it into the back of the vehicle when we left our campsite at Seronera but now it was nowhere to be seen.

Next morning, the Phillips kindly looked after my three children while I took the Land Rover to drive back along the road we had come on. Adrian was sceptical.

'You haven't a hope in hell of finding it,' he said reassuringly.

'I'll have to try.' I just couldn't face the idea of returning to Nairobi *sans* tickets, money and passports. I wasn't even sure the Kenyans would let us back into their country.

I had been driving back along the dusty road for a couple of hours when I saw a signpost: 'Olduvai Gorge 18 kilometres'.

Olduvai! The name rang a bell. This was the place where, famously, Dr Louis Leakey and his wife had discovered what were then the earliest remains of the human family. *Homo habilis*, as I recall.

As I slowed, I noticed that a paper had been attached to the sign. I stopped, got out and examined the notice. To my amazement, the message read: 'Found one briefcase. Apply Dr Mary Leakey, Olduvai'.

It took me less than half an hour to reach the Leakey Camp at Olduvai. As I drove down the escarpment into the gorge, I could see a figure coming out of a hut towards the entrance of the boma, the circle of dried-up thorn bushes that surrounded the place.

It was Dr Mary Leakey. Drawing nearer, I could see she had something in her hand. It was my briefcase. Somehow it must have bounced out of the Land Rover along the way and, by a stroke of luck, the world's most eminent palaeontologist had found it.

As I got out of the car, Mary Leakey smiled. 'Stanley, I presume?' She handed me the briefcase. 'I found your passport inside so I knew your name.'

I have seldom felt more relieved.

'Have you got time for a cup of tea?' Mary Leakey asked.

Had I ever!

The Leakey parents have now passed on but the Leakey children carry on the good work. From time to time I meet Richard Leakey, one of the sons, now a world-renowned environmentalist. Richard lost both legs in a plane crash in Kenya but remains as ebullient as ever, driving himself on when others would have sought a comfortable retirement. Whenever and wherever I see him, I can't help remembering how – back in 1976 – his mother saved my bacon.

Stanley, I presume? I can still see the twinkle in the old lady's eye.

TWENTY-NINE

'LONG LIVE ETERNAL FRIENDSHIP!'

Towards the end of July 1975 I finally had an opportunity to visit China. As I have already described, in September 1961, almost fourteen years earlier, Michael de Larrabeiti and I had come tantalizing close to the Chinese border, as we pushed north on our BSA motorcycle from Kabul in Afghanistan, following Marco Polo's route towards the Wakkan Corridor, a narrow tongue of land running through the High Pamir mountains.

But that project failed to reach its destination. China remained a closed book to me – and indeed to most of the rest of the world. In 1975, though Mao – the self-styled 'Great Helmsman' – was still nominally in charge, he was a sick man. The Gang of Four ran the show, creating chaos and mayhem on a grand scale.

Of course, there were some straws in the wind, presaging the end of China's isolation. President Nixon's visit to Beijing took place in February 1972, following several reconnaissance missions by Dr Henry Kissinger. Though no one doubted the truly historic nature of the encounter between Nixon and Chairman Mao, the visit had its banal moments. For example, as he visited the Great Wall of China, Nixon solemnly proclaimed: 'I think you would have to conclude that this is a great wall and that it was built by a great people.' Britain's Prime Minister Edward Heath had visited China in 1974 and returned with two giant pandas, called Ching-Ching and Chia-Chia, which he presented to the London Zoo. A few months later, the European Commission, anxious as ever not to miss a trick, sent Sir Christopher Soames, the Commissioner responsible for the EEC's external relations, with the objective of establishing full diplomatic relations between the EEC and China.

When I heard, a year later, that a group of Commission officials was planning an 'informal' visit to China, I quickly presented my credentials. The trip, I learned from the group's Italian leader, Corrado Pirzio-Biroli, would be an extended affair. After visiting Beijing, we would first go north to Manchuria, then south to Jinan, Nanking, Wusi and Shanghai, before heading for Canton, Hong Kong and home.

Most of the other members of the group came from the Commission's development cooperation department, known then as DG 8. There were around a dozen of us altogether, mainly French, Italian or German.

Thinking about that trip over thirty years later, I am struck by how ready we all were to swallow the pap our Chinese hosts fed us. Nowadays, of course, we have had the benefit of Jung Chang and Jon Halliday's brilliant book on Chairman Mao, the antithesis of a hagiography if ever there was one. Never have the monstrous excesses of a monomaniacal tyrant been so faithfully revealed. Time and again as I read the book a couple of summers ago I found myself literally blushing at the memory of our 1975 visit. We might not have known, back then, all that Jung Chang and Jon Halliday discovered when they were researching their biography, but we had eyes to see and ears to hear. How could we have missed so much?

One of the reasons we bought into the myth so readily was, I suspect, our own vanity. All right, we weren't an official EEC delegation. We were just a group of individuals from the EEC on a private trip. But we knew, right from the start, that our Chinese hosts didn't really see it that way. Wherever we went there were great red and gold banners: 'WELCOME TO HONORABLE EEC DELEGATION!' 'LONG LIVE ETERNAL FRIENDSHIP BETWEEN EEC AND CHINA!'

I don't blame the Chinese for the efforts they made. The interest they expressed at our arrival was understandable. At the time, China's distrust of both the United States and the Soviet Union was profound. The EEC could prove a valuable trading and even political partner. But I do blame *us* for our naïvety.

When I dug out my papers from that trip, as I began to write this memoir, I found no hint that I ever possessed, let alone used, my critical faculties. I reproduce here part of the entry in my diary for Tuesday 29 July 1975, the first day of the Manchurian leg of our journey.

'Shenyang is in Liaoning province. The Ching Emperor made his capital here. It was also the capital of the Japanese puppet government. It is an industrial town, in fact one of the key industrial towns of China. On arrival, by overnight train from Peking, we went straight to the hotel, which is off the main square, facing an enormous red statue of President Mao exhorting the people forward in their glorious tasks. A quick breakfast and, by 8.30, we are on our way to see a machine tool factory.

'There is a sign outside the entrance to the factory painted in big bold two-feet-high Chinese characters which, we are told, says WELCOME TO STAFF MEMBERS OF BELGIAN COMMON MARKET TO OUR FACTORY.

'The factory was built in 1935 under Japanese imperialism in order to squeeze resources out of China. At the time it was run on a small scale with low-level equipment. It was severely damaged during the Kuomintang regime, which also stole and sold the equipment. Then it was liberated and brought within the people's hands.

'Now the factory has 421 teams for the study of the work of Lenin, Marx and Mao. There are 4,000 members in these groups and 1,000 activists to study Marxism, Leninism and to criticise bourgeois ideas. All of the workers are full of confidence that they can fulfil the State Plan and the goal set down in the Fourth People's Congress regarding full modernisation.'

Rereading this, I realize that I must have scribbled down what we were told virtually verbatim. My notes cover 110 (double-spaced) A4 pages and much of it reads like the extracts given above. Our Chinese hosts showed us what they wanted to show us. We lapped it all up and panted for more.

The odd thing is that, though there were certainly some left-wingers in our group who seemed to become positively orgasmic at the thought of visiting yet another factory, yet another commune, most of us were probably ordinary middle-of-the-road products of the consumer society.

Of course, it wasn't all an unrelieved diet of propaganda. On 31 July, for example, we visited the Institute of Traditional Chinese Medicine in Anchang. Our host for the morning was the Vice-President of the Revolutionary Committee of the Institute. My diary records: 'The vice president of the Committee tells us what our visit is for the day. First, we are going to see how teeth can be pulled out without anaesthetic. Next a tonsillitis operation by burning. Finally an operation on a broken leg which will involve acupuncture as an anaesthetic.

'First, we go to see the operation on the teeth. An old man, maybe 60 or 70 years old, sits in the dental chair. We crowded round him and watched as the doctor pushed the man's head back and pressed hard, it seemed on his cheekbones and the side of his mouth. He did this for maybe 30 seconds and then took out a tool and whipped out two teeth from the bottom jaw.

'Ricardo Perissich, who is one of the Italians in our group, says there are two theories. Number One theory is that the number of teeth the man has is inversely proportional to the number of groups visiting the hospital. Theory Number Two is that the rate at which he loses his teeth is directly correlated with the importance of the group visiting the hospital.'

Ricardo went on to have a brilliant career in the European Commission, serving as Director-General for Industry before leaving Brussels to become Pirelli's Vice-President for Public Relations. In the latter capacity, he used to send his friends each year the famous Pirelli calendar with its wholly tasteful photographs of nude female models. Around 1995, the Pirelli calendars stopped dropping through our letterbox. I wondered about this at the time. Maybe Ricardo had left Pirelli; maybe I was no longer on his list; maybe my wife hid the calendar before I could set eyes on it. As Ricardo himself might have said, there were a number of possible theories …

To get back to our visit to the Institute of Traditional Chinese Medicine, my notes continue: 'We also watch an operation to treat tonsillitis using the burning as opposed to the cutting method. There are long instruments with arrow-shaped heads and these are heated in the flames. Children then say "aagh" in their throat and as they say "aagh" the doctor puts in the arrow-shaped tool and burns away at the infected tonsil for a few seconds. He treats it point by point. We can see the two children undergoing this treatment and it was apparent to me that they were not suffering in any way.'

It is when we get to the acupuncture ward that things go wrong. My notes record: 'We were then taken up actually to watch an operation, the setting of a fractured leg, using acupuncture as an anaesthetic. The doctor on duty, a tall impressive-looking man, explained: "this worker has fallen, he has a multiple fracture. We use the acupuncture to produce the effect of an anaesthetic. This we achieve by electrically vibrating the needles that are stuck into the area around the wound for about 30 minutes. After this the anaesthesia takes place. We can take out the needles."

'We watch the operation as it is performed. A team of nurses and assistants clusters round the man, manipulating the bone – there is an X-ray pinned up on an illuminated board which shows quite clearly exactly where the multiple fracture is.'

For once things obviously aren't going to plan. I write: 'The man is suffering, there is no doubt about that. His eyes are wide open and he is banging his head on the back of the bed. I couldn't help wondering whether, if it were not for our presence in the room, he would have cried out.'

As we all piled back into our bus, Ricardo Perissich had a theory about this operation too. Ricardo had – and probably still has – an astonishingly subtle mind.

'They knew we were coming, didn't they?' he said. 'They knew they had a leg-resetting operation on the schedule, but maybe there wasn't anyone available with a broken leg that morning. Perhaps they had to go out into the street and actually break someone's leg! Then, to make up for the delay, they decided to cut down on the length of time the needles were in. Hence the man's agony.'

'Oh no, Ricardo! Surely not!' we all chorused, hating to believe our Chinese hosts could be so wicked.

With hindsight, I think Ricardo may have been right.

We worked hard during those few weeks. If the days were full of official visits, the evenings were also packed with entertainments in which the propaganda element was at best thinly disguised.

Here is another extract from my notebook: 'In the evening we go to see another performance by acrobats. This time it is the Shenyang municipal troop who, a year or two ago, apparently toured the United States with great success. It is even better than the performance in Peking. There are the usual scenes with bicycles, chairs, plates and mock lions. As we enter to take our seats two minutes before the curtain there is applause from the audience. They all stand up to clap us and we sit down in one of the best rows a few yards from the front. When it is time for the interval, we are ushered into a special reception room and we sit with tea and cigarettes until it is time to go back in.

'The last item of the programme is a conjuring trick. There is a large Chinese bowl which is empty, and which the audience can clearly see is empty, but all sorts of things sprout and grow in this bowl by magic. Flowers, ducks, aquariums filled with goldfish; there seems absolutely no limit to the contents of the bowl. Nobody knows how the things get into the bowl or how the trick is done. In the end the lid is taken off for the last time and we see a quantity of red material inside. The girl pulls one end and another girl pulls the other end and they run round the stage and the material still pours out of the bowl and finally they stand at either end of the stage and stretch out the huge banner between them and of course it is a revolutionary banner with a revolutionary slogan which incites the people to: "UNITE TO WIN STILL GREATER VICTORY!" So that's the end. Everybody claps – more vigorously than they ever did in Peking – and we all go home.'

We went to the opera too. On 2 August, for example, we were in Jinan, a large city on the Yellow River. We spent the morning visiting a thermos factory and the afternoon at a museum, returned to our hotel for a twenty-minute break, then headed back into the city centre.

I wrote in my diary: 'In the evening we go into town to see a Chinese opera called *The Two Heroic Sisters of the Steppe*. As we get off the bus and walk into the opera building, the people line up on every side and clap us. It takes me back to my school days and running onto the rugger field for the First XV at Sherborne. The whole school had to watch.'

With all the visits to factories, communes, conjuring displays and operas, we still managed to do our share of sightseeing: the Forbidden City and the Temple of Heaven in Beijing, the Ming Tombs and the Great Wall of China, the mausoleum of Sun Yat Sen in Nanking, the canals and lakes of Wusi, the Bund in Shanghai.

I got into trouble in Wusi for jumping off the deck of the boat into the lake while we were going for a cruise. I just felt I needed a swim. That evening our guides, Mr Chen and Mr Chou (they stayed with us throughout), called the group together and, looking at me pointedly, scolded us about the need to have 'a correct revolutionary attitude' at all times.

On 14 August 1975, we left Canton (now Guangzhou) for Hong Kong. It was a two-hour train journey in an air-conditioned coach, blissfully comfortable. Mr Chen and Mr Chou came with us on this last leg too.

As always, the music of the Internationale was piped in an endless loop into our compartment. There was no escaping it, short of wearing earplugs, so we made the most of it, singing lustily along with Chen and Chou as the train passed through the paddy fields of southern China.

> 'Arise ye prisoners of starvation
> Arise ye wretched of the earth
> For justice thunders condemnation
> A better world's in birth ...'

When the chorus came, we all gave it some welly, like the prisoners released from the dungeon in Beethoven's *Fidelio*.

> ''Tis the final conflict
> Let each stand in his place
> The Internationale shall be the human race!'

At the border station, we climbed down out of the train, went through the Chinese border posts, changed all our Chinese money into Hong Kong dollars and had the currency form stamped, gathered our hand luggage together and finally walked a hundred yards or so up the road which ran alongside the railway track to the bridge. At the far end of the bridge the Union Jack hung limply in the soggy air.

Since 1975, I have been back to China on several occasions. The most recent visit was in May 2001 when Jenny and I visited our daughter Julia, then teaching English in Hangchow during her gap year. As China rapidly acquires superpower status, I am glad that I had a chance to see the still slumbering giant. Today, for example, I find it almost impossible to recognize the Beijing I knew thirty-five years ago. The hutongs we wandered around then have been bulldozed to make room for super-highways. Bicycles are giving way to cars. Industrial pollution, which was bad enough in 1975, is probably ten times worse in 2008. If I didn't know what I now know about Mao and his regime, I might almost find myself regretting the old days.

As far as my literary career was concerned, that Chinese jaunt in August 1975 was absolutely crucial. My third novel, published by Macmillan in Britain as *The Urbane Guerrilla* and by Doubleday in the US as *God Bless America*, had not been a blistering success. A review in the *Chattanooga Times* began 'even a semi-literate monkey could have done better than this'. I had been momentarily at least discouraged.

But that China trip changed all that. A week after we returned to Brussels, I started work on another novel. It was more of a skit than anything else, a *jeu d'esprit*. I tentatively called it: 'A Chink in the Armoire'. Nowadays, a publisher would probably be prosecuted under the Race Relations Act if he (or she) produced a book with such a title. As a matter of fact, the author could probably be prosecuted for just coming up with the idea. In practice, matters were never put to the test. I had no sooner finished the book than I put it away in the bottom drawer. I realized it wouldn't do. But the point is: it got me going again.

Twelve months or so later, I had completed a thriller called *The Doomsday Deposit*, where much of the action takes place on the Sino-Soviet border. Toby Eady arranged a large advance from Dutton in New York ($20,000 in those days seemed large to me, at least) and Felicity Bryan, a friend from Washington days who was now a literary agent in London, elicited £5000 from Charles Pick, Heinemann's managing director.

The Doomsday Deposit was an 'alternate' Book of the Month Club choice in America. I was very pleased about this. I felt it was something to write home about.

By coincidence, the other 'alternate choice' that month was Rachel Billington's *A Woman's Age*. Rachel, née Pakenham, one of Frank and Elizabeth Longford's daughters, was – and remains – Charlotte's oldest friend. The Fawcetts and the Longfords both lived in Park Town, Oxford, during the war. Rachel is also Alexander Boris' godmother. As the authors of the 'alternate choices', Rachel B. and I found ourselves promoting our respective works in New York at the same time. Our publishers both gave parties for us. The next day, when I picked up the *New York Times*, I could find no mention of *The Doomsday Deposit*. Instead, I read the neatly alliterative banner headline: 'Last of literary Longfords lionized'.

I knew then that an 'alternate choice' was not really a big deal and that my literary career still had a long way to go.

My letters to my parents, still on the farm on Exmoor, I am ashamed to say, became less frequent than they once had been. Telephoning was not so good. My father did not enjoy talking on the telephone and my mother was increasingly deaf. But I remember one day writing home along the following lines.

'Dear Mummy and Daddy,' I began. 'Charlotte and I and the children are well and enjoying life in Brussels. Alexander and Rachel are both doing well at the European School, so is Leo. Jo is a delight and soon he will go to a nursery school. Charlotte's painting is going extremely well. She has just had an exhibition in a gallery in Brussels. Lots of our friends came and she sold almost all her paintings. Apart from people who work in the Commission, and the journalistic community, we are lucky to have many Belgian friends too. They all came to the Sablon, which is where the gallery is, and had a good time. By the way, my new novel about China, *The Doomsday Deposit*, is an alternate Book Club selection in New York. I do hope you enjoy it, now we've sorted out the problems with the dog!'

I had sent my mother the galleys of the American version of my novel. My mother enjoyed proof reading. I suspect she got a real kick from finding a typo or, better still, a grammatical error. As it turned out, after she had bumped down the Nethercote track in her battered VW Beetle to pick up the parcel I had sent her from Brussels, she really hit the jackpot.

The hero of *The Doomsday Deposit* is a steely American, John McGrath. And McGrath has a dog, a Labrador. That was what got me into trouble.

A few days after I had sent the parcel of proofs to Nethercote, I received a stinging letter.

'I cannot believe that a son of mine,' my mother witheringly began, 'can write about a Golden Labrador! You either have a Yellow Labrador or you have a Golden Retriever!'

Ouch! In those pre-email days, I had to send a full-rate telegram to E. P. Dutton in New York: 'For Golden Labrador please read Yellow Labrador passim'.

The Latin word *passim* – as any competent proof reader should know, I imagined – means 'throughout' or 'wherever and whenever it occurs'. So I thought I had made my meaning abundantly clear.

How wrong I was! When the page proofs arrived, McGrath's dog had acquired a new name: Passim!

I sent another full-rate telegram to New York: 'Please delete Passim *passim*!'

We sorted it out in the end but, as the Duke of Wellington said of the Battle of Waterloo, it was a 'damned near-run thing!'

Even if my mother enjoyed finding howlers, she enjoyed – even more – feeling useful and needed. She always wanted to help. To the end of her life, my mother retained an almost unquenchable optimism, even when, in her declining years, she sometimes had good reason to be despondent. She came out to stay with us several times in Brussels and her visits were always a joy.

My father, I have to say, was always more reserved than my mother. Enthusiasm was not his default mode. But perhaps because his own early life, in Canada and Egypt, had been full of adventures (though he didn't talk much about it), he was quite excited about my efforts to write a decent thriller. He appreciated a good story.

In the mid-seventies Charlotte and I and the family had moved into the big farmhouse – West Nethercote (the house with the Three Kitchens) – and my parents had taken Nethercote Cottage instead. My sister Birdie was in the middle farmhouse, East Nethercote, and worked for the Exmoor National Park in Dulverton. When Charlotte and I drove from Belgium to England with the children for the school holidays, my parents as well as my sister frequently came over for a meal.

I remember my father saying one day at supper: 'Maybe they'll make a film of one of your books, Stan, like Ian Fleming and James Bond.'

I laughed at the idea at the time. But they *did* make a film of one of my books. In 1987 Century Hutchinson published *The Commissioner*, a thriller set in Brussels. I wrote the novel soon after returning to work in Brussels in the mid-eighties, once again for the European Commission, after a five-year stint as a member of the European Parliament (MEP) which I shall come to shortly.

As a matter of fact, I didn't actually write the novel – I dictated it in twenty-minute bursts as I drove to work in the morning. Whereas Charlotte and I had bought a large house in the Brussels suburb of Uccle in the seventies, Jenny and I a decade later bought an even larger house (with a tennis court!) in a neighbouring Brussels suburb known as Rhode-St-Genèse. And whereas in my earlier incarnation as a *fonctionnaire* I usually cycled to work, ten years down the line I must admit I most often drove (still the same lovely *trajet* through the leafy beech woods where Wellington's troops bivouacked on the eve of Waterloo).

Every week I used to send a collection of the tapes off to a typing agency in England and after a while a bulky typescript would plop through the letterbox at 3 Avenue Boesdael.

I was agreeably surprised at how well the first draft turned out. Though I usually had to wait weeks before being able to check what I had 'written', the book had an undeniable coherence. Occasionally, I muddled up the names of key characters and once one of them inadvertently changed sex halfway through. But as soon as I had the complete text in front of me, I was able to sort out the minor blips. More to the point, the book seemed to ring true. I suspect the real reason *The Commissioner* worked was that I was writing about a world in which I was deeply involved on a personal basis. Roy Jenkins, the Commission's former President who had left Brussels to 'break the mould of British politics' by co-founding the SDP, gave me a splendid puff for the jacket. '*Strong on authentic detail,*' Roy wrote. And I think he meant it.

The film rights were sold to a German company, and in due course a film of *The Commissioner* was actually made, with John Hurt playing the lead role.

Before it went on release in Europe (it had been co-financed by Canal Plus) *The Commissioner* was shown in the competition section of the Berlin Film Festival in 1998. Walking onto the stage in the giant Zoo Palast Cinema on the Kurfürstendamm to shouts of 'author, author!' was certainly a moment to be treasured.

We were quite a party of Johnsons in Berlin that night. Jenny and I arrived with our two children, Julia and Max, and made our way to the posh hotel where reservations had been made (and paid for!) by the Film Festival organizers. As we took the lift up to the seventh floor, we noticed that *The Commissioner* posters were stuck on the doors and walls. The corridor leading to our suite was also lined with posters.

Julia and Max guessed immediately.

'Leo is here already!' they pronounced.

'Leo!' I exclaimed. 'Surely not!' Leo was in Washington, working for the International Finance Corporation, part of the World Bank Group.

As we were debating the point, Leo emerged laughing from behind a pillar. Having flown in that morning, he had visited the Film Festival offices and grabbed a huge bundle of posters which he had put up all around our hotel.

Jo, too, flew in from Paris where he was working for the *Financial Times*, so that was a double bonus. Okay, so it wasn't a full house as far as the Johnson children were concerned. Alexander Boris and Rachel couldn't make it to Berlin that night. But when you have six children, as I do, a two-thirds turnout is certainly a quorum.

I am particularly sorry that my father wasn't still alive at the time of the 1997 Berlin Film Festival. He didn't have much time for my political ambitions, believing that all politicians were scoundrels. And I don't think he had a great deal of sympathy for my work as a civil servant, given the amount of 'paper-pushing' he imagined was involved, although I think he appreciated the case for action on the environmental front. But I would have liked to have taken him with us to Berlin. I think he would have enjoyed, as I did, seeing the credit 'based on the novel by Stanley Johnson' roll up on the giant screen. It would probably have rated a 'Good show, Stan' which, from him, was high praise indeed.

As I say, my father liked a good story, and *The Commissioner* definitely had a good plot line, full of sex, scandal and intrigue. Just like everyday life in the European Commission's huge starfish-shaped Berlaymont building in Brussels.

THIRTY

The Whip and the Slipper

But I am getting ahead of myself.

Charlotte and I separated at the end of 1978. I blame myself entirely for the breakdown of our marriage. Charlotte calculated that we had moved house thirty-two times in fifteen years. While she had successfully combined her career as a painter with her vocation as a mother to our four children, the strain had taken its toll.

I drove her to Brussels airport on a grey afternoon a few days before Christmas. After I had seen her to the plane, I came back to our house in Uccle and sat rather glumly at my desk in my study overlooking the garden. The other day I found the poem that I wrote on that occasion.

Here it is:

> On this first grey afternoon
> I think of the good times.
> The rain blots out the view
> But still, I think of the good times
> We had together.
> You ought to know
> That even if we cannot live with each other,
> I have loved you and will still.
> The roots go too deep
> For this tree to be blown down.
> So even though I smile and smile
> And pretend not to mind
> When I think of the good times
> I shall miss you.

I do not in any way wish to minimize the distress that can be caused to a family by separation and divorce. I felt desperately sorry for the children. Happily, Charlotte and I have tried to keep our relationship on the friendliest footing possible. Charlotte went on to marry an American professor, Nicholas Wahl. Though Nick has now died, I know she found a happiness with him that must have eluded her with me.

From a practical point of view, things might have been worse than they actually were. Our three oldest children were by then at boarding school in England.

After a few years in Brussels at the European School, Alexander Boris had gone to Ashdown House, a prep school in Sussex, where the headmaster, Clive Williams, and his wife, Rowena, ran – as far as I could tell – a very happy ship.

In due course Alexander Boris won a scholarship to Eton. Clive was particularly thrilled because Alexander Boris had only been at the school a term or two before he had to sit the Eton exams.

Rachel followed Alexander Boris to Ashdown. She was the first girl ever to go there as a boarder. With one other girl joining up (as a daygirl), the local newspaper reproduced the school photo with the headline 'Boys 110–Girls 2!'

Rachel is convinced that, thanks to her, Clive gave up beating pupils at the school.

'I'd persuaded some friends to raid the larder with me one night,' she told me, when I was working on this memoir. 'Clive caught us. If we had been boys he would have beaten us without question. But because I was a girl, he gave me a choice: either be beaten or miss seeing your parents next weekend. Well, you and Mama were coming all the way from Brussels to see me, so I told Clive I'd go for the beating. Clive decided he couldn't go through with that, so he stopped beating the kids completely. It wasn't fair to the boys, he argued, not to beat the girls, so he wouldn't beat anyone any more!'

Rachel won an exhibition to Bryanston, though she later went on to St Paul's Girls School for her sixth form years. While Rachel was at Bryanston, there was, as I recall, some complaint that she had bought a bottle of Cinzano in Blandford Forum, which she and some friends then consumed on school premises. At any event, I remember getting a letter from the authorities at Bryanston, politely enquiring whether I had had 'any luck finding Rachel a new school'.

By the time Charlotte and I separated, Leo was also at Ashdown House. He was Captain of Cricket in his last summer term. This meant that I was invited to be captain of the Father's XI in the Fathers' match. When Leo came in to bat, I put myself on to bowl and knocked out his middle stump first ball with a sizzling yorker.

I can still see the look of mortification on Leo's face. But he bit his lip and called out: 'Well bowled, Dada!' At that moment, I would have given my right arm to have been able to take that wicked ball back and bowl a gentle lob instead.

Clive Williams invited me to give the speech on Sports Day that same summer term. Since Clive had just won the sack race with a splendid display of athleticism, I began my remarks by congratulating him warmly on his victory.

'It has long been rumoured,' I said, 'that Ashdown House's head-master is good in the sack. Now we know it's true!'

I am not sure that Rowena enjoyed the joke, though it went down well with the assembled parents.

I went down to Ashdown House a few years ago to visit Rachel's oldest son, Ludo, who was at the time a pupil there, as his mother and uncle had been. Though Clive is no longer headmaster, he and Rowena are still very much part of the picture. Their joint portrait, painted by Charlotte, hangs in the hall.

Harsh though it may sound, I believe that having three children at boarding school made the practicalities of splitting up that much easier. Jo, who had his seventh birthday only a few days after I took Charlotte to Brussels airport that grey December afternoon when she left Brussels for good, went first as a dayboy to The Hall in Hampstead before following his siblings to Ashdown House.

Since we had already sold our house in Regent's Park Road to Simon Jenkins and Gayle Hunnicut, Charlotte was able to buy a flat in London.

The Johnson family's centre of gravity having clearly shifted to the other side of the English Channel, I decided that the time had come for me too to pack up my things and return to England.

By some happy chance, at precisely that moment I was selected as a Conservative candidate in the first ever direct elections to be held for the European Parliament. I had been on the official Conservative candidates' list for some time. Indeed, by the spring of 1979 (with the European elections scheduled for June that year) I had already had one or two interviews.

I had, for example, been 'long' shortlist for both Leicester and Surrey.

As far as Leicester was concerned, I recognized that the selection panel might consider me a touch deficient in local knowledge, so I decided to confront the problem head-on.

The Duke of Rutland being in the chair, I began my five-minute speech on the alotted theme, 'Why I should be the Conservative candidate for Leicester in the Euro-election', with what I thought was a disarmingly frank admission.

'Your Grace! I have never been to Leicester before, but I have been several times to Leicester Square!'

I was not invited back for the 'final' interview.

Surrey's 'long' shortlist consisted of (a) a Marquis, (b) a Peer of the Realm, (c) a Baronet, (d) a Dame, and (e) me. In other words, I was the low card in a straight flush. I was convinced, however, that being the odd man out might play in my favour.

Unfortunately, I blew it again. This time we had ten minutes to make our set speech and I wasted three of them telling a complicated joke which I don't need to repeat here about a cow, its udder and the nearby church clock. I could sense my audience becoming increasingly restless so, perversely, dug myself even deeper into the hole.

'Shall I tell you anudda' udder story?' I asked defiantly.

I wasn't invited to the Surrey final either. For the record, the Marquis (Charles Douro) was selected as the Conservative Euro-candidate for Surrey, was duly elected by a massive majority and went on to serve two distinguished terms in the European Parliament.

A week or two after the Surrey debacle, my luck changed. I was invited to appear before the selectors for the Isle of Wight and East Hampshire. The venue was a hotel in Gosport, a town on the south coast not far from Portsmouth.

As it happened, I had a great deal of local knowledge as far as Gosport was concerned. In the by then far-off days when, as I have already described, I was being trained by one of Britain's secret intelligence organizations, Gosport was one of our principal stamping grounds. Many an afternoon had I spent peering into shop windows in Gosport High Street to check whether I was being followed (bending down to tie up a shoelace while glancing backwards between your legs is another good counter-surveillance technique), or leaving messages stuck with chewing gum to the underside of benches in grim, wind-swept municipal parks.

The chairman of the Isle of Wight and Hants East Euro-Constituency Conservative Association was a man called Jack Bedser, who in real life worked for British Rail. Jack led off the questions at the final selection meeting.

'How well do you know this area?' he asked.

'Tremendously well,' I replied confidently.

'How so?'

'Well ...' I began, and then I paused, realizing that whatever I said was going to land me in trouble. If I said I knew Gosport like the back of my hand, they would be bound to ask why.

It was not a good start, but things improved. I answered some questions from the floor reasonably well. There was one about New Zealand butter. I was passionately in favour, which seemed to be the right answer. Then the bowling got rougher. Bedser polished the ball on the inside of his thigh. He had obviously been told by Conservative Central Office to weed out any potential mavericks, people who wouldn't do what they were told to do.

'If you are elected, Mr Johnson, will you accept the leadership of the Conservative Party,' he asked.

'I certainly will if I'm offered it,' I replied.

This raised a titter in the audience. Bedser pursed his lips. 'I mean, if elected, would you follow the lead of the Party, accept the Tory Whip in other words?'

Having done my homework before the meeting, I knew that the local Conservative agent – the man who would be looking after me if I made it – was a Mr Slipper. Norman Slipper. As I spoke, I could see Norman over to one side, scribbling notes.

'Yes, I would accept the Whip,' I replied. 'The Whip *and* the Slipper!'

This time the laughter was much more forthright and I felt I was really winning them over.

The clincher came when Bedser, like his famous namesakes – the Bedser twins who played so brilliantly for Surrey at cricket when I was growing up – bowled a really fast one.

'Well, Mr Johnson, if you are selected here today, and if you are elected in June this year, will Mrs Johnson be coming to live with you in the constituency?'

I knew I was on tricky ground. I was the third and last candidate to be interviewed that day. Sir John Peel, a former MP, had already appeared with Lady Peel by his side. Bill Cash (yes, *the* Bill Cash, Eurosceptic *extraordinaire*), whom I had known at Oxford, had been accompanied by his wife, the delectable Biddy. There was a vacant chair at the top table clearly reserved for candidates' spouses as their husbands faced the music. Having a spouse was an important part of the package a candidate put forward. Yet I had entered the room with no apparent escort and the reality was that Charlotte and I were in the throes of a divorce.

I decided to come clean, explaining the situation as best I could.

Bedser pressed the point. 'Do we take it, then, Mr Johnson, that Mrs Johnson will not be coming to live here?'

I took a deep breath. There are times to go for the winning shot, and times to push forward with the pads. I decided to go for the shot. Either they could take a joke or they couldn't.

'Mrs Johnson may or may not be coming to live in the constituency,' I replied. 'That is something for her to decide. But it certainly will not be with me!'

Later, Norman Slipper told me that my responses on the difficult issue of my marital circumstances swung some crucial votes my way. In the event, I won on the second ballot and drove back to London that night knowing that, unless the Conservative Party's estimates of voting intentions were wildly wrong, I would in a few weeks time become a Euro-MP.

My Euro-job would be mainly in Strasbourg and Brussels, but I would need to have a home in the constituency too, like an ordinary MP. Indeed, I would receive precisely the same salary as a British MP, which in those days was less than £10,000 a year.

As Winston Churchill might have put it: some gravy, some train!

Lord Bessborough, a big cheese with the local Conservatives, allowed me to rent a cottage on his estate at Stansted Park, near

Rowland's Castle. Soon after that final selection meeting in Gosport, I went back to Brussels and stuck little coloured spots on the furniture in our house in Uccle. Blue spots, for the items to be delivered to Charlotte's newly acquired flat in Notting Hill; red spots, for the items to come to me in my Hampshire cottage; green spots for the things which were destined for Nethercote.

'Piece of cake!' I told Charlotte by telephone from Brussels. 'I've talked to the movers. I've explained about the red, blue and green spots, like the ones Indian women wear on their foreheads. I'm afraid I won't be able to be in Brussels when they come, since I have to be in the US to talk to the Americans about toxic waste. But it can't go wrong, believe me.'

'What about the piano?' Charlotte reminded me. 'Make sure you leave the piano behind.'

I should explain that, apart from our own furniture, we also had a large upright piano in our house in Brussels. It had been 'lent' to us a few years earlier by the previous owner of our Brussels house, a Madame Nagelmackers, when we bought the place. This was a convenient arrangement. I still had hopes of learning the piano properly one day – going beyond *Three Blind Mice*, for example – and it saved Madame N. the trouble of moving it. As we organized our departure, I telephoned Madame N. and explained the situation. She was naturally keen to have the piano back so I promised to leave it behind in Belgium in the otherwise empty house, to be collected by her in due course.

By some mischance, I must have stuck a blue sticker on the piano, or else the movers – always keen to oblige – decided to shift it anyway. While I was still in America, I received an anguished call from Charlotte to say that some men had tried to deliver the piano to her fourth-floor flat on Elgin Crescent. They had managed to get it as far as the third floor, but could go no further. It was now blocking the whole stairway. She couldn't get out and no one could get in!

It was not a good moment. In fact, I would say the incident of the piano represented the only discordant note in the otherwise civilized and well-tempered process of our separation and divorce. In the end I managed to have the Nagelmackers' piano rerouted from Notting Hill to Hampshire. There wasn't enough room in my little cottage at

Stansted to take it but Eric Bessborough sportingly agreed to house it in his aviary until I could arrange for it to be repatriated.

The aviary! I can hear Madame Nagelmackers' Lady Bracknell voice now, as I telephoned her to give her the news. Well, I did my best to clean the piano up before sending it back across the Channel to Belgium but twenty peacocks can make a great deal of mess in a very short space of time. Of course, I wrote a grovelling letter of apology to Madame N. but I'm pretty sure I went down in her estimation.

Compared with the problems created by my misdirection of the piano, the European election itself, which took place in June 1979, was a doddle. Mrs Thatcher had won a stonking victory for the Conservatives the previous month in the general election. There was no reason to suppose that this triumph couldn't be repeated in the European elections in June.

The 1979 European election campaign lasted three weeks. Most days I went around banging on doors, as candidates do. In the evenings I made speeches at various venues. Norman Slipper had my election address printed and distributed in accordance with electoral law. Basically, I believed in a 'Strong Britain in a Strong Europe!' I thought that hit the right note.

I left the Euro-Constituency only once during the campaign and that was to visit Alexander Boris at Eton on the Fourth of June. Alexander Boris, already perhaps foreseeing a political future, went around slapping 'Vote Johnson' stickers on the Rolls-Royces and Bentleys parked by Agar's Plough.

On polling day itself, all four children were given exeats from their various schools. That evening, after a day visiting polling stations up and down the far-flung Euro-Constituency, we all gathered at my cottage in Hampshire. I roasted a chicken for dinner (one of my few culinary ventures in a lifetime of avoiding the kitchen – my motto has always been 'if you can't stand the heat, stay out of the kitchen') and next morning we piled into the little Fiat I had brought over from Brussels, aiming for Portsmouth Town Hall where, from 11 a.m., the counting of the votes would take place.

As we left, my cleaning lady arrived. 'If anyone rings, Mabel,' I said, 'tell them I'm out for the count.'

Unfortunately, it wasn't as simple as that. The Fiat for some reason actually caught fire on the motorway. We managed to put out the flames but alternative transport had to be arranged. By the time we arrived at Portsmouth Town Hall, counting had been under way for some time.

When he saw the five of us enter the room, our Conservative rosettes blackened by smoke, Norman Slipper rushed up.

I thought he was going to scold me for being late. On the contrary, he had a satisfied smile on his face. In those days there were no new-fangled electronic systems for tabling the votes. They did it all by hand. Norman had been watching eagle-eyed as they stacked the bundles in the trays. Experienced as he was in such matters, he already knew that I was way, way ahead of my Liberal opponent, Lady (Nancy) Seear.

'I am delighted to tell you, Stanley,' he chortled, holding out a congratulatory hand, 'that your piles are much larger than Lady Seear's piles and they're growing all the time!'

Though his choice of words was possibly unfortunate, Norman proved right. I ended up with 110,000 votes, 95,000 more than Lady Seear gained for the Liberals, who came second. My majority was in fact the second largest in the country, being exceeded only by my good friend Madron Seligman, in the neighbouring West Sussex Euro-Constituency.

THIRTY-ONE

Ode de Cologne

The newly elected European Parliament met for the first time in Strasbourg in July 1979. Ian Paisley, as an Ulster MEP, did his level best to reduce the opening session to chaos.

When Mrs Simone Veil, the Parliament's President, banged her gavel to announce the start of business, Paisley jumped to his feet and roared out in that stentorian voice of his: 'On a point of order, Madame President, if you go outside this building, you will see that the flag of my country is flying upside down. This is a gross insult. I propose that the session be suspended until the matter is put right.'

Of course, as loyal subjects of Her Majesty, we Britons knew that the Union Jack – the flag the Rev. Paisley was of course referring to – should always be flown with the broad stripe on top, nearest the mast. But could those who were in charge of hoisting the flags outside the European Parliament be expected to know that too? Did it matter anyway?

Poor Madame Veil. She had survived a Nazi concentration camp (she still had the tattoo on her wrist). Could she survive her time in the European Parliament? It wasn't just Paisley who made her life hell. Marco Pannella, for the Italian Radical Party, was fiendishly clever in laying traps for her. Emma Bonino, one of his principal allies, who later became a European Commissioner, was equally adroit.

On the whole we Brits left it to the others to make trouble. We reckoned we had a serious job to do. Sixty-one Conservative MEPs altogether were elected in the June 1979 elections, as against seventeen Labour MEPs who, owing to some internal party squabble, did not arrive to take up their seats for several months. Two Danes also joined our group, so that – with this streak of Danish Blue added to the mixture – we were officially called the European Democratic Group (EDG).

One of the practical consequences of being a multi-national, multi-party (sic) group was the status we acquired in the parliamentary pecking order. We were awarded seats on important committees, as well as chunks of speaking time in the debates. The Parliament paid for staffers to assist us in our work. Our group's leader, Jim Scott-Hopkins, a former MP, was allocated a large white Jaguar.

Presumably bearing in mind the work I had done in the European Commission, Jim very kindly nominated me for the post of vice-chairman of the European Parliament's Committee on Environment, Public Health and Consumer Protection. In that capacity, I was able to follow closely the proposals which I had helped to develop while in the Commission and which were now wending their way through the Parliament. I tried to make sure they received a fair wind.

In those days, of course, the European Parliament's opinion was largely advisory. The Parliament had to vote on a Commission proposal, but there was absolutely no need for the Council to take any notice of what the Parliament said.

Still, it was interesting work. I enjoyed it. I liked the sense of being surrounded by people from very different parliamentary traditions. You saw some real stars too. The French, in particular, had sent some of their most senior politicians to Strasbourg for the first session of the newly elected Parliament.

One day, I once found myself sitting across the aisle from Jacques Chirac.

'*Bonjour*, Monsieur Chirac,' I said.

'*Bonjour*,' he replied.

That was as far as our conversation went. But at least I got to shake the great man's hand. There was a lot of hand-shaking in the Parliament. It was part of the Gallic tradition.

Of course, as far as the French were concerned, the length of time the 'gros fromages' spent in Strasbourg could be fairly short. Once the election was over, the big names soon stepped down to be replaced by substitutes.

I made my first speech in the Plenary towards the end of 1979. The subject was the pollution of the Rhine, that great river which flows through Strasbourg on its way to the sea at Rotterdam.

Even if you were speaking in 'group' time, i.e. on behalf of your political group, as opposed to making an intervention as an individual, you never had long. The clock started ticking the moment you stood up. You could see it above the podium, a huge red digital display denoting how much time you had already used up as well as how much time you had left. It wasn't like the House of Commons where an MP could chunter on for hours.

So when I heard Simone Veil, the President, say: 'I now call Mr Stanley Johnson for the European Democratic Group', I jumped smartly to my feet.

'"The River Rhine, as is well known", I began,

'"Doth wash the city of Cologne.

But tell me, nymph, what power divine

Can ever cleanse the river Rhine?"'

In the European Parliament, as at Westminster, members address the chair at all times. So Mrs Veil interrupted me to protest: 'I am not sure it is right to address the President of the Parliament as "nymph".'

'Please forgive me, Madame President,' I apologized. 'I was quoting a famous poem by Samuel Taylor Coleridge. Actually, we call it the "Ode de Cologne".'

This witticism earned me a mention in the William Hickey column of the *Daily Express*. I felt my Euro-parliamentary career had made a good start.

It's hard to imagine a prettier town than Strasbourg. And if you had time, you could drive out into the surrounding countryside and have lunch or dinner in any one of a dozen little villages along the '*route des vins*'.

The great 'Asparagus-Fest' took place in May each year at one of these villages, with around three tonnes of this succulent juicy vegetable, accompanied by lashings of *sauce hollandaise,* being consumed by a huge gaggle of Europhiles consisting of MEPs and their increasingly numerous hangers-on: researchers, lobbyists, wives and even – on occasion – mistresses.

The Plenary Sessions of the Parliament were in Strasbourg, or occasionally in Luxembourg, while the Committee sessions were in Brussels. Since we had sold the house in Uccle, I rented a studio near the Place Madou, near the centre, and stayed there whenever I was in town. With many friends in Brussels, I didn't have to make my own meals.

As far as my UK arrangements were concerned, though I had a cottage in Hampshire, I felt I needed a London base too. In Brussels Charlotte and I had been good friends with Crispin and Penelope Tickell (Crispin became Roy Jenkins' *chef de cabinet* when Roy was nominated President of the European Commission in 1976). The Tickells, still in Brussels, very kindly lent me their flat in Blomfield Road while I looked around for something more permanent.

I didn't, as it happened, have to look very far. Blomfield Road runs along one side of the Grand Union Canal in Little Venice. Maida Avenue runs along the other side. An estate agent sent me details of an 'upper maisonette' available for rent from the Church Commission on that 'desirable road' in London W2.

Penelope Tickell, who happened to be in London, came to look over the flat with me.

We were, I suppose, making quite a lot of noise clumping around in the empty rooms. At all events, someone downstairs started ringing the flat's door bell angrily. I poked my head out of the door. At the foot of the stairs, I saw a dark-haired, extremely attractive young woman, staring crossly up at me.

'What on earth are you doing?' she asked.

There was something about the way she put the question that got under my skin.

'I'm a burglar,' I replied icily. 'I have broken in and quite soon I am going to start a fire.'

I signed the lease on the upper maisonette in August 1980 and moved in a few weeks later. Not long afterwards, a notice arrived from the EDG secretariat. It had been arranged, so I read, that the members of the European Democratic Group would shortly be received in audience in the Vatican in Rome by His Holiness Pope John-Paul II.

'*Biens, je jamais!*' I thought. Well, I never! Meeting the Pope, particularly this Pope, would be quite something. With hindsight, of course, we all know what a crucial role the former Karol Wojtyla played in the collapse of the Soviet Empire at the end of the eighties, but even at the beginning of that decade the Pope's dynamism and charisma were unmistakable.

At the end of the notice from the EDG secretariat, I read: 'Wives are also invited to the audience with the Pope.'

Taking soundings, I discovered that several wives were indeed likely to be going to Rome. Charles Douro (Surrey) would be accompanied, for example, by his wife Antonia. Fred Warner (Somerset) was bringing Simone. Serena would be with Neil Balfour (Yorkshire North), Nancy-Joan Seligman would be accompanying Madron (West Sussex) etc.

I had a sudden idea. What about that dark-haired, extremely attractive young woman who lived in the flat downstairs and who had been so sharp with me when I was first thinking of moving in to Maida Avenue?

Jenny and I flew to Rome with other members of the European Democratic Group, together with their wives, on 10 November 1980. On 11 November, there were official meetings between the EDG and the Italian Christian Democrats, one of the like-minded parties with whom we tried to cooperate in the Parliament. On the 12th, we were to have our audience with the Holy Father.

In due course, around 11 a.m., we arrived at the Vatican, were escorted into an inner sanctum, and seated on gilt chairs waiting for the Pope to arrive. At last he did so, gracing us not only with a brief homily but with a blessing as well.

After that we lined up to be presented. Jim Scott-Hopkins, standing next to the Pope, did the introductions.

'This is Sir Fred and Lady Warner, Holy Father. This is Lord Bethell. This is Sir Jack and Lady Stewart-Clark. This is Lady Douro ...'

Soon, too soon, it was our turn. I was the first to be presented.

'This is Stanley Johnson,' Jim said. Then he saw Jenny standing just behind me, next in line. She was wearing, as instructed by the Vatican's protocol officers, a black lace mantilla. Glancing back at her as she waited in line behind me, I thought she looked very fetching.

I could tell that our leader, Jim Scott-Hopkins, was in trouble. He told the Pope, 'And this is ... er ... um ... Mrs ... er ... In point of fact ...'

Whenever Jim Scott-Hopkins used the phrase 'in point of fact' you knew he was floundering.

Fortunately, the Pope came to his aid. He peered at Jenny under the mantilla and obviously liked what he saw: 'Well, this must be Mrs Johnson, I suppose,' His Holiness pronounced.

Considering that we had had in some sense received a papal blessing, if not an actual command, Jenny and I were married in London a few weeks later, on 27 February 1981.

Alexander Boris, Rachel, Leo and Jo were once again granted leave from their respective educational establishments to come to the wedding, while my mother and father drove up from Nethercote. Jenny's mother, Lois, and her stepfather, Edward Sieff, were present, as well as Jenny's father, the composer Richard Arnell, and her brother, Adam.

Looking back, I must say that I have been particularly fortunate as far as the selection of in-laws is concerned. I remained friends with Bice and James Fawcett, and the Fawcett family, even though Charlotte and I had long since separated. When Bice and James, in retirement, lived in a flat on the Banbury Road, Oxford, Bice told Jenny that she would 'look out for Max', our son – then only six or seven years old – in the Greycotes School playground. She meant 'look out' in the literal sense, since the Fawcetts' balcony actually overlooked Greycotes.

And with Teddy and Lois Sieff I really 'lucked in', as they say. When Jenny and I were married, Teddy and Lois had a house in Ferring on the Sussex coast, where the family would gather at the weekend. In the early seventies Teddy Sieff survived an assassination attempt by Carlos, the 'Jackal'. Carlos's motive, and that of his paymasters, the Popular Front for the Liberation of Palestine (PFLP), was undoubtedly related to the fact that Teddy, at the time chairman of Marks & Spencer, was one of Britain's leading Zionists.

Having survived the attempt on his life (the bullet hit him in the mouth and broke several teeth, before missing his jugular vein by a hair's breadth), Teddy Sieff lived to see Jenny's marriage (to me) and the birth and first years of our daughter, Julia. He did not, alas, live long enough to greet the arrival of our second child, Max, in 1985.

Par contre, Jenny's mother, Lois Sieff, is happily still very much with us. Though she is now in her eighties, she is still full of vim and vigour, as well as pep and fizz, and is immensely supportive of her children (Jenny and her brother, Adam, whose rock band Tony Blair used to manage before he became Prime Minister). And Lois's two grandchildren, Julia and Max, have for years now basked in the warmth of Grandma's evident love and affection. As far as 'grandparenting' goes, Lois sets the bar pretty high.

Lois is one of the few people I know who enjoys jokes, including colossally bad puns, as much as I do. She is, in other words, pretty quip on the draw.

As a practical matter, even after we were married Jenny and I kept both the upstairs and the downstairs flats in the house on Maida Avenue. We would ring each other up several times a day. But this, possibly ideal, arrangement didn't last for long. Having decided not to stand for a second term in the European Parliament, in the summer of 1984 I returned to Brussels to work once again for the European Commission.

On arriving, or rather re-arriving, in Belgium, we bought – as I have already mentioned – another of those large, leafy villas in the suburbs and we lived there with Julia and Max, until in 1990 I decided, once again, that the time had come to move on.

When Jenny and I were married in 1981 I was forty years old. By the time he was forty, as Tom Lehrer reminded us, Mozart had been dead five years already. So this seems to me to be a good place to bring this particular narrative to a close. I had, after all, as the saying goes, passed quite a lot of water under the bridge by the time my fortieth year to heaven came around.

But, just for the record, I should add that I am not dead yet. I have, since leaving the European Commission for the second time, continued with various careers. I have gone on writing books (eighteen so far: nine novels, nine non-fiction), while also working as an environmental consultant, journalist and, briefly, as a television presenter. I have retained an interest in politics, standing unsuccessfully as a Conservative candidate for Parliament in Teignbridge, Devon, in the May 2005 elections. I actually got over 21,500 votes, which is more than many MPs received.

I travelled a lot in my early years, as must be apparent from this story, and I've travelled even more since. In fact, I'm hard pressed to think of a part of the world I haven't been to, usually on some ecological mission to do with endangered species: seals, whales, turtles, sharks, tigers, elephants, gorillas, orang-utans, Komodo dragons etc. I've been twice to Antarctica and once to the Galapagos. There are worse ways of earning a living.

My mother died in 1987. To say that I, and my brother and sisters, were saddened by her death would be a colossal understatement. If today I retain a generally positive and optimistic view of life, it is my mother I have to thank. She set us all a wonderful example. The other day, out of the blue, a letter came to Nethercote. It was from a Swiss au pair who had worked for my parents on the farm in 1961. She wrote that her year with us was 'the happiest time of her life' and enclosed a snapshot of my mother, surrounded by sheep in the meadow next to the house. My mother is carrying Tiddles, a Jack Russell terrier, under one arm, and a newborn lamb under the other.

My father died in 1992. He was cremated in Taunton, but there was a service afterwards in Winsford church. This was followed by a well-attended gathering in the yard at Nethercote. Next day, I sent a poem to Victor Bonham-Carter, the editor of *The Exmoor Review*. I mentioned in my cover letter that I had won the Newdigate Prize in 1962 with a poem about Dunkery Beacon, hadn't written much poetry, if any, since then, but hoped another short piece on an Exmoor theme would meet with his approval. It apparently did.

The poem, entitled 'In Memoriam Wilfred "Johnny" Johnson (1909–1992)', reads as follows:

> The day dawned bright and clear
> With a touch of frost.
> Had he been there,
> Most probably he would have ventured
> A confident 'It'll be warm
> By noon.' It was a good day to go.
> The valley had seldom seemed
> More beautiful. In so many ways
> It was his valley, stamped
> With his mark. After all,
> He had lived there forty years.

After the funeral,
They came back with us for a drink
And stood around in the yard.
In our farming days, it used
To be full of mud and muck
But now the grass has seeded itself
And it's more like a lawn.

Most of the village was present,
As well as the family, of course.
One of the local huntsmen
Who had ridden through often enough
In the past doffed his cap
As he took a glass of beer from the tray.
'If I'd had my horn with me,' he said,
'I'd have blown "Gone away."'

We still have Nethercote. My sister Birdie lives in Nethercote Cottage with around eighty acres of land from the old East Nethercote holding. My daughter Rachel now owns East Nethercote with her husband, Ivo. Jenny and I still have the old farmhouse, West Nethercote, which my parents first moved into in November 1951, and around 400 acres of land. Foot-and-mouth movement restrictions prevented us celebrating fifty years in the valley but we shall make up for this in 2011, when the sixtieth anniversary comes round.

Recently, with the aid of a wonderful Greek architect, Dona Korneti, Jenny and I have built a house in Greece, on the Pelion peninsula which was once the home of the Centaurs. You can walk down through the olive groves to the sea. The Fairweathers have a house nearby, which is a great joy. It's thanks to them we found the land to build on.

When I failed to be elected for Teignbridge, Ian Katz, then in charge of the G2 section of the *Guardian*, very kindly offered me a weekly column. I did sixteen articles for it altogether, before the *Guardian* 'downsized' and I lost my slot. Several of my *Guardian* pieces were sent from Greece, actually from an internet café in Milina, our nearest town. I have Turkish blood in my veins, but I am a classicist at heart. Greece inspires. From our terrace, we can see Mount Parnassus the other side of the Pagasitic Gulf. We look west. Recently, I said to Patrick Fairweather as we sat on the terrace reminiscing about those far-off days when we worked together: 'We are all facing the sunset, one way or another, so we may as well get some practice!'

Though I can still read Homer in the original with a bit of effort, I have made shamefully little progress in picking up modern Greek. Maria Fairweather, half-Greek herself, tells me this doesn't matter. She has an English friend on the Greek island of Siros who has been married to a Greek woman for forty years. 'The other day I asked him: "How is your Greek?" and he replied, "She is very well, thank you!"'

On the family front, I have observed with pride and satisfaction the progress of my first batch of children (Alexander Boris, Rachel, Leo and Joseph) from my marriage to Charlotte, with whom I remain on the friendliest of terms. (Charlotte still lives in Notting Hill and continues to paint, though increasingly affected by Parkinson's disease. In the sitting room of our London house, we have a large portrait she painted of Julia and Max in the mid-nineties.) Alexander Boris is a politician/journalist, recently elected Mayor of London, an event which has been fairly widely reported and which has brought tremendous excitement to the whole Johnson family. I'm only now, several months later, getting used to being called 'Father of the Mayor!' or even 'First Father'. I know I must be on my best behaviour in future, mustn't let the side down.

Rachel has a weekly column in the *Sunday Times* as well as being a successful novelist. Her *Notting Hell*, set in London, has recently been followed by *Shire Hell*. Though the shire in question is meant to be Dorset, there are quite a few similarities with Exmoor. Leo is an environmentalist and entrepreneur. He also created, wrote, financed, produced, directed and even acted in a feature-length film in which a Bulgarian chef called Stanko goes to New York and wins an international cookery competition. Jo has worked for the *Financial Times* for several years and has served as that paper's correspondent both in France (based in Paris) and in South Asia (based in New Delhi). Author of a biography of the French tycoon Jean-Marie Messier, he has recently returned to London to take charge of the *FT*'s Lex column.

Julia and Max, the two children I share with Jenny, are also rapidly making their way in the world, though obviously the others have had a bit of a head start. Indeed, Julia has already begun to make a name for herself as a singer with the band Second Person, with two CD/albums already released and a third on the way. Max, having graduated in Russian, is halfway through an MBA at Tsingua University in Beijing.

Christopher Wren's memorial is inscribed inside the dome of St Paul's: *Si monumentum requiris, circumspice.* If you want a monument, look around you. I feel a bit like that. Of course, I am inordinately proud of all six of my children. They all went to good schools, and they made the most of their opportunities at those schools. Five of them went on to Oxford. Julia, showing a rebellious streak, first went up to Cambridge before switching to University College London. As they all make their way in life, I find myself wishing I had half their talent. People tell me this is an immature and childish reaction but there it is.

All four of my children with Charlotte are happily married. Alexander Boris is married to Marina, a barrister, daughter of the BBC correspondent Sir Charles Wheeler and his wife, Dip. Rachel is married to Ivo Dawnay, a former *FT* journalist who is now public affairs director for the National Trust.

Leo, as I have already mentioned, is married to Taies, an Afghan–American, whom he met when they were both working for the World Bank Group in Washington. Jo is married to Amelia (or Milly) Gentleman, herself an award-winning journalist.

As a result of all this marrying, there has been a good deal of begetting. I have – so far – the following grandchildren who are (just to prove I can count them all out and count them all back): Lara, Milo, Cassia and Theo (Alexander Boris and Marina); Ludo, Charlotte Millicent and Oliver (Rachel and Ivo); Lula Muska and Ruby Noor (Leo and Taies); and Rose and William (Jo and Milly). I can't yet remember all the birthdays, I admit, but I am working on it.

By my reckoning, the grandchildren currently add up to eleven. Fortunately, I do not feel any need to compete with them. Perhaps one day they will take on Ashdown House or some other school at cricket. If so, I would be proud to be an umpire.

Twenty-seven years after that visit to the Pope, I am still happily married to Jenny, who has pursued her interests with singular determination, while still being the anchor and bedrock of the family. When I left Brussels in 1990, after my second stint with the European Commission, we settled in Oxford. Jenny was admitted to Oxford University's Manchester College (now Harris Manchester College) where she took a BA degree in Philosophy and French. In 1994, we moved to London where Jenny gained an MA from King's College and, for good measure, completed a B.Sc. from the Open University. Now, she is on the Development Board of the National Portrait Gallery as well as being a lay member of an NHS advisory committee on medical ethics.

The above summary, I fear, is totally inadequate. It only hints at the truth. The reality is that Jenny keeps the show on the road. My part is wholly ancillary and, I suspect, mainly disruptive.

I am sure that Jenny is extremely grateful, as an intensely private person, that this memoir has concentrated on my early years. Though there have been occasional 'fast forwards', the narrative in any detailed sense effectively ends with our visit to the Pope in Rome in November 1980 and our subsequent marriage. Since I very much doubt if there will be a sequel to this book, this is the moment anyway to say how lucky I was to meet her that morning, now more than twenty-seven years ago, when I came to look at that flat in Maida Avenue, Little Venice.

I owe her more than I can say.

'May Morning'

Soft on that hilltop we awoke
And in each other saw the world below;
Soft had we climbed, spoke
Not a word, made no sound though
The morning cried aloud for praise.
Yet on this, most glorious of days
Silence was the only God we might invoke.

Questing the sun through a drench of dew
We made our way to the beacon mound;
Wet, happy we burst through
To the paean of spring-time, found
That here at last on the morning-moor
We might know something pure
And altogether new.

Perversely precarious, determined to cheat
Topographical delimitation,
We climbed up the cairn till our feet
Surmounted all terrestrial equation.
We were high, we were free, we were proud
And all our emptiness was a crowd
Filling what was beneath.

The breath of our love floated away
On the wind of red hair;
Turned into mist in the frosty air
It wisped the blue eyes of the sea.
Sojourners of a moment.
Yet filled with a great content
We felt glad that we were there.

For in this new contracted world
Before so vast and unhomogeneous
All complexities were now resolved
All myths, all magics found a place
In a central radiance,
In a complete unquestioned brilliance
Where nothing was, save one May Morning face.

And I myself, a dubious thing of youth
Changeful as the sunlight on the hill
When scudding clouds make a roof
Of light and dark, I at last could feel
Myself existing immemorial.
One small unnoticed freckle
On the larger glory of that truth.

Caught, transformed, broadcast again
In a Sunday peal of eye and hair
Agamemnon's warning flame
Hand-in-hand with the sea-blown air
Swept over the promontories
Alerted all Hellenic signatories
With the news that Troy was taken.

Passing thus from height to height
Steeple, tower, hilltop took that light
And sent it on its way.
Until at last this great expansion
Became coterminous with creation
And one ecstatic vast compression
Made past and future all one day.

That day was ours, uniquely and alone.
Standing together our love had grown
In silence sterner than the sea.
Subsumed beneath eternity,
It became itself eternal, reborn
From some vague insubstantial form
Into a thing of great glory.

All Hellenic signatories rejoiced
In one pure symphony of assent.
Cathedrals, arched like lambs, voiced
Their praise. The peaks of man's intent.
Those rare moments of deep feeling
That are sometimes actualized in being
Joined in the universal argument

To show the existence of the truth.
And so we stood, silent on the moor.
We knew nothing, yet we were sure
That somehow we ourselves were proof
That knowledge was irrelevant to life
That life consisted wholly of belief
In one another.

All past emotions then were seen
To be illusory. But even though
Remembered sunsets pale before the glow
Of present day, they have been
Themselves earnests of some greater flow
Of light and colour, born
Not there but with the dawn.

So once in Mykonos at dusk,
I thought May Morning came;
And once upon a Persian Mosque
I felt I knew some name
Of God, when in the tiles of Holy Writ
It circled one whole minaret
And streamed to heaven again.

Such feelings were not false but part
Of a greater, more complete emotion
Which we now felt. Our heart
By some agreeable confusion
Became at once the world's and ours.
We lived and for a few brief hours
Enjoyed our sweet delusion.

Oxford, May 1962